SIN-THESIS

The Compelling Power of Sin and How to be Free from It

CHUKWUMA AGU

WESTBOW
PRESS®
A DIVISION OF THOMAS NELSON
& ZONDERVAN

Scripture taken from the King James Version of the Bible.

WestBow Press books may be ordered through booksellers or by contacting:

WestBow Press
A Division of Thomas Nelson & Zondervan
1663 Liberty Drive
Bloomington, IN 47403
www.westbowpress.com
1 (866) 928-1240

ISBN: 978-1-9736-0874-5 (sc)
ISBN: 978-1-9736-0875-2 (hc)
ISBN: 978-1-9736-0873-8 (e)

Library of Congress Control Number: 2017917986

Print information available on the last page.

WestBow Press rev. date: 07/05/2018

CONTENTS

PREAMBLE

When my teacher at the Redeemed Christian Church of God School of Disciples approved the topic "Winning the battle against sin" for my graduation term paper, little did I know that I would end up with more than a trainee's paper. As it is easy to understand, I was afraid of the topic because I considered myself unqualified to take up such profound issues, particularly given my personal failings on the matter of handling sin. But shortly after, I perceived God would have me expand the discussions and circulate same. It has taken many years of unwarranted hesitation and distractions but finally, God who knows how to use weak instruments helped me to get it out.

This book is not meant to deliver anybody from the grip of sin – it has no such power. It merely aims at alerting us on the potency, subtlety and deceitfulness of sin and showing us that sin would not allow us to see it for what it is, thereby distracting us from God's offer of salvation. Throughout the pages that follow, we try to illustrate that sin IS NOT WHAT WE DO, BUT WHO WE ARE. It is only after we have dealt with who we are that we can also deal with what we do. The book discusses the **personality** inside us that is at enmity with God and behind most of our failings and its diverse manifestations. It maintains that there is only one person and one means through which deliverance from sin can come – Jesus and the atoning work of His blood, made effective by our carrying the cross DAILY. The book does not preach steps for obtaining deliverance from sin. Rather, it insists that victory is obtained and experienced through a life of daily personal intimacy with God through the scriptures and prayer.

My primary aim as a believer is to lay a firm hold on Christ for myself. I do not forget my long and tedious slavery to sin but for the

Lord's mercy. It is also my burden to awaken a yearning in your heart to pray and search the Scriptures so as to know Christ. In addition, I am aware a number of brethren have had deeper dealings from the Lord on the subject matter of this book and have insight that we all can benefit from. If this book awakens interest in them to share their experiences and insights, it would have partly succeeded in its mission. As you read the book, I sincerely desire and pray that the Holy Spirit will draw you into the closet to pursue proper equipping to live above the sin monster.

ACKNOWLEDGEMENTS

All the glory to the Lord Jesus, whose mercies saved me from sin and whose grace sustains me in the faith and for the privilege of writing this. I appreciate my wife, Chioma, who earnestly desired, consistently pressed and quietly prayed for the completion of this work. She proved a dear help-meet in meticulously reading and editing every page of the work. We also thank our Pastors – Gbenga Aroge, Johnson Anifowose and Ernest Okoye – each one a man of God in the workplace. We appreciate Henry and Lizzy Nwamadi for their infectious burden for the glory of God as well as Vin and Chinenye Onodugo, who have been so much support through thick and thin. The D-NEP brethren – Ken, Amaechi, Uche, Emeka, Ezeanata and the entire crew – have over the years provided immense support for our faith, and for which we thank them. Tochi has come to mean so much to us as a dear daughter; it is difficult telling all we have learnt from her; so also all the 'children' that have lived with us in the house – David, Ugochi, Nkechi, Florence, Chisom, Uche, Grace, Nazo, Prince, Chidi, Elijah, etc – whom the Lord has used to chip rough edges off our lives as they rubbed (some very roughly) on us. To each of these, we owe a part of our lives. The Peace House Team in Enugu has shown us in practical terms what victorious Christian living means. Hard to single out, but we must thank Bro Ralph and Sis Ngozi, Bro Ben and Sis Anwuli, Bro Eva and Sis Chinyere and all those quietly bearing the burden of spreading the message of the cross in South East Nigeria. We appreciate Obiageli, Oge and the Westbow Team who painstakingly went through and edited the entire manuscript. Several brethren, way too numerous to mention, have made inprints on our lives and helped the course of this work. For these and many more, we remain very grateful.

DEDICATION

To all those who daily grapple with the sin monster, who do not yet 'feel' delivered, but have refused to settle for anything less than complete victory. The Lord knows and identifies with your struggles. Do not let up on your cry because the rest He promised in Christ is real; He will give you victory over sin and grant you that rest.

PART I

UNDERSTANDING SIN, THE ENEMY

CHAPTER 1

SIN: WHY BOTHER?

a. The Pervasiveness of Sin

Every nailed coffin is evidence of a sentence on mankind. Every dug grave is a demonstration of fierce determination to wipe humanity from the face of the earth. Every stillborn child is a manifestation of a grand plan not to even allow human life a chance upon the surface of the earth. Every sick adult is an evidence of the fact that ultimately the destination of flesh is dust as God pronounced. Every violent death demonstrates a frenzied urgency to crush and cut off humans, the material creation and inheritance of God, from the earth. Every social, political, religious, psychological or spiritual confusion around and within us points to the desperation to coerce man to chase shadows and get eaten up by time rather than see the liberating light of God.

Since the pronouncement of punishment upon man in Eden, no man is spared physical death and only the few that find the deliverance are spared spiritual death. Over the years, the ground has swallowed countless billions of souls. With the exception of two men, Enoch and Elijah—and of course the Lord Jesus Himself – the worst of sinners and the most righteous of people have had to partake of mortality. Decay overtook the world, and the finest of creatures and inventions start the process of decay immediately it is born into the world. A child starts the journey to the grave from the day the child is born. Humanity has fought decay and death, produced drugs against sickness, researched into aging, and tried myriad means of prolonging life, but the sentence of death remains potent against mankind. Despite mind-boggling scientific progress, the mystery of death remains unraveled just as the definition and knowledge of the content of life remain elusive. None of us likes it; we wish things were otherwise, but they are not. We know that it will be our turn one day, but often, it is safer (or seemingly so) to turn the other way, pretend that day does not exist, and just live today for what it is worth. The thought that we would die always brings fear, but only rarely do we sit back to listen to God as He shows us the way out of death and its attending fear. In fact, often times we become engulfed in feverish workload so as to escape the reality that "for dust you are and to dust you shall return," (Genesis 3: 19 King James Version). But this reality stares every one, the weak and the powerful, in the face – daily!

Other creatures are not spared the ordeal. "For the creature was made subject to vanity, not willingly, but by reason of him who hath subjected the same in hope …for we know that the whole creation groaneth and travaileth in pain together until now…" (Romans 8: 20 & 22 King James Version). Does the storm happily and willingly blow down the house, killing all lives inside it? Is it of its own accord that fire breaks out in a factory, roasting all trapped therein? Was it part of the original purpose of God that lions make meat out of men and women or that viruses dwell in the blood, attacking the immune system until it completely breaks down and we die? Were cells designed to grow out of proportion, to become cancerous, to create pain, and to weaken the body till it collapses? Is it possible that when a snake bites out of fear for its own life and the person dies, the snake itself is uncomfortable? Was one animal originally created to be food for another animal with all the associated cruelty that goes with hunting and being a prey? Is it possible that all these are the unwilling subjection of the creatures to vanity? "For the creature was made subject to vanity, not willingly … (and they) groaneth and travaileth in pain together until now." As people die, so do animals and plants. Indeed, for animals and plants, life is often a lot more gruesome, unpredictable and typically shorter (except for some trees). Animals are often instruments and victims of destruction, either of one another or of humanity. Both living and non-living things regularly cause death and stumbling to one another and to man. This is because when the king of any kingdom is subdued by another force, his subjects are not free from that subjugation. These creatures are subjects in a kingdom whose king has been made subject to corruption. Man, who is supposed to be lord over the earth, was made subject to Satan, sin, and death. All other creatures were, by the same token, automatically made subject to corruption. When man became subject to sin and destruction, creatures also became subject. Originally, as seen in the Garden of Eden, creatures were meant to be at peace with one another and with man. Now they find themselves contending with and harming one another. They have all been made subjects unto Sin.

There is problem with mankind. We have all sinned and fallen short of the glory of God. There is no (natural) man on earth who likes all parts of himself and the things he does. There is this great contradiction mirrored by Paul in his letter to the Romans which every man born of woman identifies with, "For we know that the law is spiritual, but I am carnal, sold under sin. For that which I do I allow not, for what I would, that do I not, but what I hate, that I do" (Romans 7: 14 – 15). Satan has managed to deceive man into classifying sins into major and minor. The rule of law also sees sins (wrongs) as either civil or criminal. Religious men also believe that this classification is extended to heaven and is the same in the valuation books of God. Deep within each of us, we know that something is terribly wrong with war; it does neither the winner nor the loser good, but we still fight. We sacrifice precious and eternal lives to make dispensable and temporal points. We want to prove our temporal supremacy by wasting lives. Helpless children, men, and women, who know nothing of the reason behind war, are butchered in it. People are consigned to animal lifestyles, living in caves, having their meals over carcasses of fellow humans, drinking urine, and eating raw flesh. Atrocities become a way of life; some favourite and heroic pastimes of wartimes relished by supposedly brave men include ripping the abdomen of pregnant women open, dashing the heads of children on stones, and killing other men by installments. Between World Wars I and II alone, an estimated 120 million lives were lost (more than 3 percent of the global population at those periods). Interestingly, when it's all over, either because we are all tired or because God in mercy intervened in some way to save us from ourselves, we sit over the table, drink exotic wines, and sign peace treaties. Men shake hands and smile, and then work side by side to rebuild. They mount flags in honor of those who "paid the supreme price" for the rest to continue their aimless and godless lives—and that is the end! Everyone returns to normal social and economic life, and tries very hard to pretend he can never harm his fellow human being. It is then assumed that the 'barriers' which led to the war in the first place have gone away or become broken down. Going forward, those alive preach love, acceptance, and accommodation of others' views and persons. After all, they were not the ones that died; they have never tasted death and it was only unfortunate someone else was the victim. They just cannot understand the pain of a life suddenly cut short.or pain of permanent physical and psychological damages. They have never experienced it themselves and so cannot sincerely empathize with others. At sober moments, we know that destroying ourselves is profitless and absolutely pointless. Yet when the animal tendency in us rises, it looks unstoppable...and we declare wars.

As we know, wars are not only fought by and among savages. For those who look to civilization and education as the hope of mankind against the inherent self-destruction, it is important to bear in mind that the Holocaust happened smack in the heart of civilization, in the most industrialized continent, a little above seventy years ago! Europe started industrializing in the late 18th century. Meanwhile, World Wars I and II occurred more than 150 years after. Just as that civilization, in and of itself, could not halt the savagery and madness of the Holocaust and two world wars, so the current 'globalized world' cannot, in and of itself, halt wars, nuclear arms race or the threat of self-annihilation. The mind boggling acts of terrorism and mass killings currently going on across several countries of the world need not come from men of stone age; educated and civilized men of today's civilization can, and regularly do provide enough of them. Arms (and the proliferation thereof) are made by people and used for and against people. Something is not right with all these; we know that, yet we engage in them all the same, all the time. We do not engage in them because we love them; we engage in them because we cannot help ourselves; we have been made subjects, sold to Sin. Inconsistency, murder, pretense, violence, and all that go with an unstable world are natural products of the entity called Sin. For those who think we can help ourselves, it is important to remind us that these things happen, not for want of efforts to behave otherwise. They actually happen despite those efforts. Are we not doing enough? One may ask. Possibly yes! But then, maybe we are either overrating the capacity of man or underrating the power of the forces against him. Some of the people directly involved in decisions that lead to such mutual violence are only unable to stop the animal hate that rises within them or the societal pressure that moves their hands to do what their will would not want to do ordinarily. When it begins, the rest of us often realize that despite our best intentions, we either kill or get killed.

Sin is also evident in micro habits. Consider a young man (educated or not), who possibly in response to peer pressure started smoking. He would find it difficult to stop the habit after a while even though he is aware that smoking is inimical to his health. With every unsuccessful attempt,he becomes more aggressive and often with worse appetite than before he made effort to quit the habit. He is completely incapable of helping himself. A greater force compels him back to the habit. At some point, he stops trying to quit the habit. Psychologists and psychiatrists may have all manner of (logically and scientifically consistent) explanations for the addiction, but all agree that whatever it is that holds him down is much more than physical. The same way, a young lady may resolve to keep herself chaste till marriage, not just because her mother taught her that this is proper, but because something within her, a quiet voice, keeps insisting that this is the only way to true happiness. But pressure comes from all quarters – peers, environment, young men, unwary elders, the force of her own passion, curiosity, etc. At some point, she is altogether unable to concentrate on important things. Then one day, opportunity avails itself and the sin that has lurked as thought manifests as self-defilement. Immediately after, she feels guilty, becomes remorseful and hates herself as well as her action and the object of infatuation. She possibly cries all day and vows never to repeat same. "No more", she says to herself. But afterwards she realizes that she had been drawn to the same life over and again – it had become an irreversible habit so to say. But shouldn't God understand? She asks. After a while, she justifies her act by looking at others; and comforting herself in the realization that everyone else does it. Then she reasons that if the habit were that terrible, it would not have been this rampant; so why worry? While this may sound familiar and even look casual, the scriptures clearly note that there is a living entity behind the compulsion that leads us into these lifestyles; and that entity is called Sin.

A counselor would come across a good-looking young man, neck-deep in an unwholesome, immoral lifestyle and tries to encourage him to clean up. But often, the response is "I have tried but cannot just stop"? And indeed, he has tried and failed multiple times. Such trial and error is not only in the 'big' sins; 'small' sins are not exempt. For instance, how many times have you told yourself that telling lies is not the best way of life? Afterall, we all hate lies and are put off by liars. And how many times have you found yourself the very next minute struggling to wriggle out of a supposedly embarrassing situation by embellishing the truth or manufacturing an outright lie? It is familiar terrain for many of us. We catch ourselves, and those of us with a living conscience, are ashamed we have done it again. We resolve not to ever do it again; but that resolution helps nothing. The lies stick to us closer than our skin and stubbornly refuse to let go. Neither the rich nor the poor is spared, not even the aged. Have you seen that quiet, strong, and aging gentleman? He appears everything we wish to be when we grow old – graceful, mature, confident, accomplished, and in charge. Yet he is everything but what we think he is. He might have built and ruled business and political empires; he might have great and enviable children; he might have commanded garrisons and led battles; but there is an entity always with him who has continued to rule him. This entity might be manifest as an appetite, a flair, a desire, a passion, a lust, a greed, bouts of emotion, anger, arrogance, irritability, whatever! It has haunted his achievements all life long and if it were possible, he would have uprooted it long ago. But no, he has lived and continues to live with it. He may seem to have succeeded in taming it with civility and education, but he knows more than anyone else that it is a potent force that could spring up anytime and ruin all he has labored for. When no other eye is watching or when in the company of those who know but do not mind the dark side of him, he indulges himself a little. We may refer to him as civilized, honorable, distinguished, amiable, gentle, and lovable, an achiever or whatever else. But he is a slave to sin and self – civilized and honorable slave; amiable, gentle, lovable, and achieving slave, yet a slave all the same. Depending on how much fear of God such person has and the light of the Word of God available to him, he would either be frustrated and ashamed, hate himself and the indulgence or he may just find satisfaction in the fact that no one knows that bit of him. If he is frustrated and cries out to God for help, then there is hope for deliverance. But many of us would not. Instead, we build walls to hide behind. We hide behind the public image that we put up, the smiles that we intend should communicate otherwise, the lying assurance that things are not as bad as our conscience may portray. But the 'demon' that threatens to embarrass us is barely under the skin. The envy, the backbiting, the self-pity and the haughtiness are all matters of opportune time. Despite all efforts and previous seeming successes at taming it, the monster remains no less a monster. And we know he is there. Some no longer listen to conscience and have ceased to care about what anyone says; they just want to be left alone. They have quit trying to save themselves or be saved by anyone; and would not want to be judged by anyone. They care less about God and man and give themselves over to the passions that rule their lives. But once in a while, gnawing fear peeps from beneath the outer camouflage they wear. At such times, the nights seem unusually long and frightening. Often without knowing it, they end up being slaves of men's opinions and company, reveling in the 'good' company of those that hold and appreciate same opinions as they do while avoiding, antagonizing or discountenancing any contrary opinion. The nights can be quite a dread; they look forward to the daytime when the company of others would reassure them. Meanwhile, they are completely oblivious to the fact that God may be very close to giving up on them.

One way or the other, we are all affected. Mine may be *ordinary pride. Ordinary indeed when it is in me!* We all know how loathsome it could be when we find it in others. I would regularly consider other people's pride and snobbery to be much worse than my little ego trips, but, at least, that means I know my ego trips are there. We get offended and sometimes enraged at the sight of a haughty person. Yet we smile smugly with this strange sense of satisfaction after we believe we have had a nice outing and proven our point, sometimes at the expense of someone else! Yours may just be ambition – self promoting ambition, definitely not as bad as your neighbour's anger. We agree. In some cases ambition is even applauded among men, especially when packaged in civil wrappings. The ambition leads us to manipulate men and materials for personal and selfish ends, doing 'good deeds' with intent to get men notice and possibly get indebted to us. Because the society admires and applauds amibition, those who ride on the back of others, often unjustly, to further their ends get away with it. Meanwhile, the position of Galatians 5:20 is that selfish ambition is a despicable work of the flesh. How often do we pause to realize that society is not – and cannot be – the ultimate judge on any matter? We die individually and give account individually, not as society. Besides, society is always evolving, both in terms of those that make it up and the position it takes on matters.

Many people blame God who, they suppose, knew things were going to turn out the way they did and yet went on to create man. In fact, many believe God deliberately put mankind in this trouble and stood back to watch our misery. So they imagine He cannot also be trusted to get us out of it. Others have become sceptical and come to think that the disorderliness in the world is evidence that God is not all-knowing as we claim and that He lost control of things at some point. Yet there are others who have come to think there is no God (and therefore no one) in charge of the affairs of the universe. But it is important to ask whether this weak and helpless image of a man as has been described so far was the frame God had in mind when he said, "Let us make man in our own image ..." (Genesis 1:26). Definitely not! It is abundantly clear both in scriptures and by experience. Something contrary is at work, something very dangerous, and also difficult to discern. It is the mother of death and decay. It is **Sin**.

Sin is very subtle and cannot be seen unless God opens a man's eyes. The same way we know that there is blood within us, but do not see it unless there is a cut or wound; so also does sin lie within us, hidden, yet very effective. It can work for many years before its outputs and outcomes are displayed. It can even lay dormant for scores, if not hundreds of years, if that would keep it from being noticed and fought against. For instance, given that the Lord said, "...the day you eat of it you shall die" (Genesis 2 vs 17), one would have expected Adam and Eve to die the same day they ate the forbidden fruit. Yet Adam lived for 930 years. By the time he was nearing death, it is possible he did not remember all the circumstances that led to or followed his eating of the forbidden fruit. But there would not have been any death without the sin of 930 years before. Likewise, by the time death comes to most people, they could hardly remember the sin that led to or sustained death in their lives, especially when such sins are cloaked in 'fun'.

In any case, even if we had wanted to make the connection between sin and death, we cannot because by the time death arrives, 'we are dead'. What made men realize the full implications of what Adam did was his death, but by then, Adam himself was already 'lying in state', dead! His kinsmen, who may have heard his forbidden fruit story may have forgotten it at the time of his death. Moreover, they were unable to make a link between Adam's death and the pattern of lives they were living. Likewise, many of us who see the dead today are unable to make a link between the wages of sin and our present sinful lifestyles.

Many times we see death as a later occurrence. "Let us eat and drink today ... for tomorrow we die; let us worry about death some other time" (Isaiah 22:13). We reason that the dead are dead anyway ... the living simply help bury them and ... life goes on. This cycle has been on since we exited Eden. Besides, man's helplessness over the matter of death makes man care less about it. Why bother when we cannot change a thing? One may ask. After all, both the good and the bad shall all die one day. This attitude ruins the vast majority who cling to a calamitous sense of liberty and self-indulgence thereby daring death.

Unknown to us, death is neither the end nor an ordinary event. It is the beginning of the long journey of man's immortal existence. One may question the authenticity of life after death. However, God has left us with signs (some of them negligible) that point to the paranormal. For example, our daily dreams are pointers to the existence of a non-physical world. But beyond dreams, every man has a spiritual sensing. Our intuitions tell us about the eternal God. It may be more pronounced in some than in others. Through these senses, we perceive things beyond the natural world. Many have even come to believe that entities in other worlds influence our world. Many appeal to such higher powers when they are in trouble. The apparent rise in the number of self-proclaimed atheists may deceive many who fail to notice the rising number of films from Hollywood and other climes that feature 'aliens'. And even if the entire human race decided to deny these things, individuals cannot deny their personal experiences – those strange things that happen when we are quiet, in the dark, alone or asleep. God has provided these pointers for the discerning heart to understand that "the created things bear witness to the fact that God exists so that we are without excuse" (Rom 1:20).

b. Sin is in Charge

Many persons are deceived to believe in their hearts that they are in charge – a deceit that they start off trying to sell to others, but end up becoming victims themselves. Sometimes a youth who is fed up with his parents' intrusiveness may burst out, "leave me alone; this is my life and I have to live it the way I want'. Other times a well-meaning counselor may tell us with condescending concern, "take charge of your life and quit whining; it's your life". Unfortunately, the fallacy that we are in charge is very far from the truth of the word of God. **Someone else** is in charge. Romans 7: 14 – 25 paints a striking picture of the helplessness of man and the strength of the captor over our will:

> *"We know that the law is spiritual; but I am unspiritual,* **sold as a slave to sin.** *I do not understand what I do. For what I want to do I do not do, but what I hate I do … **As it is, it is no longer I myself who do it, but it is sin living in me** … What a wretched man I am! Who will rescue me from this body of death? (New International Version).*

Does that not look like you, like me, like us all? We can admit it openly or do so secretly; it really makes no difference. We are as affected by this plague as the madman on the street possessed of legion demons and as culpable to penalty as the decomposing dead body lying by the roadside, shot during a robbery operation. We are **all helplessly sold as slaves to sin and are never in charge.** No man is more (or less) sold than others; everybody is sold to sin in equal measures. **This is why despite our efforts to hide it, sin** clings to us like a second skin, and pops up to disgrace us at the slightest opportunity. Sin, the slave driver is not always a civilized entity. It could make us do what we don't want to do. When you see an educated and quiet gentleman in a fit of rage, you should not be surprised that such person could fight in the open. He is merely a slave at service incapable of saying no to his tyrannical master – Sin.

Indeed someone is behind all these; "an enemy has done this …" declared the scriptures (Matthew 13: 28). The enemy is the one behind the wreckage of man. Yet he confuses us and makes it difficult for us to make the necessary connections and identify him as the one at work. It is difficult to trace the cause of man's failure to sin because the enemy comes in a form that appears innocent and makes him look like an angel of light (2 Corinthians 11: 14). We focus our attention on death, decay and the devastations that have come upon man and the earth, but see little of the sin behind them. We either excuse or blame our poverty, our illiteracy, our lack of finesse, our poor mannerisms, our uncouth culture, our social background, our economy, our leaders, our profession, our forefathers, our genetic make up, our lineage, our health, our personalities, etc. All that we decry on earth is death, but really the source of all the desecration is sin. Ironically, we fear death but welcome and enjoy sin. We cry out at the physical, spiritual, psychological and material manifestation of death, but are snug, lukewarm or uninterested at all appearances of sin. Those that pray at all spend whole nights in prayer vigil binding all demons and purveyors of sickness, oppression and death in their lives, but go back to meddle in lies, backbiting, and all manner of 'fun' during the day. We hardly see the link between what we pray against and the way we conduct our lives. We fail to realize that our lives breed evil that haunts us, and which we pray against. The sharp pain, grief and tears that accompany the visitation of death stand in sharp contrast to the lethargy demonstrated towards the indwelling sin. But there is no death without sin. Sin is responsible for all the woes, hurts and limitations of man. Sin has put man into bondage to the elements of this life, to principalities and to self.

Sin is not limited to wrong doings. It also includes all the 'good acts' emanating from self-will and lack of faith in and obedience to the Word and will of God. The Bible plainly declares that '...whatsoever is not of faith is sin...' (Romans 14:23). Many people devote their entire lives to doing well, in the hope that the good they did would yield eternal lives for them. But how deficient such thought is! A rich young ruler approached Jesus to know the requirements for eternal life (Matthew 19: 16 – 26). Like many of us, his eyes were fixed on 'good'. He began by calling Jesus 'good' and then proceeded to ask what **good** thing he shall **do**, that he may have eternal life? As is common, many people think that fighting sin boils down to **doing good.** Regrettably, the sin personality that is holding man captive is happy to have it so because, that way, we will never be able to get to the root of sin. This sin entity does not mind if a man is bogged down looking for what is good to do and what is bad to avoid. This is because humanity is already evil and cannot deliver anything good. An evil tree can never bear good fruit. It is the tree first before the fruit. We cannot produce pure goodness anymore. We had received a mix nature of good and evil in Eden. Therefore our righteousnesses are as filthy rags (Isaiah 64:6). While a rich young ruler was looking for the good to do and the bad to avoid, Jesus was looking elsewhere. He began with the regulars with which the young man was already acquainted – *keep the commandments...,* *thou shalt do no murder, thou shalt not commit adultery, thou shalt not steal,* *thou shalt not bear false witness, honour thy father and thy mother and,* *thou shalt love thy neighbour as thyself"*. For many, these are the end of righteousness. Strikingly, the young man insisted he had kept **all these** from his youth up and Jesus did not insist otherwise. Many are not able to come close to this sort of boast.

But one good thing was that the young 'righteous' man knew he still lacked something, which was a big leap over many who do not know they lack anything. Most are content to simply quieten their consciences with the good they have done. So when the young man pressed for what was lacking, Jesus gave him the requirement – *go* *and sell that thou hast, and give to the poor, and thou shalt have treasure in* *heaven: and come and follow me* (Matthew 19:21). It was at this point that the old nature, the will of the natural man that had hidden within the man and behind those 'good works' jumped out. Jesus was asking a man who had acquired all the world could offer, who was at the peak of control, to give it all up and come and do nothing else than follow Him *lazily* from morning till evening daily. That sounded anathema to the **doing** tendencies of the man. Suddenly, the young man was no longer as excited about eternal life as he appeared initially. He was now sullen and sorrowful. His will, the major anchor of sin, and which God insists we give up, was under test and he could not bear it. He turned and left. Perfection is not in doing good; it is in giving up one's will to follow Jesus. *If thou wilt be perfect, go and sell that thou hast...: and come* *and follow me (Matthew 19:21).* Whether Jesus would want the person following Him to do anything or not remains His to determine. This is the demand for righteousness and it has not changed over time. Doing good with the will of man and the fallen human nature is unacceptable to God as it merely serves to entrench the rulership of the flesh.

Sin has subjected everything to decay and destruction (1 John 2:17).

The man of the flesh is a sentenced slave. Esther succinctly captured the essence of the slavery and trouble of man when she approached Ahaseurus to make a plea to overturn Haman's scheme against the Jews. She told the king, "If we had just been sold as slaves, I would not have bothered, because it would not have been sufficient to warrant disturbing His Majesty. The challenge is, "for we are sold, I and my people, to be destroyed, to be slain, and to perish..." (Esther 7:4). If sin were merely a matter of being under slavery and not doing what we wish to do, it might have been a different matter, probably not worth elaborate emphasis, and definitely not worth Jesus paying a heavy price on the cross for. Sin is potent and deadly. It is the reason our great grandfathers are not here with us today; it is the reason we may not be here in the next 80 years despite our desires for longer lives; it is the reason many of our loved ones died under such painful and terrible circumstances that made us angry with God; it is the reason for so much frustration, pain and uncertainty in life; it is the reason for the absence of the peace of God in our hearts and its attending pervasive mutual fears among men and nations (the latter leading to accumulation of nuclear weapons); it is the reason for the decay of the body, diseases and sicknesses, natural disasters, pains, traumas, fear, hate, insecurity, and all those extreme and baffling wickedness we see people exhibit; it is the reason behind the continual emergence of new and deadly diseases; it is the only power in heaven and earth that can stop the hand of God over someone's life (Isaiah 59: 1 – 2). Sin is the reason multitudes will spend eternity in agony, total darkness, hopelessness and far away from God in what scriptures called the second death (Revelation 20:14).

Adam and Eve did not have to go looking for death. They merely found sin and death came as part of the 'sin contract' they signed. Death is a part of the sin-package, the **sin-gift,** which man received upon entering into a treaty with Satan in Eden. Death is not a result of sin in the sense of an indirect relationship. Death is actually wrapped up in sin; it comes through sin and both are inseparable. *"Therefore, just as sin entered the world through one man, and death through sin, and in this way death came to all men, because all sinned ..." (Rom 5:12).* So it is impossible to deal with death, remove it or avoid it wherever sin exists. One is woven into and found in the other. For as long as sin is found in a man, death has power over him. The scriptures say, "The wages of sin – the natural reward for any manifestation of disobedience to God – is death". So sin ends in death. Sin can also be called death-in-progress. "...and sin, when it is full-grown, gives birth to death" (James 1: 15). Every tendency to death and decay; every corruption and destruction, failure and disease; every damage to the fabric of man, whether physical, mental, psychological, social, spiritual or material; the condemnation to temporality, all point to one evidence – the existence of sin. Wherever sin is not present, death and the devil have no power. The devil was completely powerless over the Lord Jesus because there was no sin in Him (Matthew 4: 10 – 11; John 14:30). Yet, Satan used sin of others – jealousy, anger, hatred and lies – to incite men to nail him on the cross. And His death was only possible because He was carrying the sins of other men. The moment Jesus finished with sin through death, the grave was incapable of holding him anymore (I Corinthians 15: 55).

CHAPTER 2

GENESIS OF THE INDWELLING ENEMY

a. Sin – A Subtle Personality

In Genesis chapter 3, Eve presumptuously listened to the serpent. By this act she (and afterwards Adam, her husband) disregarded God's instruction concerning the fruit of the tree of knowledge of good and evil. God judged all parties in the rebellion. But He was careful not to curse man whom He created in His image. Instead, He cursed the ground for Adam's sake, multiplied Eve's sorrows in child birth and made her a perpetual contender for Adam's heart and place. We really do not understand in full what happened in Genesis 3. But by the time we get to Genesis 4, God mercifully tried to x-ray the nature of the man living under sin through the story of the sacrifice of Cain and Abel. The events leading up to the murder of Abel present food for thought.

In Genesis Chapter 4, we were introduced to the first fruits of iniquity – the children born to Adam and Eve. Cain was the first to remember God and to remember sacrifice. The scriptures say that"… in the process of time it came to pass, that Cain brought of the fruit of the ground an offering unto the Lord". We are not told that Cain was either instructed or compelled to do so. He, of his own accord, took an offering to God. But for some reasons, God did not honor Cain and his offering; Cain's sacrifice meant very little to Him. There have been numerous speculations as to why God did not accept the sacrifice of Cain. But one thing, shown by subsequent events, is clear; Cain's heart was not right before God in the first place. When eventually his brother took an offering to God and God accepted it, Cain was very angry. We know God was not arbitrary in accepting Abel's sacrifice. Yet He did not altogether reject Cain. Instead, being merciful, God waded in to see if He could stop Cain from the self-destruct path that he was in and deliver him from the entity that had taken hold of him. God saw something Cain was not able to see and kept warning him to bring him to his senses. But the man was already a captive of sin and sin would not release him until he killed his brother and made himself a vagabond. When that happened, God could no more come in with warnings but judgment.

Cain probably thought he had every right to be angry and to express it. First, he was the firstborn but his younger brother was stealing the show. Cain reasoned that by his position, he was entitled to respect (including from God as many of us presume we are today). Cain was the first to think about offering a sacrifice to God. There is no mention anywhere in scriptures of anyone offering sacrifices to God before Cain. Intellectually, Cain was a pioneer per excellence; he held the "copyright" or "patent" over sacrifices. But ideas have more to do with the head than with the heart and it could be dangerous when a good head is not supported with a good heart. Unfortunately, God was more interested in the heart and brother Cain failed in it.

Most men are abundant in sacrifices. We are full of good and religious ideas like Cain. We are eager to spend our time in the house of the Lord, rather than watch our hearts' attitude towards God and fellow men. Severally, we have wished our perceived competitors evil. How many times have we secretly rejoiced when things turned ill for someone who wronged us in the past or with someone who appeared to be doing better than us? Have we ever found ourselves coveting our brothers' gifts and wishing we were in their shoes? Have we ever been angry even at a good work simply because we were not the ones that initiated the work or the ones at the centre of its execution? Some of us who are very competitive in nature sometimes find it impossible to empathise with someone's ill-luck because (s)he used to outshine us. Now this is food for thought for all those who put so much faith in sacrifices. We disobey God in the secret and think we can placate Him in the open by giving fat offerings or doing some good to another man in the name of God. It is important to note that all the men God applauded in the scriptures were men of faith and obedience. Samuel captured it perfectly when he observed, "It is better to obey than to sacrifice" (1 Samuel 15:22).

We also saw that Cain was very wroth and steamed within himself; but God was proactive. In His mercies, He did not wait for Cain to understand the implications of an evil heart; it was almost certain Cain would not. God confronted him. *"And the Lord said unto Cain, why art thou wroth? And why is thy countenance fallen?* (Genesis 4: 6). God saw that the anger was simply a prelude to a major disaster that Cain needed to be warned about. Just like many of us, Cain did not understand the danger of the precipice he stood upon, but God did. Cain simply thought that he was expressing himself. He was unaware that someone else, a much bigger monster was on the stage and wanted to act out his personality. But God knew the monster and his intentions. God also knew how he intended to work it out and spoke out to Cain. He told Cain, "If thou doest well, shalt thou not be accepted? And if thou doest not well, **sin lieth** at the door. And unto thee shall be **his** desire, and thou shall rule over **him**". The Amplified Version of the Bible puts it thus, "...and if you do not do well, sin **crouches** at your door; its **desire** is for you, but you must master it". The New International Version renders it as "...if you do not do what is right, sin is **crouching** at your door; it **desires** to have you, but you must master it". Let us consider what this testimony of God means for our understanding of the nature of sin.

His, him, crouch, desire and have are all active words associated with living things. The first implication, therefore, is that sin is a living, active being. We undoubtedly know of some animals that crouch – mostly carnivorous animals of the cat family. Most animals that crouch also pounce. In the same way sin crouches (as it did when Cain was merely downcast and angry), and pounces (as it did when it led him to murder his own brother). God warned Cain that sin desired to have him, but that he must master it. A deeply profound statement – *sin desired to master, conquer, devour and swallow man*! The idea we get out of this is that like a wild cat, sin crouches and waits patiently for its prey. After God warned Cain, he obviously did not take heed to himself. Therefore, he fell into the net of the beast waiting by the door. And it pounced, devoured and had him, leading him to lure his brother away to the field for the first record of bloodshed. It is important to note that we are unaware that up to this point, Cain had ever seen a dead person let alone seeing a murdered person. Who then taught him to kill by murder? Well, sin did. The bidding that Cain did at this point was no longer his, neither was it God's; it was sin's.

The fact that sin is a living, active being stands in sharp contrast to the idea that many of us have that sin is an abstract entity. By no means! We are not sinners because we commit fornication; rather we commit fornication because we are sinners. A man is not a sinner because he tells lies; he tells lies because from birth he is steeped in sin. Often preachers make the mistake of giving unregenerated men the impression that the problem is what they are doing. We tell them to stop cheating and gossiping, to do away with drinking and womanizing, to do well and make their ways straight. But this falls short of the whole story. No matter how much a sinner tries, he just does not have the capacity to overcome sin. David said "Behold, I was shapen in iniquity; and in sin did my mother conceive me" (Psalms 51:5). We are shapen in it. Our structure arises from it. We can help our sin only to the extent with which we can help our bones and blood. It is a part of us and our actions simply emanate from its being. A man thinking of stopping a particular sinful act as a means of becoming free from sin is akin to one planning to pluck the fruit of a tree as a way of removing the tree. As long as the tree remains alive and in good condition, at the right season,, the fruits will come forth. Sin is NOT an act, definitely not an inanimate act. It is a personality, a force and a potential captor which has intertwined itself with us. There is apparently no difference between us and Sin.

For many Christians, the fight against sin boils down to nothing more than what we do or say. Many kind-hearted teachers and leaders of virtually every religion in the world teach their followers to do well and avoid evil. Hence, renowned men of all climes and ages claim that there is no difference between Christianity and other religions. Many Christians believe that. The reason is that our own Christian teachers also taught us that to do good deeds and avoid evil is the framework upon which the faith of Jesus Christ hangs. But that is one of the greatest fallacies of Sin itself. Such teachings have managed to simplify our enemy to one inanimate, abstract concept that we can easily overcome by more attention and obedience to the law. But this is contrary to the witness of God in the story of Cain and Abel and in the rest of the Bible. Indeed, this teaching amounts to rubbing balm on a man whose throat has been slit with the hope that the balm would heal the flesh and cause the man to come back to life. But the truth we perceive after listening to God talk to Cain is that sin is an intelligent, active and tactful being. This understanding is also supposed to shape how we interact with and position ourselves against sin. When fighting an inanimate object (assuming it is plausible to do so), one does not need to guard against a counter-attack because an inanimate object does not have the capacity to retaliate. There is no need to fear while cutting down a tree that it will hit back in retaliation or that a stone being quarried might get angry and fire back at the worker. Apart from accidents, no such thing can happen. But it is not so with sin. Sin thinks, acts and pounces in response to whatever actions we take against him and indeed, he does not wait for us to take action against him. Sin is usually the one on the offensive. Paul said that after teaching others, he is quite stringent upon himself, lest he be a castaway (1Corinthians 9:27) He was actually referring to sin turning around to make him odious before God.

Sin does not crouch everywhere; it crouches at the door! It is not difficult to know which door because in Revelation 3:20 the Lord announces "Behold I stand at the door …". It is the door of our heart. Sin crouches at the door of our heart, implying that it does not live outside us. Sin is by the heart (the innermost part of man) and so is intricately interwoven with the man. No matter how close another human being may be to us, they have no access to our hearts. But sin does. And he does not stand at the door; he crouches at the door.

Even the Lord, when he comes to our heart, stands and waits. But sin crouches, and pounces from the door of the heart. The Lord waits for permission. Sin does not; it acts of its own volition and against the will of the man. One does not crouch unless one is after something and wants to hide his presence while doing so. Anyone that crouches does so on intention to catch its prey or victim at unguarded. As expected, the victim is usually overcome by surprise, suddenness, unpreparedness and fear.

Sin can come in the form of civilization and smartness. Like the servant in Luke 16, when conscience asks us, 'How much do you owe your master? We will ordinarily reply, 'I told a lie'. But sin, taking advantage of society and civilization, would not allow the victim to call it a lie. It will rather tell him like the deceitful servant: "Now take up your pen, and write 'I was smart'. So we replace 'telling lies' with 'being smart'. Likewise, where we see fornication and adultery, we are told to replace them with 'love and flirting'. Where we see covetousness and greed, we replace them with 'appreciation for good things of life' or better still, with 'being focused and ambitious'. Where we see cruelty and hatred, we replace them with 'self-defense, tact and realism'. Where we see faithlessness and doubt, we replace them with 'using our heads and being rational'. There is no manifestation of sin that has not been coated in societally acceptable regalia. In reality, these coatings merely help to fortify the deception of sin, but they do nothing to reduce its potency and ultimate deadliness. Until we are in the firm grip of death, sin will make us believe that we are in charge and that there is really no serious harm in fiddling with it. But God is not mocked. He never has been; nor ever will be, "He that soweth iniquity shall reap vanity ... (Proverbs 22:8).

Describing this same deception and covering that characterizes sin, the Holy Spirit says in 2 Corinthians 3:15, "But even unto this day, when Moses is read, the veil is upon their heart ..."Veil upon their heart? The curtain that makes it difficult to see things clearly lies over men's hearts. I am sure a regular fellow walking down the street will consider a preacher mad if the latter tells him that there is a veil over his heart. It never occurs to an unbeliever that a veil is over his heart.

This is simply because the carnal man knows nothing about the veil being there in the first place. It sounds like delusion to talk about a veil over a man's heart when the same man can reason well, logically put things together, analyze issues, come to conclusions and take decisions. But this is the witness of the Holy Spirit and we know it is true that upon every heart, that is yet to turn to the Lord, there is a veil - the veil of sin.

Most men believe they know. But man acquires knowledge only from searching and observing things, then logically coming to conclusions. That sort of head knowledge, which is what many are acquainted with, is only useful for the material, physical life and is completely different from spiritual knowledge of God which is the knowledge that gives life. Spiritual knowledge ascribable to God comes by 'opening up'. A matter simply opens up and we know that this is it! There may not be any logical sequence to arriving at this 'this is it', but the one to whom it is opened simply knows and is convinced that 'this is it'. Sometimes, he may not even know or be able to describe how he knows, but he knows that he knows. There is a world of difference between the knowledge that comes by observing and the knowledge that comes by revelation. Jesus said to Peter, "Blessed art thou, Simon Bar Jonah, for flesh and blood has not revealed this to you, but my Father which is in heaven" (Matthew 16:17). How did Simon Bar Jonah know that this is the Son of God? It was not by evidence, not by observation, not even by his having hung around Jesus; it was by revelation.

No man clings to God without this revelation. Education does not place advantage on individuals in knowing God and the lack of it is not a disadvantage to anyone either. Being a professor of theology does not make a man more capable of grasping and manifesting the truth of God any more than those who are unlettered. At some point in His ministry, the Lord Jesus said, "I bless thee o Father, for thou hast hidden these things from the wise and revealed them to babes..." (Matthew 11:25). Those that are wise have a particular kind of knowledge, but the Lord was thanking His Father for giving revelation, not to these wise men, but to babies. It means that what the Father gave to the babies was different from what those we consider wise have. Those wise men nailed Jesus to the cross and persecuted the Church as they tried to establish their traditions, but the babies that received the revelation went on to bear fruit, make disciples and grow the kingdom of God. What the Lord gave to the babies was all that was required for eternal life; the wisdom of the wise profited them nothing.

The effectiveness of sin is in its ability to deceive. That is why the first point of salvation for a man is the realization that he is a sinner. The moment a man knows and acknowledges that he is a sinner, he is able to see through the deception of sin, see his helplessness and cry out to God for help. Then, and only then, is hope on the way for him. Sin only triumphs when a man is deluded from this truth.

b. What Really Happened in Eden?

We have made the point that all of today's troubles emanate from sin. And we are told that sin came into the world through one man, Adam, in the Garden of Eden. It is possible that many, like me, have read the simple account given by Moses about the fall of man in Eden and in their minds wondered how the simple symbolisms, interactions and descriptions given there about the origins of sin could be in sync with the cruelty, decay, tortures, troubles, and death we see today. Many believe there is more to the story than is given out in the Genesis 3 account. Some have reasoned that if what is written is correct, then God overreacted. Else, how can you associate the terrible pains of today's life with the fact that two persons ate a fruit (probably a grape)? How can the misdemeanor of a couple come right through the generations and affect us in the 21st Century to the point of death, pains, sicknesses and the persistent calamities of daily life? Were there other issues that we do not know of and what could they be? If there were, why were those things not explicitly outlined in the Genesis account? If Adam and Eve really sinned against God and He was so cross with them and would not forgive (despite what we know of His mercies), why not punish them and let the rest of us alone? Is it really true that Eden marked the beginning of sin, punishment and death or was the story contrived to give credibility to the scriptures? Was the serpent-eve-fruit story a parable or not? Was the fruit actually a fruit or did it represent something deeper, which the Bible would prefer not to call by name? Many questions! Really many questions!! And the way the Bible simply tells the story does not seem to help matters. It summarizes everything in just one chapter and then ... it's all over. And the rest of the big volume is dedicated to diverse incursions and repercussions of sin, as well as efforts to rescue man from the damages of sin.

So what really happened in Eden? For the believer reading Genesis 3, it is important to bear in mind that spiritual things are spiritually discerned (1 Corinthians 2:14) and because it is not a story book, the scriptures present spiritual truths in condensed language. That was why men often went away because "the teacher was teaching in parables". Therefore, for us to understand what happened, we have to fall back on the Holy Spirit who authored Genesis 3 to explain it. And He did explain it. Roman 5: 12 – 14 says, *"Therefore, just as sin entered the world through one man, and death through sin, and in this way death came to all men, because all sinned – for before the law was given, sin was in the world. But sin is not taken into account when there is no law. Nevertheless, death reigned from the time of Adam to the time of Moses, even over those who did not sin by breaking a command, as did Adam, who was a pattern of the one to come* (New International Version). First we note that *"**Sin entered** the world ..."* Entry implies getting into a place that one originally was not in. Sin *entered* into the world at the fall in Eden means sin was not originally in the world prior to then. That means that something bigger than just exchanging and eating fruits happened. **Sin entered the world. There were only two men in the then known world. Impliedly sin *entered* man; enveloped him; became part of his nature, mingled with his blood and got entrenched in his heart**. The nearest analogy to this is to imagine a cup of poison poured into a bucket of water. It enters the water; mixes up with the water and makes the water permanently unusable. This is not easily discerned by reading the story of the fruit eating, but it is there throughout the pages of scriptures. Sin entered; sin did not touch, it did not brush, it did not wave. It entered! When such entering happens, it changes the nature of what it has entered. The poison that enters water changes its nature. In most instances, such change of nature can only be reversed by complicated processes. For instance, just sieving water cannot make it pure when there is poison in it; a more complicated process like heating and distillation may be required to make it safe for drinking again if possible. This can help you understand why moral instruction, lecturing and sermonizing (including the Sermon on the Mount) are not enough to deal with the redemption of man from sin. It is the reason Jesus had to go to the cross and pay a heavy price. The man formed in Eden was permanently destroyed and made useless for any form of spiritual work by the contamination. God could find no way of using the old carcase; the only option left was to dump the old entity and build something new – Jesus, the last Adam.

Significantly, this is where many religious leaders miss the point. Most religions, including some segments of Christianity deal with sin through instructions and penance, In giving the instructions and penance, it is assumed that adherents might be allowed to inherit heaven if they stick very close to good, keep their involvement in evil very minimal or completely abstain from sin. Others go one step ahead to teach that God would compare our good with our evil and reward us based on the net outcome. In that case, it is important to rack up as much good as possible so that they would cancel out the evil we could commit in our lifetime. Yet some others rely on enforcing strict codes and laws to keep the sinful man in check. How useless all these are in dealing with the sinful nature! What these approaches fail to appreciate is that sin **entered** us. It is not just what we do; it is not just what we say; it is not just what we think; it is us; it is who we are. Sin mixed up with man and became a part of him. The sort of entering discussed here and throughout the scriptures is that which changes the state of the person it entered. The same way God breathed the breath of life into man and man became a living soul, so did sin enter into man and man became *'dead in trespasses and sin'* (Ephesians 2:1). The enterance of the breath of God turned a lifeless entity into a living being; the enterance of sin turned a living entity into a dead object. In both instances, the nature of the entity changed structurally and permanently. What turned up after the enterance was completely different from what existed before sin entered. Thus, for God to restore the man He created in Eden, He must first re-infuse life into the lifeless object that was left after the enterance of sin. That is also why Jesus would insist severally and at diverse times "I am the bread of **Life**" (John 6:48), "I am the Resurrection and the **Life**" (John 11:25) or "I am the Way, the Truth and the **Life**" (John 14:6), "This is **life** eternal, that they might know thee, the only true God and Jesus Christ, whom thou hast sent" (John 17:3), among many other declarations of the kind. These words were meaningless to the Jews whom Jesus was speaking to because it takes revelation to appreciate them. But those who stuck with Him till after His resurrection and many more through several generations have proven how utterly profound and life-changing these simple statements are. Whoever is able to see beyond Jesus the Son of Joseph and Mary, Jesus the great teacher and prophet, and all the other condescending appellations that men have given to the Lord and goes on to touch Jesus the **life** bears witness that He transmutes men from death to life. This transformation is experiential for all willing to ask for it.

Sin resides in our hearts and thoughts. The scripture says, "And God saw that the wickedness of man was great in the earth and that every imagination of the thoughts of his heart was only evil continually (Genesis 6:5). This was God's conclusion about the working of sin in man as far back as the first generation, before the destruction of the first earth. And it is noteworthy that it was not just about the acts of man. Issues about the **thoughts** and **imaginations of the heart** seem to be more prominent in that verse. Unfortunately, these are so deeply engrained within that no amount of lecturing or enforcement of codes can get to them. The thoughts of a man are locked up so deep within that except a man permits, no words, action, or threats of others can ever get to them. When a man decides to close his mind, it is only God that can get across to him. Man was created in such a way that no one, by whatever means, can reach the innermost recesses of another except the listener grants him access. Codes enacted to check indecent dressing, bullying, gossiping, extremism and the like are wholly incapable of dealing with the deep recesses of the heart, the spring-source of thoughts. Scriptures called men 'inventors of evil' (Romans 1:30). Most of the homilies and laws that we give merely deal with the superficial, outward part of the challenge. They are of no use in dealing with the highly sophisticated and compromised source of the sin, the heart. Attention to legal codes and instructions is similar to trying to keep the surface of a pavement clean by sweeping away dirty water when there is a stream of flowing gutter water underneath pouring endlessly on the pavement. And that is why in the plan to deal with sin, the Lord Jesus would not stop at the Sermon on the Mount and go back to heaven. He knows it is not enough, so He proceeded to the cross to effectively provide a solution to sin. Consequently, without leading a man to the cross and helping him understand its place in redemption, we cannot help a man under the slavery of sin.

There is yet another perspective to this. When sin entered, the human entity became 'dead in trespasses and sin' (Ephesians 2:1). He stepped down from his lofty image-of-God position. There was something man could see, feel and hear before sin came that he stopped seeing, feeling and hearing immediately he had contact with sin. He entered another world. The first world of spiritual light (image) and capability (of God) got lost the moment man contacted sin. A thick blanket, so to speak, came over him separating him from the world of light and leaving him in darkness. His heart and understanding became darkened and he lost sight (Romans 1:21; Ephesians 4:18). His capacity to hear spiritual language and have spiritual feelings ceased. The only way the Genesis 3 account could describe what happened was that 'the eyes of them both were opened...' (Genesis 3:7). Interestingly, when their eyes were opened, what they saw was nakedness. It is strange that a man, whose eyes opened, would only see his nakedness. They had been (at least physically) naked prior to this moment and all the while, they had eyes and saw other things or rather, saw things in other realms. When their eyes were opened, they became limited to seeing nakedness, self-consciousness and the world around them.

The same process that suddenly got their eyes to see what they could not see before also automatically closed them from seeing the things they could see prior to this time. There would have been no opening to something unless there was a closing to another.

'The eyes of them both were opened', even in day-to-day parlance, connotes there was something they can see now that they were not able to see before. Such language is often used of someone who was led astray and who suddenly came to his senses. It can also be used to relate to either an insane or drunk person who 'came to' himself from his insanity or drunkenness. When a drunk or mad man wakes up from his drunken state and realizes that there is no clothing on him, he quickly grabs one. But it would have been difficult to get him put on a cloth if the influence of the wine or madness was yet to clear. This is because he lives in a world that is completely different from where the regular person lives and sees things that are different from what the regular person sees. He is comfortable with his environment. When the influence clears, the same person comes to a different environment and sees from a new and different perspective. His sight and speech all change again and become consistent with the real world. It is the same personality. The only difference is the environment in which he lived at each point.

As we see the depth of effect alcohol and madness can have on their victims, it becomes easy to appreciate in a little measure the sort of changes that happened in Eden as Adam and Eve 'came to'. Unfortunately, they came from the positive to the negative. The brilliant and powerful world of God's presence they lived in suddenly shut down and their eyes opened into another world. All spiritual capabilities vanished and in their place were impotence, darkness, and an empty world without God. Then they noticed…they were naked! Naked to the elements and hazards of nature, to animals they no longer had control over, to sin, the devil and his demons, naked to hunger, lack, sickness and death. They were overcome by fear. What followed was natural – they hid. They hid behind leaves and ran behind trees as there was nothing else to hide behind. They became ashamed of and afraid for even their bodies and sewed leaves to cover them. They could no longer face the animals and heard sounds of invading spirits that had overtaken the world. It must have been a very fearsome experience for the two. Suddenly, they heard the sound of God approaching – and ran even more vigorously. They definitely noticed a difference between the world they had been in and the world they had entered.

They noticed the difference between the two worlds because they had been in both. But children born to Adam who never saw the first world their forebears lived in would never appreciate the difference between the two. All they know is the one they inherited after the fall, which we all live in. They may imagine that first world, but they have not experienced it. They do not know how much real that world is or by how much it is better than the one they are in. Thus, a man may live in the present dark world and genuinely not believe he is in darkness because he has never seen the world of light. Everyone who ever went on evangelism, taking the responsibility of pointing men to the Light will attest to the fact that the natural man responds with arguments and reasonings. He may even take offence the moment you try to point out to him that there is darkness around him. He simply does not know and severally does not care because he does not know of that better world of light.

The darkness that enveloped man also cut short his spiritual sight. Before sin, God could trust Adam to name millions of animals. Adam most likely did not have to go round the entire earth to find and name the animals. He probably sat at one spot and from there could see each animal, and automatically conceive names for each of them. God did not alter the names not only because Adam was authorized to do that work, but also because Adam was in tune with God in the naming. This is spiritual sight and capability. But Adam lost that at the point of fall. The fall implies that he fell from a realm of height and started operating at a lower one, what Romans 3:23 calls falling 'short of the glory of God'. Unfortunately, this came with lots of constraints. The realm of light where he operated with God was quite different from the realm of darkness into which he came after the fall. Spiritual darkness and a blanket fell over Adam and he became constrained. He could no longer see God and what He does. He could no longer effectively have contact with the spiritual world which he originally belonged to. He was ostracized, cast out and made incapable of returning. The Cherubim and Flaming Sword were there to ensure he never did. And except the One who placed them at the gate removes them, Adam is helpless. Likewise now, except God removes the Cherubim and Flaming Sword at the Gate, no man can come into experience of Life.

Prior to the fall, God was the centre of Adam's existence. God could come in the cool of the day for communion. He saw and was seen by Adam; they interacted. There is no record of God coming in the cool of the day after Adam's fall. Adam got into a realm where neither he nor God could meet each other. God's hands could no longer reach him (Isaiah 59:1). Adam became like a ship at the harbor whose rope was cut off while the engine was switched off. The life of God could no longer flow into Adam or flow out of him to his environment. Meanwhile, Adam was not structured to be self-sufficient; he had to have an anchor. Therefore, when the heavenly anchor was cut off, Adam had to search for anchor elsewhere. That was when and how his environment, mere things and other men became important in his life. What is now known as society became influential in Adam's life. He was created to please God, but he could no longer see and reach God. What he saw and could reach was his immediate environment. So he promptly replaced the pre-eminent position God occupied in his life with resources and men in the environment he could see and touch. Today, men and women consider career, money, relationships and societal norms and opinions, among others as critical for their survival. They may not publicly admit to it, yet they lean on and defer to these mundane items because the hollow created by the absence of God has to be filled.

The fall terminated man's right and power to rule the earth, and made him impotent before spirits and physical creatures. God said He needed to make man so he could "**rule** over the fishes of the sea, the birds of the air, livestock, all the earth and all creatures..." (Genesis 1:26). When man was finally created, God instructed him, "Be fruitful and increase in number, fill the earth and **subdue** it, **rule** over the

fish of the sea and the birds of the air and over every living creature"
(Genesis 1: 28). Altogether it is obvious that God meant for man to
bear the rule. He used the word 'subdue' to buttress His intention.
'Rule' and 'lead' are synonymous, yet they do not mean exactly the
same thing. To understand why He wanted **rulership**, it is important
to realize that man was the only creature made in the image of God,
capable of communicating with and receiving from God and passing
on to the rest of creation. Everything God created had been certified
good. But the devil had already sinned, been chased out of Heaven
and was probably responsible for the voidness of the earth reported in
Genesis 1. He could 'hijack' any creature (as he did the serpent) and
use same against the purpose of God. The creatures did not have the
power to resist the devil. Therefore, since God purposed to commit the
earth to man, it became important that, to stand effectively for God,
man would be given the same nature and dominion as God. To take
charge, man had to draw instructions and authority directly from God
and use same to rule. Man's government should not be by consensus
because none of his subjects had the capacity to receive directly from
God. And he could not govern of his own accord because he had no
inherent power of his own and the enemy he is up against is older,
subtle and more knowledgeable.

The 'ruler' man must continually be in submission to the direction
of God and draw life from Him (God) for his kingdom to be both
effective and capable. The instruction to rule came with clearly
outlined responsibilities consistent with the gap God wanted man to
fill. The Scripture says, "And the Lord God planted a garden eastward
in Eden; and there He put the man whom He had formed...to **dress** it
and to **keep** it" (Genesis 2:8,15). Other versions of the Bible use similar
terms: "to tend, guard and keep it" (Amplified); "to work it and take
care of it" (New International Version); "to tend and care for it" (Living
Bible); "to cultivate it and guard it" (Good News). Adam had two jobs
in Eden. The first was captured by the words translated *dress, tend,
work, etc* by different versions of the Bible. The Hebrew root word
used here is *abad* which means to work, to serve and to labour. It is
a generic word that could be applied to work on things. God asked

Adam to work the Eden ground or offer service to man (as Jacob served Laban) or service to God (in terms of delightful worship service with joy). So which of these does the reference to dressing, working and tending here imply? It could not be to Eden; Adam had no obligations to Eden. Besides, Eden was in perfect shape and needed no further improvements at the time God put the man in it. In fact, from accounts of the scriptures, it was yet to rain. So God was referring to delightful worship service. Eden was to be a dedicated worship centre where God could meet with Adam, where God would come down in the cool of the day and fellowship with man, empowering man afresh to fulfill the responsibility of being his representative on earth and rule over the creatures.

What God was referring to when He asked Adam to tend Eden was not a farming occupation or service of labour on the land. We read in the earlier part of the same chapter (Genesis 2 : 4 - 8), "This is the account of the heavens and the earth when they were created. When the Lord God made the earth and the heavens – and no shrub of the field had yet appeared on the earth and no plant of the field had yet sprung up, for the Lord God had not sent rain on the earth and there was no man to work the ground, but streams came up from the earth and watered the whole surface of the ground ... the Lord God formed the man ... Now the Lord God had planted a garden in the East, in Eden; and there He put the man he had "formed". So Eden was fully planted, cultured and nurtured with trees that were already yielding fruits before Adam was put in it. The implication here is that God did not design farm work for Adam as some have suggested. Adam did not need to add anything to God's design. Everything he needed for food, including the tree of life to live forever was in Eden. Rather, God intended Eden to be the comfortable operational headquarters of His ambassador, a place where He (God) could come down to, fellowship with him and pass on necessary grace with which the man would move to the rest of the earth and keep things in order.

It is against this background that we begin to grasp what was intended in the second assignment that Adam was given in Eden namely: to "keep it, take care of it, guard it, keep it in order, etc." The root word here is 'shamar' meaning hedge, watch, protect, attend to, preserve, reserve and save. Each of these words connotes that Adam was like a guard and organizer, saddled with the responsibility of maintaining order on the earth, beginning from the vicinity of Eden. He was to preserve the deposits in Eden, hedging against intrusion by any unauthorized entity. The verbs used to describe Adam's function in Eden convey the possibility that someone could creep into Eden and spoil things if Adam was not watchful and careful. In fact, it was this person that God instructed and equipped Adam against. In the book of Revelation the consequence of the defeat of the devil and his angels in heaven is described in these words: "...But woe unto you inhabitants of the earth and seas, for the devil is come down unto you, having great fury, because he knows that his time is short (Revelation 12:12). So Eden was supposed to be the beginning of the extension of the defeat in heaven upon the earth. So his responsibility was not necessarily like that of a farmer as much as it was like that of a warrior; a military guard. But he was also instructed and empowered to 'be fruitful, multiply and replenish'. That way, Adam was supposed to multiply his kind and from Eden take charge of all the earth, as mankind obeyed the instruction to 'subdue and have dominion'. Because he was carrying the life of God, Adam (and consequently his offspring) would take over the earth, preserving and securing every part of it from any form of defilement and insurrection of the devil. That also explains the reason why deceiving Eve and taking mankind off that lofty, divine and powerful height that he had occupied was the devil's first responsibility; a do-or-die battle that he must win or forever lose relevance and future on the earth.

c. Disobedience – 'To DO' or 'To BE'?

In Genesis 3 Satan told Eve, "You will not surely die ... for God knows that the day you eat of it (the tree of knowledge of good and evil) your eyes will be opened, and you will **be** like God, knowing good and evil". To a large extent, Satan was correct. As usual, his lies began with some elements of truth; their eyes were indeed opened! But subsequent events showed that Adam and Eve never imagined the implications of their eyes being opened. They obviously did not expect whatever was to come to be as dire as it turned out to be. As the serpent correctly indicated, their nature was changed; they actually **became**. But they did not become like God; that which they became was completely contrary to what God is. All the capabilities, wisdom and righteousness of the Godhead were gone from them. Instead of a powerful representative of an all-knowing God, wearing the image of God, they became slaves to sin, the world and the devil. But at least, they became something different from what they were and to that extent, the devil was correct. Once again, the devil has managed to tweak the truth to produce lies that seemed believeable but which outcome was drastically different from what those that were entangled were made to believe. Adam and Eve's shock at the turn of events after they ate the fruit is better imagined. How would they have known that such a simple acquiscience to the serpent was going to produce such dramatic fallouts? How would they know have known that they would become completely incapacitated, thrust out to darkness and made objects of such grim violence as we see today? How would they have known that it was not only death that would occur but that long years of suffering, including working on cursed land, and battling sicknesses would follow from the consideration they gave to the words of the serpent?

So it becomes important for us to consider the contents of that enticement. The enticement was not for man to start acting in a particular way, it was for man to **become** some particular thing, something like God. It was for man **to be**, not **to do**. To **be** like God! The enticement may have started with what the man should do, but the ultimate aim is what the man should become. Of course we know there is a difference between what the devil told man he would become and what man eventually became. There is also a wide difference between what man is and what God is, but the devil was correct when he informed Eve that they would become something different. They became something different from what God intended and what they were before they ate the fruit. So what did they (and eventually us) become? The Scripture has several descriptions for it. Ephesians 2:1 and Colossians 2:13 call it 'dead in trespasses and sins' while Ephesians 2:2 calls it 'children of disobedience'; Romans 6:17 and 20 call it 'slaves to sin'; with the spirit of disobedience working in them (Ephesians 2:2).

In effect, sin pounced on us, drove right through us, took up our nature, enfolded us, became part of our lives and nature and made us take its own nature as well. It demobilized what we were to make us what it was; we died in it. We took the nature of sin and became interwoven with it so much so that there was no difference between us and sin. In summary, we did not just commit sin, we **became** Sin. This is the tragedy of the fall, the less discussed, less known part of the great outworking of the man of iniquity in all flesh. But it was at Adam's instance, through obedience to Satan. Remember a man is a slave of whomsoever he obeys (Romans 6:16). The moment Satan got the nod from Adam, he promptly jumped into him and took over his nature and his faculties. In effect, Adam ceased to exist independent of Satan. Adam became a captive of the enemy in his thoughts, decisions and actions. Christ's teaching ministry could not redeem man because it was not about what man has done. Instead, Jesus Himself **had to become sin** so as to be able to save those whose nature was sin. In becoming, He had to die and in His death incorporate and bury the sin of man out of sight so that the empty carcass that remained could be refilled with the life of God and used for His purposes.

Even Adam's desires were taken over such that he no longer did what the original Adam would have been interested in doing. He longed for and did what this invader in him wanted him to do. He was overpowered and suppressed to the point of dormancy and incapacitation. His own desires became overwhelmed by the more pronounced and aggressive desire of the new landlord. Each of us understands how this works in his own life. For instance, severally we are overwhelmed to desire or do wrong things we would ordinarily not have wanted to do, sometimes after we have condemned such things in others. Sometimes, we fantasize about the thought or go right on to perform the action. But Jesus warned that it is not just about those that sleep around but that those that fantasize about fornication are not guiltless either. So the questions arise - who is it that wants to commit those evil acts, who is fantasizing about those iniquities and who is behind the pleasure we seem to derive from thinking about the indulgence? The reality is that there is someone underneath who regularly has the better of us. It is the man of sin in us and those things we cringe from are his delights. That is his nature.

Hydrogen and oxygen are both gases. However, when under given influences they fuse, water emerges, and water is completely different from either oxygen or hydrogen. We learn in science that there are two kinds of such fusion – the mixture and the compound. For a mixture, the separation is easy and reversible, but not for a compound. The substances that come together to form a compound 'partially' lose their individual identities or are at least not easily identifiable in the new material. Sometimes, what appears as the end product is completely different from what either of the two materials was before the fusion. That might serve as an instance of what happened to man, but it is still an insufficient analogy. In the fall of man, sin retained its substance and originality, but man who was subsumed lost a significant part of his original character. As such, the prominent characteristics manifested by man are those of sin that subsumed him. Even though we still see some fine prints of the original glory of God on man once in a while, they are so subdued that their manifestations are usually sporadic and weak. In addition, even when they do manifest, they are hijacked by sin such that the end product itself is considered a filthy rag before God (Isaiah 64:6). Consider a man who sees a helpless, poor person on the street and stretches out his hands to help and to make something good out of his life – noble act! But when he goes home and is alone, his heart goes through all that happened again, and he thinks within himself 'what a nice man I am! How helpless and worthless that man's life would have been without me!' Later he runs into a conflict with the one he helped. Anger wells up in his heart as he wonders who this 'rat' thinks he is. At that point, he fails to see how ordinarily helpless he himself is and that his very life is free gift from God. By thinking in this way, what started as the manifestation of good ends up an abomination to God.

The random shots of *righteousnesses* that we see in our lives could becloud us from seeing our dire need of holding unto the redemptive work of Calvary for the washing of our souls unto salvation in Christ. In fact, many people think that if only they can behave better, act in a little more civilized way, be generally good, then they will enter into the kingdom of God. Many in the church of Jesus Christ preach Jesus as the only way, the truth and the life. They preach the necessity of salvation, but do not sincerely believe that piousness on its own cannot take a man to heaven. They see the 'good works' of the unsaved and conclude that God cannot be so mean as to throw men of such good behavior into burning fire for eternity. We abhor sin and believe God should punish us for it, but we think that the way out is to counter our sins with good works. In several instances, gruesome penalties like crawling on the knees for kilometers on sharp stones, sitting in the dung for days taking in stench, being flogged with metal coated canes, starving for days, etc. are regularly prescribed to atone for sins. But how helpless these things are in saving man! They amount to self-punishment for the acts of sin and not the destruction of the nature of sin. Paul said "such regulations indeed have an appearance of wisdom (semblance and indication of sensibility), with their self-imposed worship, their false humility and their harsh treatment of the body, but they lack any value in restraining sensual indulgence (are useless in dealing with the tendency of the flesh to self-indulgence)" (Colosians 2:23 – New International Version). If the fall was anchored on what **we did** either before or at the advent of the devil, then we could seek redress in the things we can do now and our present or future good intentions. But it was anchored on what **we were,** what we sought **to become** and of course what **we finally became**. All through the Bible, references are made to what we were, how we were born and what we were made of. It is about the nature and constitution of the individual. And a wrong understanding of the issues at stake leads to a wrong therapy and a wrong approach towards solving the problem of sin. David declared that he was (and all of us were) shapen in iniquity and conceived in sin (Psalms 51:5). The Jews told the man born blind whom Jesus healed in John 9:34, "...thou wast altogether born in sins ..." These passages refer to the nature of all men and reinstate the fact that we are moulded of and in sin. Since the fall of Adam, our shapening, conception and birth as indicated in those passages happened in the laboratory of sin. The raw material and the machine with which we were formed all came from sin. So the blood flowing in our veins and the thoughts flowing from our hearts are all those of sin. Our surname by birth is **sin** and we are *incapable* of pleasing God, not by our nature and definitely not by our acts. In effect, trying to undo sin by doing good does not help a man get nearer God. This does not mean God has absolutely no regard for sacrifices. But when God senses the sincerity of the heart of a man, how he is struggling with good works, He treats the man the same way He treated Cornelius. In Acts 10, God told him to send for Peter, who will tell him what he should do. Peter's preaching generated faith in Christ, which was immediately followed by salvation and then the outpouring of the Holy Spirit. That salvation encounter that leads to cleansing through Christ is a pre-requisite for any meaningful thing that must follow in a man's relationship with God. And it is free; it can never be earned!

The Bible describes what we currently have as "the sinful nature" – a nature; not an outcome of nurture. The difference between two dogs – one trained and the other wild – cannot be the same as the difference between a dog and a man. Two dogs have the same nature even if the other is better trained, but a man and a dog have different natures. A dog, even with the best of training, can never have the capabilities of a man. The difference between the man before and after the entry of sin is as stark as the difference between a dog and a man. It was a complete change of nature. The new personality that evolved after the fall was no longer a living soul, but 'dead in trespasses'. There was no change in the outward form, and so those that judge by the outward miss the point. Nebuchadnezzar's experience was something similar to Eden. When Nebuchadnezzar would not humble himself after much warning, God gave him the soul of an animal but made him retain his entire body and physical appearance. The highly revered and powerful king could have been discussing with his cabinet when God suddenly handed him the soul of an animal. He was still looking same, but could no longer understand human language or reason like a man. He had acquired a new nature and this nature does not drink tea; it eats grass. It does not mind the sun or the rain; it thrives in the bush. No amount of preaching, rationalization and explanation would make Nebuchadnezzar sit on the dining table or address a press conference at this point. He would have to head to the bush. His nature was changed and the things that appeal to man no longer appealed to him. We see this altering of personality also in smaller measures in mad persons.

The change in Eden was holistic. The man who moved out of Eden was structurally different from the one inside it. That is why scientists who refer to man as species of animal may not be altogether incorrect. In the original nature in which God created man, that would have been a complete derogation. But in man's current nature, such reference is close to the truth. The poison spread to all tissues of the body and soul of man to the extent that even God did not have a purification process that was capable of healing and restoring man to what he was. So the only way out has remained to kill and discard the old man, remove everything that is of the old stock and pour Jesus into the carcass. The personality, mentality, nature and nurture of the old man are all decaying material and God had to now take the pure stock of Jesus and put into the empty vessel as a way of now creating a 'new man'. This is the why a tinkering Christianity that tries to get something better out of the old man is no use. All those teachings about 'the giant within', 'the better you in you', 'the power of the inner self', are mere shams. Within each unregenerate man lies a monster that has made himself manifest a number of times as he took man on a rampaging spree. When, as has been the case through the ages, man wields power without checks, we see wholesale carnage. Think of all the Idi Amins, the Hitlers, the Maos, the Stalins and Lenins, among several others who were railroaded by ambition and societal silence. Every man is like them. Indeed, what differentiates us from them are training, societal norms, access to power and other external pressures that have the capacity of restricting and civilizing the demon in us. Without the Spirit of God in regeneration, man is but a beast.

d. Sin and the Two Deaths

In the eyes of man, Adam and Eve did not die the same day they ate of the fruit. Instead their eyes merely opened in line with Satan's prediction so to say. This stood in contrast to the threat of God's word, "...in the day that thou eatest thereof thou shalt surely die" (Genesis 2:17) as both of them lived for hundreds of years after being driven away from Eden before they finally died.

One would wonder, was God economical with the truth? Was the devil correct in mentioning to them that their eyes would merely be opened and they become like God? Could it be that their eyes being opened amounted to the same thing as being dead? Of course! We know God told them the truth because He does not lie. The difference, however, is that while God called that opening of eyes 'death', the devil deliberately made no mention of death in connection with it. Note the devil's words, 'ye shall not **surely** die. For God doth know that in the day ye eat thereof, your eyes shall be opened, and ye shall be as gods, knowing good and evil' (Genesis 3: 4 – 5). The "surely" was the trick of the enemy; the foundation of the entire falsehood and deception. Being as gods (all the other fallen angels) and knowing good and evil served as the baits of the enticement into sin. To God, the eating of the fruit was already death in process – a denaturing of the man He created and an eternal separation between God and man in time and eternity; but the enemy deceitfully blindfolded them from the progression of the death they had contracted.

Adam and Eve died immediately after eating the fruit according to the word of God. That death was initiated by and as sin – a monster that jumped into and took over their lives, killing the original personality instantaneously. That was the death God was referring to which we do well to refer to as spiritual death. In Adam's word, they were naked and afraid, but in God's sight and definition, they were dead, 'dead in trespasses and sins' (Ephesians 2:1). However, there is another death, the death of the physical body (the physical death). This latter death, though more obvious to and feared by the spiritually undiscerning, is really not the main death. It is merely an outcome of the first death. It may take its time (and it regularly does take a lot of time), but for as long as the spiritual death has occurred, it will surely come. Part of the reason why all men must partake of the physical death is that all were born into spiritual death in the first instance. The Lord Jesus has been the only person not born into spiritual death as He did not carry in Himself the seed of man. It has been a puzzle to many that God allows 'the righteous' to also die. But reality is 'there is none righteous, no not one (Romans 3:10). For all have sinned (Romans 3:23), beginning from the womb, into infancy and all through life.

But right there in Eden, we also see God initiate the process of redemption of man. While He declared His verdicts on the man and his wife, He also notified the serpent that the seed of the same woman would bruise his head. It seemed to the devil that he had won the war when he felled man, but God's wisdom was way ahead. Contrary to the expectations of the devil that the corruption of man in Eden would be the end, God announced to the hearing of all parties that He was not going to completely destroy man and start all over with a new agenda. His plan to have man oversee the earth remained unchanged. Indeed, the devil did not know that the creation of Adam was only God's plan B, but which He thrust forth first, knowing the enemy would make a dash to destroy it. His plan A has always been the slaying of the Lamb, which was concluded before He even laid the foundation of the world (Revelation 13:8). In that plan A, God would fuse Himself into man and lead a generation of those that willingly choose His ways, crush all rebellion and establish a kingdom where man will govern the affiars of the earth. That fusion was to be in and through Christ, the Seed of the woman. Christ will be at the head of that generation of mankind and all that shall partake of the era should have willingly and willfully submitted themselves to God.

CHAPTER 3

THE TASKMASTER PER EXCELLENCE

a. The Enemy is Driven by Fear of Man

Unlike God, sin is violent and compels compliance from man. It tries to get a man to act contrary to his convictions, using force or any form of coercion. Sometimes, the compulsion may not come from force, it may just be a psychological coercion or a subtle threat to socially ostracize a man for refusing to comply. For instance, many among the Jews believed in Jesus when He was on earth, but because the leadership of their day had already made it clear that whoever confesses Jesus as the Son of God will be thrown out of the synagogue, some that believed kept it to themselves. That is coercion and it is the nature of sin. Sin uses such coercion because it knows it can never obtain willing compliance from man. Every man is under the rulership of sin by compulsion.

Sin is the greatest taskmaster ever. It distresses the life of the man living in it. The Bible captured it succinctly that "there is no peace for the wicked" (Isaiah 57:21). He does not exaggerate; every word there means exactly what it says. There is no peace for the man who hobnobs with sin. Elsewhere in John 16:33, Jesus told His disciples "In the world ye shall have tribulation ..." That sounded like persecution, and indeed, that was what He was directly referring to. But also, by that sentence, He outlined the guiding rule that sin and the world are all about tribulation. Sin is a heavy burden for the the bearer. In referring to it, Christ said, "Come unto me all ye that labour and are heavy laden" (Matthew 11:32). We see a typology of the relationship between man and sin in the experience of the children of Israel under the hand of Pharoah in Egypt in the book of Exodus. At the onset of the book, we are introduced to the Israelites that have now become a numerous (what the Bible would call mighty), yet weak and oppressed nation in the land of Egypt. Note the counsel Pharoah took with his people:

> "Look the people of the children of Israel are more and mightier than we; come let us deal shrewdly with them, lest they multiply, and it happen, in the event of war, that they also join our enemies and fight against us, and so get up out of the land." Therefore they set taskmasters over them to afflict them with their burdens. And they built for Pharaoh supply cities, Pithom and Raamses. But the more they afflicted them, the more they multiplied and grew. And they were in dread of the children of Israel. So the Egyptians made the children of Israel serve with rigor. And they made their lives bitter with hard bondage – in mortar, in brick, and in all manner of service in the field. All their service in which they made them serve was with rigor (Exodus 1: 8 – 14).

From the above passage, we find out that Egypt had no problem with the Israelites except as it relates to the latter's multiplication. The afflictions, burdens, bitter bondage and rigorous services were all because the Egyptians feared that the Israelites may someday gain freedom from their slavery. Likewise, Sin and its allies (the principalities in charge of the world system) have a potent fear of man – the fear of God's mandate on mankind. Nothing else could have made Satan more envious than that a living soul made from the dust of the ground (Genesis 2:7) could possess the image of God and have dominion over every creature, and replenish and subdue the earth (Genesis 1: 26 – 28). Which earth again? "I thought I had been cast down to the earth", Satan wondered (Revelation 12:12 -13). This was sufficient reason for the devil to attack humanity so viciously with the intent to steal, kill and destroy the man carrying the seed of God and with the mandate to 'be fruitful, multiply; fill the earth and subdue it', just as the Israelites in Egypt carried the seed of God and therefore were multiplying because of God. And just as Pharaoh urged his people; so does Satan. There is a note of urgency in his voice as he shouts everyday, 'Let us deal shrewdly with them, lest they multiply'. So also, sin is minded on immediate annihilation of mankind. Indeed, if not for the mercy of God that saves us despite ourselves, the whole essence of sin is to completely wipe mankind off the face of the earth as quickly as possible so as not to give a chance for the purpose of God to be realized in man. The enemy continually devises new methods to oppress man. But in nearly all cases, the success or otherwise of the methods depend on man's limited understanding of what is at stake, and consequently his inability to resist the allures and oppression of sin. When he is ignorant of his placement and generally remains in rebellion against the only power that could rescue him from the power of sin, he will not understand his worth nor the fear in the heart of the enemy. Had the Israelites known that the Egyptians' numerous whips and multiplication of their sufferings were only expressions of innate fears for the emerging heroes, they would have used their comparative advantage against Egypt; their reaction to the oppression would have been different from mere tears and pleading. When Moses appeared with mandate to take them out of the land, Pharaoh's response was to first increase their hardship. The elders of Israel then met with Pharoah to plead and when that failed (as it always will), they turned on Moses and Aaron saying *'the Lord look upon you, and judge; because ye have made our savour to be abhorred in the eyes of Pharaoh, and in the eyes of his servants, to put a sword in their hand to slay us' (Exodus 5:21)*. Likewise, man does not know the fear in the kingdom of darkness, which is the reason behind the frenzy of oppression. So man's reaction has been that of defeat to sin and expression of helplessness.

b. Busy ... Multiplying Sin

The means of oppression are legion. Satan's priority is to capture the mind of man. Given that the mind is the navigator for everything else in life, capturing it makes the devil able to control man's perception of everything, holding him captive through subjectivity. The moment the mind is captured, the rest is easy. He puts man under physical and emotional pressure all the time. The Egyptians set taskmasters over the Israelites who forced them to build store cities – Pithom and Ramsees. But think about it: since the famine in Egypt was over, what did Pharaoh and the Egyptians need storehouses for? What were they storing and for what reason? The truth is that there was nothing specifically to store! But it was important to keep these men busy and not allow them think and grow. Every morning, the men gather as slaves and work rigorously until late and they become so exhausted that they are unable to also reproduce and grow. They could no longer sit back and ask questions or even organize. All other forms of productive action were tedious. Meanwhile, what they built was neither needful nor meaningful.

The same way, humanity is kept busy building storehouses for sin, for a Pharaoh that knows neither Joseph nor the God of Joseph. We are always under pressure, stressed out and burned out. Many run out of their houses before the first light of the day and return long after dark. No one is at rest, we all just keep working; and it is severally difficult to specify what it is we are pursuing. We are worked up and out, sometimes just to meet the most basic needs of the body. And should we seem to have met the basic needs of the body and therefore want to stop and ask questions, the taskmasters will arise on our backs. They remind us that the family would all die off; that we would leave the table where we are currently eating from and eat from the floor; that we would be left behind by time, that we are yet to meet our targets, etc. So we are kept busy, working, and restless. Nearly all men on earth are victims of this pressure. Interestingly, none of the things we work for are ours. All we have to show for all the labour is our daily meal and even that comes with lots of sorrow and pain for many people. Many of the things that we gather often dissipate while we are still alive. The rest dissipate after we die. But even where they do not dissipate, we still die empty-handed. We are forced to leave them, sometimes to irresponsible descendants and sometimes to an irresponsible society; either of which hardly recognizes the labour we put in. So we are all so buried, busy and engaged, yet unable to take any lasting thing out of the busyness. We have been sold to sin, which captures our minds, does not allow us to ask questions and is not prepared to answer the questions if we ask them. But this is just an aspect of the enslavement of sin.

Many men may think they understand why they work. But do they? Some believe they are working for their children or working for their retirement. For some, it is the love of their jobs that drives them to work. Some work for 'humanity', thinking to leave the world a better place than they met it. These all sound attractive and ideal. But are these reasons really as logical as they sound? Instances abound where the children for which many worked would have had more peace after the parent is gone but for the wealth left behind. The children get at each other's throats and scatter all the wealth in the process. Often, when we see these, we tell ourselves that there was something the man did not get right which must be responsible for the lack of order in his house. But this is not always so. Sometimes, the children could all be great friends, and the father could have drawn a great will, but somehow, an unanticipated spirit of greed takes hold of one of them and everything goes wrong from there. But even where there is no problem, the children might just not be great managers of the wealth such that in less than one generation after the man is gone, all he labored for vanishes. In retrospect, the man lived for nothing; all he thought he lived for had scattered. Likewise, it is great to work for one's retirement. But as we know, the financial system everywhere is one of the most unstable things ever built by man. So one could scrupulously do his own part only for the system to collapse just at the time he needs to start drawing from it. 'Working for humanity' seems quite appealing. But who is this 'humanity'? While it may seem difficult to fault the man who wants to leave the world a better place than he met it, it is important to remember that whatever is not done in and by God does not endure. Sometimes, a man finishes working for humanity in his active days only to see all he has done reversed or dismantled by others who do not share his convictions. Nothing endures, and humanity does not have the capacity to know (and want) what is good for itself. We should work for men, but we must also acknowledge the limitations of such 'good intentions' especially when they are not based on explicit instructions from God.

c. A little Sin-burden for Every Man

Sin is a great taskmaster in more ways than one. There is no (natural) man on earth who likes all aspects of his life. There is this great contradiction mirrored by Paul in his letter to the Romans which every man born of woman identifies with, "For we know that the law is spiritual, but I am carnal, sold under sin. For that which I do I allow not, for what I would, that do I not, but what I hate, that I do" (Romans 7: 14 – 15). Most of such things which we allow not, but which we still find ourselves doing constitute the things that we would never like to be brought into light. We sometimes feel sorry that we do them, but we get back to them at the next possible opportunity. The reason is simple: we are sold under sin, and our master is a terrible taskmaster. He dictates to all men and does not care about our wishes. Once in a while, he will appeal to our desires and aspirations. But when such appeal fails, he resorts to commands and compulsion. For him, the end justifies the means. So when he is not able to convince the young lady by appealing to the elegance and intelligence of the young man who has been hovering around her, he would whip her body with passion and make it impossible for her to concentrate on anything else until she crumbles. Often, it is only after crumbling that we 'come to our senses'.

The interesting thing about the compulsion of sin is that the Sin entity does not load every man with every sin habit or sin manifestation. That will be deadly. And in any case, it is really not necessary. Any one sin is alright; sin is content to just get a man to manifest any of the parts of the body of sin. No one man needs to manifest all of them; the important thing is to be put the victim on the wrong side of God. Is it not He that said 'do not commit adultery' that also said 'do not kill' (James 2:11)? According to that scripture, if someone commits only one sin, but does not commit others, he is a transgressor of the (whole) law and an enemy of God. The issue here is not about how many things wherein a man sins; it is about participating in the sin project, no matter how seemingly small such participation is. It is about disobedience to God; any disobedience will do. And Sin understands this. And indeed, overloading any man would make the need for help from God obvious and that might defeat the whole aim. It is important that the man does not even know he has a problem. So Sin finds it unnecessary to load any single man with many sins; he just leaves each person with few (at times just one) major sin (some prefer to call it fault), a couple of minor faults, and of course, several good attributes. The role of the few good attributes is to consolidate the veil on the man and make him oblivious of his need for God's righteousness. That is why that gentleman does not need to be a drunkard or robber; it is enough that he merely keeps anger. Another person inherits instability in character and speech; that also is enough. Indeed, the more 'civilized' the society is, the less the need for very obvious manifestations that could place the bearer at odds with others. At such times, pride and vanity can solve all the problems. But in less enlightened societies or during periods of crisis, it becomes obvious that most persons carry all the basic manifestations of sin in about the same degree. Men who would ordinarily knot a tie and sit in well-furnished offices for corporate board meetings in normal times may have no qualms raping a lady or maiming a fellow man during an armed conflict, riot or war. A man who would shudder at the thought of telling lies at normal times would have no moral challenge cheating another to meet his needs during a crisis. Sin is rebellion against God and the nature of manifestation of the act of sin at any point in time is simply unimportant, irrelevant.

But that is also where Sin and the Devil have managed to score a major point in deceiving man. They have made man to believe that there are major and minor sins. In civil courts, we have managed to classify sin into those that are criminal and those that are civil. This would not be a problem if it ended in human courts, but most often the pulpits have left worshippers to believe that this classification is extended to heaven and is the same in the valuation books of God. Indeed, such classification could be considered welcome and important to maintain minimum law and order. But in the court of God, it has no place. The place God is preparing for those that love Him accommodates only those without spot or wrinkle – nothing that defiles can get into it (Ephesians 5: 27; Revelation 21: 27). God has prepared only one place for all sins and all that are sinful. The account of those that will go into eternal condemnation in Revelation 21:8 starts with the sort of sin none of us ever classifies as sin in the first place, let alone as minor or major. Scriptures say, "But the *fearful*, the *unbelieving*, the *abominable* ..." before it goes on to the more obvious ones " ...murderers, whoremongers, sorcerers, idolaters, and liars ..." and insisted that they all shall have their part in the lake which burneth with fire and brimstone: which is the second death. The issue at stake with God is the nature of man, which produces those manifestations, and not necessarily the manifestations themselves. The reason why even the fearful will enter the same place as murderers is that both are birthed by the same nature – the sinful nature of man – and both need to be wiped off if the purity of God has to reign at all. For God is light and in him is no darkness at all, neither major nor minor darkness (1 John 1:5). All sins, minor and major, proceed from the same source – the carnal mind (the seat of sin) "...which is not subject to the law of God, neither indeed can be" (Romans 8:7). But for the devil and his cohorts who are in control of the body of sin, it is both safe and comforting to see man classify sins arbitrarily. The arbitrary classification permits us to also be selective in the ones we attend to and the ones we let go. And he knows that for as long as we take such positions, we cannot really fight for complete liberation nor can we totally abhor and fight the root cause of all sins. Meanwhile, he is happy enough if he is allowed to keep just a little part of us, because big or small, such part makes us his and keeps us in enmity with God.

The very purpose and essence of sin is to dominate man. From several references in the Bible, it is easy to see that the main issue at stake between man and sin is dominion: the complete overpowering and subjugation of one over the other. Romans 6:14 notes, "For sin shall not have dominion over you ..." Fact is, no natural man (one under sin) is in charge of anything though it does not often look like it. A man may have issues with gluttony and drunkenness even though he ostensibly has firm grip of himself in other areas. Or a lady may merely be vain, but is otherwise very kind and patient. This appears to be a contradiction. Every man is either wholly under sin or not at all. At any point that sin engages a man on a matter, it is merely the part that is convenient or that sin requires of him at that point. It does not mean that sin cannot engage him in other ways if need be. How many times has a man who is known to be very gentle, straightforward and even fearless been involved in a major scandal? People are often baffled that such a man has such tendencies? Neither his past nor his present is a pointer to this character flaw. At such times, the devil is blamed. And it is not wrong to blame the devil because, indeed, sin (which is of the devil) is responsible. But the fact is, sin actually chose to engage him in that role for that moment even though it has not been doing so in the past. When it became necessary, sin forced the man (against his own will) to do things that would lead to scandal. This is what dominion is all about. When people are under subjection, their lords do not go about everyday managing their day to day lives. It is enough that each party knows the relationship. When the lord wants anything, he simply demands it and it is done. The same goes for sin. He does not need to manifest everyday and in every way. It is enough that when sin wants any man under his dominion, he gets him. As long as the Israelites were busy building, the Egyptians need not be anywhere in sight. But the moment they stopped work, the taskmasters appeared and then the whip.

So what could be driving this insane torture garage that the Egyptians set up or the larger torture system set up by the devil? The whole purpose of sin is to destroy the work of God. The Lord Jesus said "The thief cometh not but to steal, to kill and to destroy ..."

(John 10:10). God created man to be 'a little lower than the Angels, (crowning) him with glory and honour, and didst set him over the works of (His) hands" (Hebrews 2:7). On earth therefore, man represents God's best. The story of Job outlines the justice question at stake following the devil's ouster from heaven. Was his rebellion typical of all creatures with free will or could God actually create perfectly free-minded creatures that will turn over their wills to God without compulsion and for no other reason but that He is God? Man was the only creature with freewill and so would have to be the only way of proving this. When God boasted about Job, Satan was swift in his response, "Does Job fear God for nothing? … " That was the research question. God's hypothesis was that Job did, but the devil's position was that it was impossible for Job to do. As costly as that research was, it had to be conducted transparently so as to put all arguments to rest. If God conducted it, the devil may yet accuse him of partiality. So it was necessary that the devil took charge of the process; hence he received authorization over Job. In Job, God overcame. In Jesus, He also overcame. And just like these two, every other man intending to receive eternal life from God has to also be tried. Only then could the eternal sentence on Satan and his cohorts pass the test of divine justice. As in Job's story also, God sets limits for the devil in dealing with those who have yielded their will to God. For those who are yet to submit to God, resisting the devil is nearly impossible; there are no limits. The devil will continue to drive such a man until he completely destroys him; there is very little God can do.

When the Lord says, "Come unto me, all ye that labour and are heavy laden…and I will give you rest, take my yoke upon you and learn of me, for I am meek and lowly in spirit, and you will find rest for your soul", He was referring to a system He knows all too well. Sin is a labour-driver. Take the example of any sin and the pattern is the same …and very predictable. Sin loads a man with hard labour. To illustrate this, we will use the more obvious sins that many of us are very familiar with. Take unforgiveness for example. Can you imagine a bigger jailer than unforgiveness? When someone is imprisoned in our hearts, we often are the ones laboring under bitterness. We have to monitor the prisoner lest he escapes and then have to always bother about the next 'deserving' torture to give him. The presence of the offender stirs up putrid gall in the heart, a discomfort that could become indescribable depending on the level of bitterness held against him. This gets more difficult when the one against whom forgiveness is withheld may be completely unaware of either his offence or the fact that someone has aught against him. So he might even be enjoying himself right in the presence of the one who is withering under pain and bitterness without even knowing the pain he is causing. Unforgiveness is a labour, a very uncomfortable labour. The story is told of the teacher who told her pupils to carry a tomato fruit for each person they bear grudge against. As they carried the tomatoes around for a few days, the pupils began to complain about the discomfort emanating from the decaying fruits, which gets worse by the day. The teacher explained to them that the same (or more) discomfort and stench ooze out of each unforgiven offence. So why carry it around? We carry it around because sometimes we just cannot help ourselves. We know we should forgive, but each time the heart recounts what was done against us, the bitterness is renewed. The renewal may result from the fact that we think the other party is not deserving of forgiveness. It may also come from the fact that we notice this mild pleasure in the thought of revenge; it would be such a delight to watch that culprit drink from the cup he prepared for us.

But there are several instances where we carry grudge and unforgiveness around because we do not even know we are carrying it around. How so many times we think we have forgiven when in actual fact we are far from having done so! Like other sins, unforgiveness can be very subtle. Many times, we imagine an issue with someone else has been dealt with until something similar happens; when the same person offends in the same way and under the same circumstances. Then this irritation or outright anger springs up. We justify it by the fact that the culprit should know better and has no reason repeating a mistake. Well, when the Lord Jesus said to forgive seventy times seven in a day, it was because He knew such recurrent offenders will always be there to touch an open sore. The challenge is not in the one that touched the sore, it is in the fact that the sore exists and remains a sore in the first place. If there were no sore, he could have touched us without the sharp reaction. And that sore is evidence that the offence remains unforgiven. Sometimes we wrongly classify these offenders among those whom the Lord said would better be served if they drowned in the sea with milling stones around their necks. But the Lord was referring to men of deliberate iniquity, not those who out of ignorance regularly offend us. He has harsher words for those who hold others in prison in their hearts even after they have received forgiveness from the Father above.

As with forgiveness, so it is with other sins. Take stealing for example. A thief is never at rest, whether before or after the crime, not even when he is not planning an operation. The planning of a robbery or break-in is usually tension-soaked. The execution is with a lot of looking over one's shoulders and standing tight to ensure nothing goes wrong. When the act is completed, the thief begins another round of watching, being on edge to ensure that his path is covered up and that the law does not catch up with him. Fornication goes with significant prick on the conscience, at least until one is able to effectively shut the conscience down. In decent societies, shutting the conscience down can be a very tedious job for individuals. Some societies, by trivializing or even accepting fornication as a norm, have made this task of shutting the conscience down easier for individuals. But of course, public opinion is of no consequence in eternal life. Pride does not allow its carrier to rest. For as long as there is some seemingly better person around, the proud man is restless. Pride is linked to covetousness (which is idolatry). Pride is not only uncomfortable with persons; it is also uncomfortable with things. It continues to accumulate, just to be in front.

d. "Being Good" Makes No Difference

It is usually a difficult task trying to prove that being a nice fellow does not make one right with God. Every person on earth needs the gospel to be saved. No man is good (Matthew 19:17). Absolutely none! But the fact is, not many (even among many professing Christians) really believe this from the depths of their hearts. We see some unregenerate people as good in themselves and do not deserve God's wrath because they appear kind, gentle, patient, temperate and possess nearly all the virtues many professing Christians are still struggling to acquire. So in our minds we ask, "Why bother them?" What else can the gospel turn them into or do for them?' Unfortunately, harmless as the question may seem, it not only questions the verity of God's word on the matter, it also dims the zeal with which we set out to pray and to preach to these good but unregenerate persons. Many have also perished because of this deceptive perception.

We hail good works in people but admit to the imperfection of man in flesh and blood. Sins of violence are clearly anti-social and they generally threaten the corporate existence of man. As such, it is easy to agree that those whose sin is associated with violence and destruction really pose a potent threat. By that same token, those whose sins do not pose a threat to the existence of others are generally more acceptable. In fact, some men's sins promote the happiness of others. For example, a man's pride and vanity (especially when backed by material means) can lead him to community service and philanthropy which benefits other members of the society. Yet, the word of God is an unbiased standard for acceptable righteousness. According to the scriptures, God wants us to be holy in all manner of conversation (1 Peter 1:15); the hallmark is, "be ye holy/perfect as your heavenly Father is holy" (Matthew 5: 48)

Man's definition of good and evil culminate in the 'ways of man' while God's definition of good and evil are 'the ways of God'. The challenge is that many people think their perception of good and evil must be the same as God's perception. Thus, when they make effort to avoid 'evil' or to do something 'good', God should be pleased. Therefore, they cannot understand all this noise about having the Holy Spirit's guide on a day to day basis. They simply try to do their best on the basis of their own defintions and perception of good and evil. But how very different the two perceptions are! Throughout His ministry, the Lord Jesus contended with the ways of man, trying in both action and word to show that His (and God's) thinking is completely different from ours. In John 4, He labored so hard to show the Samaritan woman that even what she called worship was not worship at all; that God's perception of worship was completely different from the practice of her day. He ordained the twelve that they should be with him (Mark 3: 14) just so they could learn in practice how different God's thoughts and actions are from man's. So day by day, as issues cropped up, He would respond using God's thinking and perception and they would watch to see the difference. When He spoke in Matthew chapters 5, 6 and 7, we come close to seeing the difference in thinking. Consider the following perceptions in Matthew 5:

Blessed are the poor in spirit (5:3); Blessed are they that mourn… (5:4); blessed are ye when men shall revile you… (5:11); but I say unto thee, that whosoever looketh on a woman to lust after her hath committed adultery with her already in his heart (5:28); but let your communication be yea, yea; nay, nay: for whatsoever is more than these cometh of evil. Ye have heard that it hath been said, an eye for an eye, and a tooth for a tooth, but I say unto you, that ye resist not evil but whosoever shall smite thee on thy right cheek, turn to him the other also (5:37 – 39). But I say unto you, love your enemies, bless them that curse you, do good to them that hate you, and pray for them which despitefully use you (5:44). He made it clear that the reason for the latter injunctions is so that we might be "children of our Father which is in heaven, for He maketh His sun to rise on the evil and on the good, and sendeth rain on the just and on the unjust" (5:45).

In content, God's ways are truly different from ours. I wonder how many of us even desire to be associated with those words. How many want to mourn? Who wants to be reviled? Who would want to be constrained from even 'ordinary admiration' of the opposite sex? Who would not once in a while give or seek affirmation to issues of contention by (at least verbal) oaths? Who would not want to resist evil? Who would turn his left cheek after the right one is smitten? Is such a person supposed to smile or cry as he goes away? How many can truly love their enemies, bless those that curse them, do good to those that hate them and pray fervently for those that despitefully use them? How many are even genuinely happy when someone that hurt them in the past gets more blessed by God? But those are a few soundbites of God's ways, thoughts and perception of good and evil. For those willing and obedient to the ones they have heard, the Holy Spirit will show more. And whoever does not want to welcome the lifestyle dictated by those words in Matthew 5 should not think that he understands good and evil. The concept of good and evil as we learned them after the fall is completely different from the concept of good and evil that God maintains. When on the cross, even while in unimaginable pains, Jesus prayed for those that nailed Him there, asking God to forgive and not hold that iniquity against them. We see Stephen repeat it at the point of death in Acts 7:60. Was God pleased with the prayers made by these two? We all know He is. These two, and several other disciples that have followed in their footsteps, transcended the mundane knowledge of good and evil that guide many of us. Neither Jesus nor Stephen had man's sense of good and evil, of justice and fairness or of any of the other positions we often take in our relationship with God and man.

But beyond content, humanity's perception of good and evil is grossly unreliable. It changes from age to age and from people to people. It is all so subjective and depends on the world view of the particular generation and tribe involved. For example, at some point in time and in some cultures, friendship between two unmarried people of opposite sex would be frowned at, in fact punished. In another clime, it is encouraged or even celebrated. In some religions, human sacrifices are welcomed; killing men in the name of God is not a problem for as long as those killed are outsiders. But in other places, they are not tolerated. Who defines these benchmarks? Each society defines for itself what to call 'good' and what to call 'evil'. People therein then proceed to judge their actions by these definitions. But as we also know, these norms are sometimes not even products of consensus but the product of force by one group who have the authority to impose their own definitions on others. Some think their own sets of definitions of good and evil are better than others', so they instigate cultural changes that force others to adopt new definitions. But all these are outcomes of the fall of man. Whatever is not based on the infallible word of God cannot be a basis for defining good and evil. Our natural senses are largely deficient in this.

Unlike the doctrine that was taught to many of us, there is no such thing as God comparing our good with our evil and accepting us on the basis of which one outweighs the other. The principle here is that if there is a dot of evil, no matter how tiny, it belongs to the devil and God does not struggle with him over his property. Whoever has an iota of sin is sinful and there is no big or small sin because He that said thou shalt not steal is also the one that said thou shalt not bear false witness. So if a man is 99 percent perfect and has only 1 percent sin, then he is rebelling against God whom he has denied in the 1 percent zone. More worrisome, he has 1 percent of the enemy's property and so is liable unto him. And the devil does not look away from anywhere his property is, no matter how tiny.

In effect, every man needs salvation, both those that are apparently good and those that are thoroughly evil. Like a chain, every man is only as strong as the weakest point of his character. And that weakest point is not about what you do as much as it is about who you are. That is the reason salvation is not an improvement on a man's righteousness; it is a complete throwing away of all that is in a man, both his good and his bad; and replacing them with the righteousness of God in Christ which does not know corruption. When many people come to God, they expect God to take away their weaknesses and improve their strengths. But the scriptures say that the righteousness of man is like a filthy rag before God (Isaiah 64:6). Of course it does not look like a filthy rag before us but that will not make God to keep them. His ways are different from our ways. That means nothing of the man is taken by God. Indeed, the body of sin is such that it is wholly corrupted and there is nothing to take from there. So God disposes of everything and then plants a new man (Christ Jesus) in the old carcass. This is what God uses and this is what is acceptable to him. Because many do not understand exactly how corrupt and useless their old man is, they often go about trying to impress God using their talents and personal profile. That is also why many of us are offended when we are told that we must be completely born again, that there is nothing good in us and that we have to humble ourselves before God. But the fact remains that any man who does not come dropping off everything that he is and has, cannot pick up what God has provided for him. Such a person has no part in the work and kingdom of God, no matter how religious and good he might be.

CONSTITUTION OF THE BODY OF SIN

a. The Body of Sin

The most potent aspect of sin, and which again is completely hidden from the eyes of mortal man, is what Paul called 'the body of sin'. Romans 6:6 says, "Knowing this, that our old man is crucified with Him, that *the body of sin* might be destroyed, that henceforth we should not serve sin". The body of sin refers to the encompassment of all sinful acts in man. It is the source or basis of sin that resides inside of us individually.

The above description is contrary to what many perceive sin to be. Men often see the individual sinful acts (or even thoughts) and judge them by their individual strengths and inclinations. It is not unusual to see a believer who is concerned over a particular weakness in his life cry about 'my lusts', 'my instability', 'my greed', or whatever other manifestations of sin that are most obvious in his life. An unbeliever may know he is bound by sin, but it usually translates to attention to a particular sin that is pronouced in him. For some, it is the abuse of the body (e.g. smoking and drinking), for others, it is unrestrained eyes (lust and greed) while for some others, it is pride or self-will. In other cases, it might be a combination of these, multiple manifestations of sin. In many instances too, the reaction of the individual depends largely on how 'obvious' the manifestation of sin is or how deep he perceives his struggle with sin is. Those whose manifestations of sin are not too obvious try to manage without much noise. Part of the reason for these diverse reactions to sin is that sin is seen as that specific act, weakness, word, thought, or whatever else we may be struggling with. Many perceive the things we do (or fail to do) as those things which get us into trouble with God. How wrong such perceptions are! We hardly see the body of sin; that integrated complex and well-managed system that incorporates the world without, the self within and the kingdom of darkness around. That system has woven rings around every man from both within and without and work together to ensure that we are held bound on all sides.

The human body, for example, is the amalgam of systems – the respiratory, digestive, nervous, skeletal, reproductive and other systems. Each system contains a set of organs, each different in make-up and specialization, but combines with others to bring about an ultimate objective. In describing the body system, Paul noted that "For as the body is one, and hath many members, and all the members of that one body, being many, are one body ..." (I Corinthians 12:12). This means that no single member of the body is the body. A hand does not make a body, neither does an ear, leg, or any other part. Likewise, the body of sin is made up of the systems and parts of sin. No one part is *the sin*, no one system is the sin. All the parts and systems have to agree for the body of sin to function effectively. If then sin is a body, our ability to see it for what it is, how it functions and the interactions among the members will help us appreciate what we are up against, what God is fighting to deliver man from and how we can cooperate with Him.

The only purpose and determination of the body of sin is to destroy all that God has put up on earth, beginning with man who is head of that creation. But for sin to achieve this purpose, it must bring every member to absolute cooperation within the body. Unfortunately, what many of us see are isolated members of sin, not the body of sin with members. This is why many of us still deal with sin contextually and specifically. As indicated earlier, a lot of people are still familiar with this problem of 'my anger', or 'the jealousy in that young lady', or 'that man's drunkenness', 'his lust' or whatever else we might be battling with. These are sin specifics emanating from the body of sin. The body of sin may need a hand to work when it gets to the farm, or it might need the feet to carry it to the place where it needs to transact a business at any time. Interestingly, every member of the body is present at all times but not all of them are needed to work at the same rate and at the same time. In fact, there are many times when some of them may not even be needed to work at all, though they are present. It is the same way with the body of sin. When we seem to be enslaved to lies, we pray against lies, take resolutions against lies, press ourselves against telling lies, confess if we tell lies and work against telling lies the next time. But telling lies is not the body of sin; it is not the system of sin. We may fast and pray to be delivered from lies, but the problem is not lies. Lies are just the manifestation from the body of sin that is still alive in a man. Meanwhile the man does not just need deliverance from lies, he needs deliverance from the body of sin. Sin only manifested as lies because that is what is needed at that point or circumstance. It says nothing about callousness which might not be needed at that point, but which all the same is there as part of the body. Nor does the manifestation of lies in him at a point in time say anything about his capacity to envy, which is latent at the moment. In effect, all men carry all sins together. There is no sin that is absent in any man. Rather, all sins are not manifested in every man at the same time, but all of them have strong roots in every man, including you.

To see how this could work in a man's life, we look at the story of David, Bathsheba and Uriah. There was apparently nothing wrong with David, the super warrior, staying home, away from war, and taking some leisure for once. He was the King of Israel, had subdued all his enemies roundabout and was really not under any threat from anyone at this stage in his life. But when he looked out from his roof and saw Bathsheba, he did not take his eyes away. Sight was therefore the easiest point of entry for sin in this case (remember the words of Jesus about looking lustfully?). It was also the point at which he would have overcome the entrance of sin with significant ease and minimal effect on any other person. Was sight a part of the body of sin? Yes and no. Looking is not a problem for anyone, but looking usually comes with some work in the heart and therein is the problem. His persistent, improper looking was with lust and when he realized she was within reach, the lust demanded that he sent for her. That was how a mere look was quickly followed by adultery. If prior to this point anyone had ever told David that he was a potential adulterer or murderer, he would have denied it vehemently. And indeed, if the devil had come to David with the temptation of adultery, he would have realized it from the onset and fought against it. But part of the work of the body is to achieve its objectives by assigning the most appropriate responsibility to the one best equipped to do it. And usually, it starts in a seemingly innocent way and at the easiest point of entry. For David, that point of entry was the eyes. The responsibility of tracking and pinning David down was assigned to lust and by the time lust was done, the field was ripe enough for adultery to come on the scene. Of course, we know that the matter did not end with adultery. David sent for Uriah in order to force a lie on him and use him to cover up. That did not work. Then he sealed Uriah's life in a letter and asked him to carry it through Joab to the Ammonites, thereby killing Uriah with the sword of the Ammonites. Again, it would have been unthinkable for David to murder one of his most trusted soldiers, one listed among David's mighty men. Uriah was a man of heroics and had deep love for the God of Israel, David and the people (1Chronicles 11: 1 – 47). Only few men have the sort of heart Uriah had. He would not as much as go home to sleep and give himself rest because the Israeli Army was in the open. But David did the unthinkable and murdered a man that adored him that much. The body of sin knows that it would have been useless to ask David to murder Uriah (or any other person for that matter). He was not a murderer. But the way of the body of sin is to entice him through the instrument most appropriate at the time and then introduce other parts of the body at latter times. The entire range of lust, adultery and murder are from the same source. They are all parts of the same body, each merely arriving at their rightful turns and working in collaboration with others towards the same purpose of wrecking the work of God in the life of a man.

Many have come to believe in the Lord Jesus, but have merely tried not to indulge in any of the obvious sins. And in many instances, when a believer is being encouraged to stay away from subtle places and situations that could lead to deeper entanglements, some would ask 'but what is wrong with what I am doing?' The answer is 'nothing!' except that it has the capacity to draw bigger and mightier members of the body of sin. It is foolish to focus on only what I am doing now and worry about what is wrong with it when I fail to see the link between what I am doing now and what may happen next.

b. Interconnectedness of the Body

The interconnectedness of the body of sin is at four levels. First, there is the interconnectedness of the different segments and manifestations of sin. All sins are connected one to another as we have described in the David example. Second, there is the connection between sin and the flesh. The flesh is the 'I' within me that holds on to its own things. It is a major accomplice of sin. Third, there is the interconnectedness between sin and the devil. The devil tempts and points us in directions far away from God. He also suggests sinful acts. Then there is the interconnectedness between sin and the world. The world is the system of dos and don'ts, expectations and norms, beliefs and processes, set up in every society and based upon which the devil directs the affairs of men. All sins are connected to one another, to the flesh, to the devil and to the world. The devil is the supervisor or administrator of the body of sin using the world system which he set up to ensure that the body of sin is functioning. The flesh ensures that the man lusts after the world and its trappings. Without these connections, it would be difficult for the body of sin to operate as smoothly as it does. Indeed, the body of sin and/or the flesh would have no potency without either the world or the devil.

No sin is alone; every sin is connected to another. Consider the case of a well-educated, fine, and respectable gentleman in a community who recently started nursing political ambition. However in an unguarded moment or rather in the course of trying to mingle, he went with some friends to a bar and after some wine, got coaxed by an attractive lady. Under the influence of wine, this gentlemanly father of two sleeps with another woman. Prior to this moment, he was known as responsible and committed to the good of the society. But now the story is different. The messy situation all started with a supposedly harmless desire to please his friends or acquaintances which by the way are important for the realization of his political dreams. So now **friendship with the world** and **the desire to please man** led him into **drunkenness** and thereafter to *lust* after a strange woman, and eventually to *adultery*. Someone gets to know of it and tells his wife who confronts him, but he **denies** it. This gentleman at normal times would never have imagined himself capable of cheating on his wife. But that has happened. When he was drunk, lusted and went in to another woman, he never thought about lies. But the sin of adultery is supported and accompanied by *lies and falsehood*. And indeed, he might have been very honest with his wife all along until this time. So he didn't even know he had problems with telling lies. Supposing this person who got to know and had evidence starts blackmailing and threatening him with exposure. First, our political aspirant friend gets **angry**, despite that he used to pride himself as being impossible to provoke. But now **frustrated**, he plays along with the blackmailer and pays up for the **fear** of being found out. Meanwhile his campaign posters boast about his courage and fearlessness, his capacity to confront any situation, especially the current ruling class, **without fear or favour.** But now, because of the body of sin, he is living contrary to that mantra.

Sin will convince him that he is merely covering this up in order to keep his family intact, which is an honorable thing to do anyway. Then one day, he decides he has had enough and thinks of a way to quietly eliminate this blackmailing nuisance so he can continue his 'normal' life. So he plots to kill. But it is impossible to *murder* without *hatred*. Well, he does not have to work up hatred for the blackmailer; it had already grown naturally within him as he observed this scum take advantage of him to make undeserved money. Under normal circumstances, this same man would have shuddered at the thought of harming a fly, but he tells himself that times are abnormal now and he is working to restore normalcy. All the while, he comes into his house acting his usual responsible self, *deceiving* his wife and children who would readily swear that he is the most responsible father in town. If he succeeds in the plan to kill, he realizes that once in a while, his mind runs to this act and the thought he might be found out someday haunts him. He then takes to *drunkenness* and *reveling* to calm himself. What started as one harmless night out ends up attracting other sins. Even the sins we consider small are not exempt from this interconnectedness. When a man *defrauds* the company, it is because he is *greedy, covetous, lustful for filthy lucre and unclean.* Then he has to make up numbers (*telling lies*) to cover it all up. All the while, he has to *pretend, deceive* and give false impressions. Name any sinful act and it is not difficult to establish that connectedness.

Many of us never know we are capable of certain sins until circumstances requiring them appear. Sin is patient, calm and generally never shows up until required. But it is there all the same and all the time – that is the crouching we discussed earlier. Every manifestation of sin waits for an opportune time. That is why many of us never knew we were capable of some of the things we later found ourselves doing.

Doing our best to stay out of sin can subdue the manifestation of sin, but it does nothing to uproot sin from us. Meanwhile, it is this uprooting of sin that the scriptures call holiness. That is why it is fatal for any person to rely only on doing his or her best to be able to get to heaven. The word of God declares that without holiness (uprooting of sin from within him) no man can see God. This also explains why God does not just judge the outside (external actions) which deal with the manifestation of sin, but the inside, where Sin dwells. The Pharisees were well-manicured, religious and externally ordered. There was hardly any mention of iniquity of the sort many of us contend with among them. They even paid tithes of cumin and anise. But the Lord Jesus continued to be so hard on them. Yet when He met a woman caught in the very act, He promptly forgave her, dismissed her case and confounded her accusers. In certain instances then, it seems safer to display gross manifestation of sin, the social stigma associated with it notwithstanding, than to be cultured and have the sin well tucked within. The former helps the man to seek God quickly; the covering of civility that accompanies the latter veils the need to run to God. Jesus said... "if ye were blind, ye should have no sin: but now ye say, we see; therefore your sin remaineth" (John 9:40 – 41). This is not to encourage sin (every sin will be judged), but to discourage hypocrisy and covering which are sometimes more dangerous because they sustain covering that makes the sin even more potent.

The entire human nature is a nature of sin. Sin goes far deeper than the blood running in us; it is as far as the marrow that produces the blood. Sin is not something to be rooted out easily. It is engrained and intertwined with all that a man is. It is the body of man. That is why sometimes it is easier to kill a man than to pluck out sin in him. Consider a man who is guilty of a particular shameful act. For the fear of the shame that will come upon him in facing his family and kinsmen, he hangs himself or picks up a knife and stabs himself to death. What is the problem here? By openly standing and confessing what he has done, the man denies sin and is made free from it. But because sin is so deeply intertwined with his life, it is easier to deny his life than to deny the sin that is standing between him and his life. So he does away with his life and keeps the sin. Many of us are guilty of secret sins that we would ordinarily not like to be associated with. We know that it is proper for us to confess such sins. But do you remember the kind of chill that runs through your spine when you think of what it means to stand before those who have held you in very high esteem to confess to having brought yourself so low? Majority would rather die than face the shame. Pastor Adeboye of the Redeemed Christian Church of God told the story of a woman with a strange sickness that was pining away and nearing death. He was invited to pray for her. He prayed without results until he enquired from God who told him to stop praying and ask the woman what she did. When he asked, she told him. It turned out that she married a widower who had two sons from his deceased wife. Out of envy and desire to create space for inheritance for her own children, she poisoned and killed the two boys. God told the pastor that the only condition for her to live would be that she confessed the act to her husband. When she was told, she responded that it was impossible for her to do that. She would rather die than face the shame. And she died. In effect, rather than get healing by making a confession, she chose to suffer eternal condemnation for fear of being exposed. There are only few men who have no dark sides that they would rather die for than stand in the public to declare. That is how tenaciously sin would want to remain hidden. It would prefer to take the life of the person than allow the person to expose him. This lady's situation has been replicated in the lives of millions over the ages. The circumstances, scene and actors may vary, but the principles and operational modalities remain the same. Several men and women (some of whom are Christians) have had extramarital affairs, but would rather die than confess these to their partners. They would live in pretense and in the same house with their partners all the days of their lives. It is sin that holds them down, kills them by installment and gives them the impression that the shame of confession is worse than the eternal condemnation which is certain should they never get to confess the sin before they die.

c. The Purpose of the Body of Sin

Sin's main objective is to destroy the image of God in man, leave the man to his own devices and ultimately ruin him. Man was not created to live independently of God; he must always draw his supply of life from God. Knowing that God cannot supply life to a body of sin, sin enters to disconnect man from God. As is always the case, when the life is cut off from any flesh, that flesh begins to decay. Sin hinders a man from reaching or being reached by God so that he will perish forever. That is why it is heartbreaking to see many persons respond casually to the matter of confronting sin. Their response is often, 'I am doing my best'. How on earth can one do his best against an enemy of this magnitude, an enemy that he has no power over? What power has a six-month old baby against an invading lion? Doing one's best is extremely dangerous because as we have seen, sin can never be overcome by a man who is already enslaved and deceived by it. Some do not believe they are enslaved, which makes deliverance for them a lot more difficult because their mindset is altogether wrong. Sin's objective at all times is to wrap up, overcome, subdue, and eat up humanity. A mortal man in the hands of sin is like a rat in the teeth of a cat. Resolutions, self-discipline and all other measures that have been, or can be, invented by man, have absolutely no effect or power over sin. Civilization and education most often merely find a way of coping with sin; they have no real and lasting effect on it. Laws are equally useless; a law points out avenues of the entry of sin, but does not empower a man to use them.

Until a man sees his struggle against sin in the light of the great might which sin possesses, it is difficult to appreciate his helplessness and why Christ is the only hope he has for salvation. It is easier for a man to pick up a knife and slowly slit his own throat than to root out sin in himself. We just do not have the power and so cannot do our best on a matter as critical as sin. It is either God is doing something for us or we are helpless and hopeless on the matter. And God does not step in to help a man overcome sin until the man acknowledges his sinfulness and helplessness towards sin. We have to come to our wits end to be able to call God to help us. We also must come to the end of our road to appreciate His help when it comes. For as long as we are tinkering with sin, telling ourselves that we are not doing as badly as the rest of the society, there is no hope for overcoming sin. And at the root of such tinkering is a complete lack of appreciation of whom we are dealing with. Sin is a powerful enemy that has bound us completely on every side. Sin is not the little tantrums we throw in the public before we quickly come to our senses and become civil again. Sin is that weapon that stabs you with pain as you think of the shame of being paraded naked or that makes you desperate about covering your innermost weaknesses and vulnerabilities. And it does not let up. There is nothing tame about sin. It acts as the situation demands. If what is required is to be calm and calculated and poised, sin will get his captive to do just that for as long as that will let sleeping dogs lie. If sin is trapped and in a dangerous situation, it can become violent in order to continue dominating the person. It flows in our blood. But because we do not even understand him that way, we think it is something we can control with time. Sin manages to live in many people all the days of their lives without being identified for even one moment. It is only when it has eventually taken them to eternal condemnation that it freely reveals itself, because then, there is no option of repentance.

There are many who believe that time can heal sin or strengthen a man against sin. We easily imagine that as one grows old, he gets wiser, understands better the damaging power of sin and therefore works more to overcome sin. But again, this is a fallacy. Interactions with the aged easily prove that this is not so. In fact, the aged face a special kind of problem. Long years of living in and being governed by sin solidifies its hold on them so much so that they are no longer sensitive to the anomalies of sin in their lives. They become so caked in sin that it no longer sends any warning signal to them. Many old sinners simply adapt to and start managing sin. Long years of practicing civility make them a lot more mature and gentle in appearance, providing a convenient mask to the stranglehold of sin underneath to which they are in bondage. They no longer rock any boats nor are they taken by surprise. But of course, none of these implies that the man has grown any less sinful than he was when he was younger. Instead, what happens is that they are less sensitive, and sometimes can even become blind to the existence of sin in their lives. Often, it is only those around them that are able to note the arrogance, self-conceit, selfishness and other weaknesses in the old man's life. Have you ever been close to one who has been made senile by old age? Many of them manifest the raw selfishness of little babies because the covering of civility is gone.

Many others harbour sin and know it is there. They work hard to eliminate it, but most times, they deal with branches, members of sin and not the body of sin. Even in dealing with the branches of sin, the method is usually to resort to penance, re-dedications, resolutions and self-denials. But these have a show of wisdom in will worship, and humility, and neglecting of the body, but they have no value against the indulgence of the flesh (Colossians 2: 23). Some get around to seeing their need, but they see more than one part (in fact, too many parts) of the body of sin and consequently feel frustrated and see themselves as incapable of doing anything. So they give up. This is usually the case with those whose sins are manifest in very many forms here and now. They seem to have too many 'sore points' in their lives that often it does not seem to make sense to try to stop and cure any of them. Why bother with any sin when many other sins (often more grievous) are also at work? They reason, quite correctly, that there is no hope trying to solve the sin problem in their lives. This is correct. But it is just one step short of the solution, which is to call upon God through Jesus Christ. We will come to this point later.

CHAPTER 5

SIN AND SINS – THE TREE AND ITS FRUITS

a. The Tree of Sin and the Fruit of Sins

At different points, the scripture uses two words – sin (singular) and sins (plural) to depict the fallen nature of man and the manifestations thereof (John 8:24, 34). The first reflects the root while the other reflects the fruit(s). The first is the reduced nature of man while the second is the evidence of the presence of Sin. The relationship between the two is exactly as the relationship between the root or body of a tree and its fruits as depicted by several verses of the scripture. For instance, Matthew 7:16 says, "Ye shall know them by their fruits. Do men gather grapes of thorns, or figs of thistles?" And later in verse 18 insists "A good tree *cannot* bring forth evil fruit, neither *can* a corrupt tree bring forth good fruit". No one is in doubt that the reference is not to trees and fruits but to the nature of man and the resultant actions. The analogy of the tree and its fruits is very simple yet so profound that even though many of us have heard and even considered it, we have difficulty understanding and appreciating it. In some cases, as men struggle to put the world in order, there seems to be some semblance of understanding that it is important to sow the right seeds in man if we are to expect good fruits from him. But then, even the interpretation of what is or what is not the 'right' seed is not easy for most men. There would be no 'sins' if there were no 'sin'. It is the nature of sin that makes the acts and tendencies of sins possible and prevalent. The scriptures indicate this in several places. Usually when the bible refers to the first 'sin', it speaks of it as though it were a personality, whereas it acknowledges the latter sins as (set of) actions. For example, in Genesis 4:7, probably the very first mention of sin, God spoke to Cain:

"If thou doest well, shalt thou not be accepted? And if thou doest not well, **sin** lieth at the door. And unto thee shall be **his** desire, and thou shalt rule over **him**.

Take note of the reference to sin as a personality as the scriptures talk of 'his desire', rule over **him**. Cain was the first person on record that sin wanted to overcome. For Eve, it was an external serpent that misled her and brought her under control. The serpent needed to first lure her. Until she agreed, the serpent was powerless, but the moment she did, it overpowered her and gave her (and her husband) a new sight. The same personality was at the door of Cain's heart seeking to rule over him.

God did not destroy Sodom and Gomorrah because of their 'sins', but because their 'sin' was very grievous. In God's assessment, it had come to a point where there was only one way of stopping the multiplication of the Sodomite nature, and that was by wiping out the accommodation of sin, the human beings. They were the media for expression of the harbinger of wickedness. Just as every parasite needs a medium of habitation and from where it expresses itself, so does sin need man to inhabit and to express itself through him.

And the LORD said, because the cry of Sodom and Gomorrah
is great, and because their sin is very grievous (Genesis 18:20)

Several other scriptures bear witness to this. The man David said of himself, *"For I acknowledge my transgressions: and my sin is ever before me* (Psalms_51:3). Notice the plural 'transgressions' and the singular 'sin'. The first is the many manifestations of his actions and thoughts while the second is the nature behind them. He acknowledged both. Undeniably, acknowledgement of sin is the first step to salvation.

In his treatise to the Romans, Paul probably did the most justice to the matter of sin and sins. One of the first issues he set out to address was the matter of 'sin'. He sought to demonstrate that sin 'reigns' over all men. All flesh is subject to one lord and that lord is sin. In being subject, there are no first and second class citizens; all are simply subject to the lord. First referring to the Jews who had the 'advantage' of belonging to God and possibly therefore had less of the baser manifestations of sin than the Gentiles, Paul said:

> *"What then? Are we (Jews) better than they (Gentiles)? No,*
> *in no wise: for we have before proved both Jews and Gentiles,*
> *that they are all UNDER sin" (Romans 3:9)*

It is important for every man that this point sinks in deeply: no man is more subjected to sin than the other. "For we have before proved both Jews and Gentiles, that they are **all** under sin" – that is the declaration of the Holy Spirit over everything that is called flesh. That a man is decent, well-behaved, well-mannered, honest, courteous, easy going and easy to deal with while another is mean, disrespectful, rude and untamed makes no difference. Both have been proven to be under sin. I have noticed (and I know many will agree with me on this) that it is sometimes difficult to preach to decent and cultured people because we often assume that civility and the manifestation of the fruit of the spirit are synonymous. Nothing can be farther from the truth. Sin can make a man gentle the same way contact with the Lord can bring about gentleness to a man as long as that would serve his purpose at the moment. Pride, education, moral obligation towards the society, and the demand for decency from other men can make a man to be apparently decent, gentle, truthful, and sociable. But none of these make him any less under sin than the man who is more openly brutal, dishonest and selfish.

The challenge is that men try to measure the existence of 'sin' by the availability of 'sins'; akin to measuring the existence of a tree by the availability of fruits. But the lack of fruit does not mean that the tree does not exist. Not at all! A tree can be perfectly healthy without fruits either because it is not time to bear fruit or because it is not mature for fruits or because for some reasons, it is simply unable to produce fruit at the moment. None of those in any way invalidates the life of the tree. If a tree is not producing fruit today, it will produce fruit tomorrow. In fact, for many seasonal trees, the times they are without fruits are longer than the times they are with fruits. Examining the tree at any of the times it is not producing fruit and concluding by such observations that it has no life is faulty, to say the least. Measuring the amount of sin in me by the number of sins I commit is equally deceptive thinking. All men have equal endowment of the spirit of sin. Everyman comes with the same measure of capacity to sin. The difference is that while some men are born and groomed under circumstances that make the manifestation of their sins easier, others are born and bred under circumstances where base mannerisms are frowned at. One goes on therefore to produce more physical fruits of sin, not because he has a greater spirit of sin, but because the circumstances surrounding him are conducive to the production of fruits of sin. Now it does not in any way mean that the man who is not producing as much fruits is less prone to sin. It simply means the demand to manifest is far less on him and in some cases; there is no need to do so. I know someone reading this may respond; 'Well you don't know me, I have made up my mind that I will have nothing to do with sin. I respect myself enough not to go into dirty things". This sort of response does nothing but validate the existence of the monster in you. The monster denies anything that tries to point a finger at it. Its major approach is to keep you in denial until it becomes too late. Unless Jesus is the one who has borne away your sin (not only in principle), but in reality and experience, all men are bound under sin, Jews and Gentiles alike. And all will perish except they repent.

b. Respectable Abomination

There is a worse situation: the tree might well be producing fruit, but the fruits are not recognized for what they are. One major reason is that whenever sin is being discussed, people's minds run to evil (in the sense of something negative and harmful). Sin is synonymous with evil, for sure, but sin does not only manifest as negative and harmful things. The Lord Jesus talked about things that are honoured among men but which are abominations before God.

> *And he said unto them, ye are they which justify yourselves*
> *before men; but God knoweth your hearts: for that which is*
> *highly esteemed among men is abomination in the sight of*
> *God (Luke 16:15)*

Can you think of things that might be highly esteemed among men, but which are abomination in the sight of God? Whatever they are, one thing is clear: they do not appear evil to men. Had they appeared evil to men, they would not have been highly esteemed. At the same time, even though they do not appear evil to man, they must have evil embedded in them, else they would not be an abomination unto God. Many men's fruits manifest in religiosity, philanthropy, support and fight against injustice or even a subtle sense of pride in one's accomplishment and achievement. Or they may be in less obtrusive forms like ambition, personal convictions, competitive spirit, self-righteousness, even tenacity and other 'virtues' that appear right, righteous and/or Christian. Many in this group have strong attachments to and appreciation of themselves, what they do and their sense of self-worth. They are often passionate and self-driven; they lead exemplary lives and are reference points in the society. They may be philanthropic and selfless in many ways, helping many and making huge sacrifices on behalf of humanity. They could even live and die for some worthy cause, speaking out for the voiceless. As such, they are esteemed among men; their actions become reference points for honour. Someone once asked me whether an internationally-acclaimed philanthropist who passed on would be denied heaven. My answer was that I do not know, as I knew nothing about the man's personal life and therefore his relationship with Jesus while he lived. But the much I know is that no amount of good work qualifies a man for heaven for it is written " ...for we have before proved both Jews and Gentiles, that they are all under sin" (Romans 3:9) ... "for **all** have sinned and come short of the glory of God (Romans 3:23). And no man can save himself. Only Jesus can save a man. Jesus stated clearly that He is the Way, the Truth and the Life and insisted that no man can come to the Father except by Him. In addition, we have evidence that all they that would be in heaven have a song and it is not the song of how they saved themselves and how they made sacrifices on earth that qualified them to be there. It is a song to someone else that redeemed them, a redemption they did not contribute to.

> *And they sung a new song, saying, Thou art worthy to take the book, and to open the seals thereof:* **for thou wast slain, and hast redeemed us to God by thy blood** *out of every kindred, and tongue, and people, and nation (Revelation 5:9 – emphasis mine).*

A man's good deeds reduce nothing of his sinful nature. You often hear self-righteous people say, "My kind of person does not get involved in such things". Their thoughts and conversations revolve around themselves, the great escapades and achievements of 'I'. The challenge is that what a man thinks he is can itself constitute a veil over his heart and hide his need of the gospel and life from God. And no one gets into heaven on the basis of what he thinks of himself. It is often very difficult to reach such individuals mainly because their hearts are already filled with 'self'. Others in this group appear humble and self-effacing. Such may even be more difficult to fault. If the humility is not deep and Holy Spirit-induced, the devil can play on it in the sense of getting the individual to be proud of his humility. That is even more dangerous and more difficult to detect and deal with. In our analogy of trees and fruits, we know that the fruits of some smaller trees, or trees with tiny fruits, are difficult to appreciate for what they are. Many trees have fruits that appear more like seeds and do not look like fruits at all, yet they are as potent and full of life as the bigger fruits. So the shape of the fruit has little to do with the life in the fruit. The packaging of sin has little to do with the potency of the sin. The sins of the Pharisees were civil, yet very dangerous. Severally, we think we know what kind of fruit a tree should bear. If only we would humbly admit that we do not know! Jesus told the Pharisees, "if ye were blind, then you would have no sin, but because you think you see, your guilt remains (John 9:40 – 41). Often, that which seems good and acceptable to man, including good behaviour, might actually be a fruit from an evil tree. For that reason, it is the Holy Spirit that must search out sin in man before it can be dealt with. Whoso relies on himself to search out his sin will make a mess of the job. Like David, we have to pray, "Search me oh God and know my heart; try me and know my thoughts and see if there be any wicked way in me, and lead me in the way everlasting" (Psalm 139:23 – 24)

In trying to understand what is wrong with men who appear and/ or act good, it is important that we bear in mind that the fruit man ate in the Garden of Eden is not fruit of the **knowledge of evil**, but fruit of the **knowledge of good and evil**. Some men produce good fruits, but it is still of the same root, the tree of knowledge of good and evil. And the scriptures concluded that "The heart (of man) is deceitful above all things and desperately wicked". It then asked the critical question "who can know it?" (Jeremiah 17:9). Even the owner of a heart, which all men are commending for humility, does not know his own heart, much less other men that surround him. One sister once said to me, "I just like you because you are so humble". I could have screamed because pride was one big obstacle to my walk with God. She had no idea how much I was fighting with the Spirit of God on the matter of pride. The scriptures say " ...all are under sin" (Romans 3:29) ... "for all have sinned and come short of the glory of God" (Romans 3:23) ... "wherefore, as by one man sin entered into the world, and death by sin; and so death passed upon all men, for that all have sinned" (Romans 5:12). All men, whether mean or gentle, harsh or mild, good or evil, sacrificial or stingy, outrightly evil or mildly good, are under sin. Not one man is excluded. So, good deeds that are not proceeding from the instruction of the Holy Spirit are merely fruits from the tree of knowledge of good and evil. This is the reason scriptures would say "whatever is born of the Spirit is spirit and whatever is born of the flesh is flesh" (John 3:6). For as long as man took the initiative in a good deed, it had no value for God because the source is the same as that which produces evil.

Man's rebellion in Eden was a rebellion to be on his own; to take initiative and decide his own fate. First, the devil told Eve, "You shall not surely die, but God doth know that the day ye eat of it, ye shall be as God, knowing **good and evil**". He was right in saying that they would know good and evil, and that particularly appealed to Eve. "She saw that the fruit was good for food, and **also would make one wise**". She most obviously explained why she took the fruit to her husband and consenting with her, he also ate. Man wanted to throw God out of his system and administer the earth on his own, which is what we have been doing for many years. But that is a recipe for confusion. As is the case today, the moment there are two men, there will be two opinions on a matter. Even when they share the same goal, want to achieve the same result; they may differ in approach. It is worse when the two men have different goals. Most times, even for very homogenous groups, agreement has to be compelled. However, if God were the source of actions, each would merely be complementing the other because they are taking instructions from one source, which coordinates all the components. It is same with our bodies: all components function together and complementarily because every part is taking instructions from the brain. Imagine a body where each member takes decision over what it does - the hand decides what it wants to do while the leg decides where it wants to go, etc. Even though where the leg wants to go is good (at least for itself), if such action does not contribute to the welfare of the whole body, it would be of little or no value.

An illustration may help here. Assuming a very excellent bricklayer sees a building site, walks in and starts laying blocks on an existing foundation. Or even worse, no foundation had been laid and he starts laying the blocks. We ask, is laying blocks evil? Definitely no! However, the site engineer or manager would not be happy on seeing the laboring man because he had not hired or instructed him to lay blocks there. Besides, the bricklayer is not privy to the building plan, which his unaligned efforts may have impeded. There is a plan, a purpose for creating the world. Only God knows how to actualize that plan and so

He is the only one qualified to administer the earth, bringing all men in perfect coordination to fulfill that purpose. Whoever acts without God's explicit direction, even though such acts may be nice, would likely obstruct the overall purpose of God. And the act of obstructing the purpose of God, whether well-intended or not, whether through a good action or bad one, constitutes sin. The fact that the action is respectable among men makes no difference.

CHAPTER 6

THE EQUIPMENT OF SIN

a. The Reign of Sin

Sin is not a democrat; it reigns…with terror! It does not interact with humanity at the level of a friend, colleague or equal, nor does it cohabit with man. It lords it over man, rules over him and forces him; and that with an iron hand. This approach in the relationship between sin and man is one of the most fundamental differences between the reign of God and the rulership of sin. Many people expect God to interact with us the same way sin interacts with us. In fact, many people cannot understand this 'seeming passivity' on the part of God and they wonder why He would turn around to hold us responsible for our actions when He could have made us do what he wants from us. Unfortunately, this is a great misconception. Whatever forces a man against his will, whether physically or spiritually, is not of God and cannot lead to mutually beneficial outcomes. God made man a free agent. Indeed any form of relationship involving free moral agents, whether they are governance or business, can only be fruitful and enjoyable to all parties when it is borne out of volition. By its constitution, this is what sin sets out to violate. Indeed, sin can only be sin, anti-God, anti-man and destructive because it violates this freewill. This is why all systems that use violence, political or religious cannot be of God. Only sin together with anything else that is borne of it uses compulsion to rule. The following scriptures point to this compulsion:

"That as sin hath reigned unto death, even so might grace reign through righteousness unto eternal life by Jesus Christ our Lord" (Romans 5:21)

Let not sin therefore reign in your mortal body, that ye should obey it in the lusts thereof (Romans 6:12)

Know ye not, that to whom ye yield yourselves servants to obey, his servants ye are to whom ye obey; whether of sin unto death, or of obedience unto righteousness? But God be thanked, that ye were the servants of sin, but ye have obeyed from the heart that form of doctrine which was delivered you (Romans 6:16, 17)

For when ye were the servants of sin, ye were free from righteousness. But now being made free from sin, and become servants to God, ye have your fruit unto holiness, and the end everlasting life ((Rom 6: 20, 22).

But sin, taking occasion by the commandment, wrought in me all manner of concupiscence. For without the law sin was dead. For sin, taking occasion by the commandment deceived me, and by it slew me (Romans_7:8, 11).

Thus, quite contrary to the perception of an impersonal set of actions, the Bible clearly demonstrates that sin is an iron-fisted lord that binds, reigns over and preys on men. It slays. It is placed almost at the same realm of lordship and ownership, with the same ruling capability as any other supreme. Consider the operational words of some of the passages above – reign (Romans 5:21; 6:12), obey, servant of sin, made free from sin (as in being previously bound by him – Romans 6:16 - 22), sin ... wrought in me, deceived me, and... slew me (Romans 7:11). Romans 3:19 which we earlier considered puts it as "they are all under sin", akin to saying, they all have one ruler, one lord and one supreme – and that lord is sin. As indicated in Chapter

3, this iron-grip tyranny and God's process for redemption of man are depicted in the book of Exodus. Pharaoh did not only rule the Israelites with tyranny, he had complete disdain for God. It took extreme measures for God to free the Israelites from Pharaoh much the same way it takes extreme measures for God to free men from sin. The same way the Israelites could not free themselves from Egypt, so can man not ever free himself from sin.

Note that what drove the children of Israel into Egypt was famine. It is also noteworthy that during the lives of the patriarchs, whenever there was famine (genuine and life-threatening famine) on all other parts of the earth, Egypt had food. Abraham ran to Egypt to avoid famine, Isaac would have done the same had God not intervened. Jacob finally took his entire family into Egypt to avoid dying out of famine. There is always food in Egypt – lots of onions, garlics and other desirable foods – but they come at a price. Most people that subject themselves to sin often do so because of certain attractions; the food, shelter, security, fame and other allures of "Egypt" attract them.

The challenge has never been going into Egypt. There is always enough incentive to go in, as well as enough pleasure for everyone inside. The challenge is in coming out of Egypt. An attraction made Eve stretch her hand to pluck the fruit of knowledge of good and evil. It was only after she had eaten it that she realized that she was into something very terrible and much stronger than her. By then coming out was not possible anymore. Like Eve, the children of Israel went into Egypt without coercion, but they could not just stand up to leave Egypt. They needed help. And indeed, in every manifestation of sin in our lives – pride, drugs, sexual pervasions, greed, alcoholism, laziness, cultism and idolatry – going in is the easy part; quitting is not. Getting out of the terrible hold of sin is altogether impossible without help.

Pharaoh noted that the children of Israel were growing mighty and broached the topic with his advisers.

> *"And he said unto his people, Behold, the people of the children of Israel are more and mightier than we: Come on, let us deal wisely with them; lest they multiply, and it come*

to pass, that, when there falleth out any war, they join also unto our enemies, and fight against us, and so get them up out of the land. Therefore they did set over them taskmasters to afflict them with their burdens. And they built for Pharaoh Treasure cities, Pithom and Raamses" (Exodus 1: 9 – 11).

Again, we will look at the above scripture: Sin needs man in captivity because every free man is a potential force that could join hands with those fighting against (and can conquer) it. Whatever might liberate man from captivity has to be fought against at all costs. Therefore, Jesus came to give freedom to man first. For without freedom, it is impossible for any man to worship God. As Paul would insist, it is important that the believer "stand(s) firm in the liberty wherewith Christ has made us free, and be not entangled again with the yoke of bondage" (Galatians 5:1). Zechariah, inspired by the Holy Spirit, noted in Luke 1:74 – 75 that part of the promise of God is, "we being delivered out of the hands of our enemies might serve him without fear, in holiness and righteousness all the days of our lives". Deliverance from the hands of our enemies must precede serving God.

The Israelites were forced to build storehouses (Pithom and Raamses) for Pharaoh. In the same way, every natural man is a construction worker, actively tasked with building storehouses for the devil. With his heart serving as a dumping ground for the devil's rubbish, he builds storehouses of hate, envy, greed, unforgiveness, to mention a few. This position is without prejudice to whatever education, civilization or grooming a person may have received. The natural man may look attractive and polished externally; yet it makes no difference. Viewed from outside, a room full of rubbish and dead bodies does not look any different from another clean room. As long as the room is locked and the viewer is not near enough to perceive the stench, all looks well. But the moment one gets near, the stench from the storehouse of evil thoughts, indiscipline and lusts becomes strong. Thus, even though as we have earlier noted, the building is for no particular eternally useful purpose, man is kept very busy building. There are taskmasters with whips, cudgels and knives compelling him to build. It is a reign of terror. He cannot even as much as raise his head from the heap that is underneath him; he must continue to either mold bricks or build with molded ones – one brick upon the other.

We admit that the devil is tasking men, placing ferocious taskmasters over them. For some, the taskmaster is a habit of sniffing drugs, drinking or smoking whether you like it or not. So even when you cry and beg, pointing out that you have been in it for many years and it has been very expensive and of no gain to you, the taskmaster behind does not listen. It compels you to take the next sniff, sip or puff. Sometime ago, on a trip to East Africa, I was chatting with a group of Britons who came mountaineering, all mostly in their 40s. Of the eight or so in the group, only one was married (or at least living with a woman). The rest were either gay or single. About 6 of them were compulsive drinkers and smokers. After the initial group banter, I closed in on one of them. He gave me the details of the rest. He could not keep off the cigarette and told me he tried marriage but it did not work for him. I understood virtually everyone in that group was educated and comfortable. "So why are you not married", I asked? I got to learn that they were unmarried because none of them could live with a lady or no lady could live with them. I asked one why he smoked when he knew that smoking was dangerous to his health. He told me he had done everything under the sun to stop. He had been through rehabilitation a number of times, but the habit simply refused to go away. Though I could not identify with him on the level of smoking, I could relate with him because of personal experience in other forms of bondage. I therefore tried to introduce him to Jesus, but the young man obviously could not understand how a Jew of distant memory could be of help to his current struggles. Many of us can identify with this very easily.

For some, the taskmaster is ambition. When a man becomes ambitious, He thinks ambition is a minor issue that can be given up anytime. But it turns out that the habit drives the victim from dawn till dusk. Even when the man admits that he has accomplished a fairly great height, he is unable to slow down or stop pursuing. Ambition takes over his life, with no possible finishing line except death. Ambition defines minimum deliverables for class and social status. Men under such compulsion cannot afford not to meet up societal expectations in virtually all areas of their life. Society dictates the kind of food they should eat, toys to keep, clothes to wear, the type of jobs they can accept, company to keep and whom to marry, etc. The unpleasant and suffocating pressure to keep up keeps such people constantly stressed out all the time. I have met many very busy persons who do not like the hyper-activity and would wish they had more time to themselves. Yet none is able to stop himself from the hustle. Some keep jobs they do not like and wish for freedom to pursue their dreams while the years roll over on them, slowly but surely dimming the possibility. It is because of the taskmaster. The taskmaster is in paid employment, relationships, housework, wherever. He is lord over nearly all of humanity and over nearly all practical aspects of human endeavour. He uses whatever is convenient for each man. Only the man over whom the Lord Jesus reigns is free.

> And the Egyptians made the children of Israel to serve with rigour: And they made their lives bitter with hard bondage, in mortar, and in brick, and in all manner of service in the field: all their service, wherein they made them serve, was with rigour (Exodus 1:13 –14)

Even now, every man is crying because the labour is with rigour. No one is without pain and tears. Many express their tears only in the solitude of their rooms, upon their pillows in the night. No man likes the servitude, but none has what it takes to rise above it or shake it off. Groupwork is useless here. No amount of coming together of men can reduce the hard labour or take it away altogether because the enslavement was concluded individually; it is not collective run. Therefore, every man also has to be saved as an individual.

But the reign of terror does not end with keeping men terribly busy with rigour and pain. When it seemed to Pharaoh that the tasking of grown-ups, terrible as that was, was not producing fast enough result, he turned his attention to infants – the male infants.

*And Pharaoh charged all his people, saying, every son that is
born ye shall cast into the river, and every daughter ye shall
save alive (Exodus 1:22)*

In most cultures, the male folk represents the future and the
inheritance of a people. The strength of a people is directly related to
the strength of its men. In olden day Israel, as in many other cultures,
women did not make the number. Wars are fought by men. Homesteads
and inheritances are named after men. Men are the burden bearers;
they are the future brick builders. So it is not difficult to understand
that even though the male children were the future slaves in Egypt,
Pharaoh was willing to do away with them. He preferred killing the
male children and doing without their great service to keeping them
and risking overthrow.

It is tragic enough that the enemy subjects mankind to rigorous
labour. Yet this is a less evil compared to the unthinkable slaying of
infant males. The enemy wants to eliminate anyone with a potential,
anyone that could pose a threat, anyone that could be relied upon
to further the course of God among men. In the fight with God, the
devil's classic approach to decimate man and bring the word and work
of God to nought was to cut off God's future plan from him. If there is
no posterity, then the command of the Lord to multiply and subdue is
made of no effect. Have you not seen the legion of able-bodied young
men and women who have no sense of direction or of responsibility?
Have you not noticed thousands of youths, who are running to drugs
and drinks to subsist? They anchor their lives on fun. Some of them sell
their bodies for daily bread while others wear violence like a garment.
Many more are aged and seemingly more responsible older people. But
they have already been eaten up by greed, lust and covetousness. They
live and struggle all life long for wealth, power and sex. Externally,
they may be well dressed, but they are wholly empty within. The
scriptures say that all these are already dead though they appear to
be living (1 Tim 5:6). In the church, Satan cuts off visions of believers
before they are even born. Those that catch any vision for God are
eaten up by secret sin before they bud. All these infant mortalities

represent the all-out war by the devil against the human race and against the purposes of God.

Pharaoh did not need to do this himself. He simply engaged the midwives assigned to the pregnant mothers. The midwives stand between the pregnancy and birthing of the child. The instruction was specific, 'If it is a male child, kill him, but if it is a female child, keep her alive'. Likewise, Satan instructs his agents:"If it is a manly vision, with seed in it and a potential to change lives; if there are possibilities that what is being brought forth will live beyond the immediate and produce the life of God and seed for future generations, kill it! If it has the seal of the Spirit of God and is likely to stand the wiles of the enemy, kill it! But if it is a useless idea, if it is based on the ideals of man, if it is only out to consume, then let it live!" How many God-inspired visions have been murdered by pastors who do not understand the vision, or are too lighthearted for serious business with God? A young brother comes to share a man-child vision with his pastor who has been placed by God as a midwife. But because the pastor does not fully understand the vision, he manhandles it and lets it die. How many zealous brethren who were determined to serve the Lord have been quenched by the apathy and lukewarmness of those around and above them? They get over-burdened by administrative assignments and menial responsibilities and receive no encouragement and support on God's calling over their lives. Some wet blankets in church would remind you that they have been there, have had such zeal in the past, but that at the end it was not sustainable. These old prophets demand moderation of zeal but do not define the terms of the moderation. More men are being killed this way than by the direct attack of the enemy. They are midwives commissioned by the devil. But the midwives of Egypt, Shiphrah and Puah, did not partner with Pharaoh on this matter. They realized that killing infants is a worse crime than putting the adults on hard labour. God respected their stand and blessed them with their own homes. May we always appreciate the weightiness of collaborating with Sin to slay young soldiers of Christ through the abortion of their visions.

b. The Equipment for Doing the Work of Sin

In Exodus chapter 5, we are introduced to the striking raw materials Pharaoh made available to the Israelites. The scriptures say they received straw. Exodus 5: 6 – 7; 15 – 18 has this to say:

> And Pharaoh commanded the same day the taskmasters of the people, and their officers, saying, Ye shall no more give the people straw to make brick, as heretofore: let them go and gather straw for themselves.Then the officers of the children of Israel came and cried unto Pharaoh, saying, Wherefore dealest thou thus with thy servants?There is no straw given unto thy servants, and they say to us, Make brick: and, behold, thy servants are beaten; but the fault is in thine own people. But he said ye are idle, ye are idle: therefore ye say, Let us go and do sacrifice to the LORD. Go therefore now, and work; for there shall no straw be given you, yet shall ye deliver the tale of bricks.

Another place where the scriptures mentioned straw (or stubble) as building material is in 1 Corinthians 3:12 – 15:

> Now if any man build upon this foundation gold, silver, precious stones, wood, hay, stubble; Every man's work shall be made manifest: for the day shall declare it, because it shall be revealed by fire; and the fire shall try every man's work of what sort it is. If any man's work abide which he hath built thereupon, he shall receive a reward.If any man's work shall be burned, he shall suffer loss: but he himself shall be saved; yet so as by fire.

Six building materials are mentioned in the passage– gold, silver, precious stones, wood, hay and stubble (straw in New International Version, Living Bible version, Amplified version etc.). Considering the fact that the testing item for all the building materials is fire, we classify the listed materials into those that can be consumed by fire and those that cannot. The three stone and metal derivatives (gold, silver, and precious stones) are in the category that cannot be consumed by fire while the three plant derivatives (wood, hay and straw) can. The raw material made available for the Israelites in bondage is in the second category – it cannot stand the test of fire and definitely cannot stand the test of time or eternity. Straw burns up; it is flammable. It is a material for today; it decays and gets consumed with the elements of this world and with time. In the same way, Sin is a hostile equipper. Nothing built with straw lasts here, nor can it enter into eternal dwellings. When a man is engaged in sin and with the world system, his raw materials are laughable, weak and difficult. Whatever is built on education, wealth, fame, political power, tribe or even humanity and other perishables are made of straw. The devil gives men straw to build with and sets taskmasters over them such that not only is the work tedious, but nothing that is built from it lasts. How many times have you met a man who labored all his life to build an empire and even before his death, watches all his life effort crumble? Men work like camels all their lives only to find out that nothing that they built can be transferred to anyone else. Institutions of the world system can speak grandiose words about men that have served them well, yet the very day the person becomes unproductive to that system, it quickly discards and replaces him. The world system equips with straw, outputs from the efforts are products of straw and the reward for the effort is equally straw. Sin and the world system perpetuate that system and retain the captives by giving the impression that any man can hold on to any of these 'rewards'. But no man ever retained the products of his labour here on earth. All the acquisitions and glories slip away from the hands of a man as he retires to the grave. Most men realize only after their lives are gone or when they are close to the grave that it is all vanity, and that after serving sin every faithful slave will receive what others received – straw! Many do not realize exactly how much vanity the world and the things they pursue are until they are incapable of reversing the things they have done. Multitudes of apparently successful men bow into the grave with tears and regrets.

And it is such a fearful thing for a man to enter into eternity where fire will test all things and all he has are flammable straw. The devil does not have the capacity to give a man raw materials that can build for eternity and that is why God ruled out the possibility of serving him effectively while in bondage in Egypt. A man must first repent and be translated into the kingdom of God through Christ before he can serve God acceptably.

Haman, for example, labored for and with straw. According to the Book of Esther, Haman was promoted (possibly beyond his widest imaginations) by Ahasuerus the Persian King. He was the prime Minister and Second-in-command (Esther 3:1-2). But Haman was also very wealthy, so rich that he was willing to commit $20 million (Esther 3:9, Living Bible version) of his personal wealth to the cause he considered important. He was willing to pay upfront into the royal bank to finance the extermination of the Jews. Unfortunately, as it is in several cases of things men chase with money, it was a cause against God, the fact that he did not realize it at the time notwithstanding. On the surface, he looked prosperous and unstoppable. It was state law that men everywhere should bow whenever he appeared. Haman was so powerful in the Persian kingdom that he could sentence a whole race to condemnation because of an offence committed against him by only one man. In terms of fruitfulness, Haman was already the father of a tribe, with ten sons to his name, not to mention his daughters. He was respected among his peers. His word was law and none could stand against his opinion on any matter. He had influence with the king and was famous.

But like all men who are enslaved by sin, they may be materially comfortable but they lack **'the blessing'** referred to in Psalm 133:3 as 'life forevermore'. One of the manifestations of this lack is discontentment. Sons of time need to acquire things here and now but sons of eternity know that they have more enduring inheritance hereafter and so are not under pressure by what they fail to get in their sojourn here. Haman was discontented. In his own words, "Yet all this avails me nothing, so long as I see Mordecai the Jew sitting at the king's gate" (Esther 5:13). Goaded by arrogance and vanity,

Haman employed his great oratorical skills to convince the king to permit him deal with a people that had done nothing to him. Haman would not just kill Mordecai; he needed to exterminate the entire Israeli race. You may wonder what would push a man to go to this length over a matter as small as one man refusing to bow to another. Reality is, it was not about Haman; he was merely a slave to Sin. He was not pursuing his own agenda. Haman's master, Sin, wanted all Israelites dead because he knew they had been chosen by God to produce the Messiah. By exterminating them, he would forestall the coming of the One who had been empowered by God to bruise the head of the serpent and liberate mankind. Haman did not need to know this; he only needed to follow the instructions of sin dwelling in him. It was the devil who is against humanity and all that God had set up that would want all those people dead. The devil has come to steal, to kill, and to destroy. But he needed Haman as an instrument, the same way many have been and are instruments in the hands of the devil. So he inflicts him with discontentment, arrogance and over-bloated ego. He could not overlook one miserable security man that would not bow and it meant nothing to him that millions of others in the kingdom were bowing. After the idea of killing Mordecai dropped in his mind, the devil convinced him that snuffing out the life of one single man was too small for a man who had so much power at his disposal.

No sin manifests alone. When Haman decided to go after the entire Jewish race, his pride and self-promotion also needed the services of lies. So he told the king, "There is a certain people scattered and dispersed among the people in all the provinces of your kingdom; their laws are different from all the other people, and they do not keep the king's laws. Therefore it is not fitting for the king to let them remain ..." (Esther 3:8 – 9). Of course, the issue under contention had nothing to do with laws, obedience, or culture. It had to do with one man's ego and his desire to demonstrate his absolute power over other lives. Haman wanted to make a god out of himself; and he needed to tell lies to achieve his goal. As is always the case with manifestations of sin, the moment the devil had gained sufficient foothold through Haman, he took the process out of Haman's hands. Events got accelerated immediately Haman got the king's approval. At that point Haman had reached a point of no return; Sin had taken over. Even if Haman, in the quietness of the night, begins to weigh and rethink his steps and decided he did not want to continue with the process, it was impossible to pull out. Stopping meant he would have to deal with public loss of face, and possibly loss of his position for leading the king astray. It would be difficult for Haman to go back to the king and confess that there were really no such people as he had described. He would also have to deal with the people that reported Mordecai to him whom, he imagined, would think he was chickening out of the process because he could not carry through. He would lose his honour, the very item he was fighting to protect. Sin (and Satan) work hard to bring a man to this point of no return, at which point it is impossible to go back and by which time whatever little control the man may have had has been handed over to the devil and his team.

At the point of no return, the man knows that should he not proceed with the rest of the requirement for bringing sin to a successful finish, he would be exposed and brought to shame. At the point of lust, David was in charge of the process; he could say no to the pull towards Bathsheba. But the moment he slept with her, he handed control to the devil. Because it would be shameful to have it on the media that the king descended to the point of impregnating the wife of one of his trusted friends, David had to make some desperate efforts using the powers available to him to try and cover the sin. That effort failed. Therefore, he had no option but to set Uriah, Bathsheba's husband, up for death and proceed to acquire his wife. Straightforward and predictable! That is the way of sin. The examples are legion, both in the Scriptures and in day-to-day life of every clime. A man, leading a public organization is pressed by need, and starts dipping his hands into the coffers of his organization. Later he finds out that the sum cumulates to the point where he is unable to repay. So he arranges with some colleague to tie the funds to one phony project, ostensibly belonging to the group. The project never sees the light of day and then he is under threat of exposure. Fearing he might be exposed, he eliminates his ally (possibly by murder). He is then in a hole where he needs to continue to cover one sin with another in order to survive. Of course, no one in this position ever gets free. Sin never gets done with any man without giving him the appropriate wages – death!

Haman was in a hole and bound to sin. So far the devil had given him three instruments for work – arrogance, self-promotion and lies. But he needed others, each to manifest in its time. So he also gave him bitterness and boasting. This particular evening, after he had fed fat on the Queen's delicacies, and unaware of the relationship between Mordecai and the Queen, he gathered his friends and relatives for a boasting party. Everybody had to attend even if they did not cherish the purpose of the gathering. Afterall the man who convened the meeting was the Second-in-Command in the kingdom. In the gathering, he made the confession which all sinners inwardly admit to, but which they hardly acknowledge openly, 'Yet all this avails me nothing ...' (Esther 5:13). How is that possible? All this wealth avails Haman nothing? All the power, all the glamour, all the cheers and hailing from friends and well-wishers in high and low places avails him nothing? All the children, flock of friends and relatives, all the men and women he could command, the power to take other people's lives, all the prostrating from others, all the laughter and mirth in the public were meaningless to Haman? Even the king's pleasure and adoration of Haman and now the Queen's banquet to which only he had the privilege of going to, were reduced to nothing by arrogance and bitterness. He declared solemnly, "All this avails me nothing..."

Sin avails nothing. It had used Haman extensively, binding him firm with straw – money, fame, power, children and the applause of men – and now he had brought Haman to the point of no return. With bitterness taking control of him, he could no longer wait till the 12th month as earlier agreed to see the end of Mordecai. Sin compelled him to hang Mordecai before the end of the next day. This seemed very good idea to the captives of Sin - Haman, his wife and his friends. Unfortunately for them, God delivers his own from the curse of death, for 'curse causeless shall not come ...' (Proverbs 26:2). But at that point, Haman himself had already become a spectator in the unveiling drama.

Still bound and blinded by sin, it was not until he was compelled to honour Mordecai that his wife and friends drew his attention to the fact that he had spiraled out of control and was heading towards a certain, looming doom. Haman could not be saved anymore. Then, the same friends that hailed him and confidently advised him the previous night suddenly seemed to know something different. Hear them, "If Mordecai be of the seed of the Jews, before whom thou hast begun to fall, thou shalt not prevail against him, but shall surely fall before him" (Esther 6:13). Was there a sudden revelation concerning Mordecai as a Jew or about Jews in general? Were they not always aware that Mordecai was a Jew or that it was dangerous to trifle with Jews? Did they suddenly realize that Jews always won battles or did they refuse to discuss it with their friend in the hope of a miracle?

When sin equips a man, it continues to drag him till it gets him to the point of humiliation and death. Haman had to die the same day. In quick succession, he lost his position, his reputation, his relationships, his entire wealth and the pride he so badly wanted to protect. His family and friends were not spared. The entire array of accomplishments that Haman boasted about and depended upon was burnt up in a twinkle. That is how sin equips a man, helps him produce bad fruits and rewards him with death. No man ever labours for sin and fails to earn the wages of death as defined by scriptures.

c. To Steal, kill, and to Destroy

Sin comes to steal, to kill, and to destroy. It is an enemy to all that is good. The imagery the Bible uses for sin is 'darkness'. And this imagery (and of course its contrast to light) runs through the scriptures.

> Let darkness and the shadow of death stain it; let a cloud dwell upon it; let the blackness of the day terrify it (Job_3:5).

> Such as sit in **darkness** and in the shadow of death, being bound in affliction and iron;

*He brought them out of **darkness** and the shadow of death, and brake their bands in sunder (Psalms_107; 10, 14).*

*For, behold, the **darkness** shall cover the earth, and gross **darkness** the people: but the LORD shall arise upon thee, and his glory shall be seen upon thee (Isaiah_60:2)*

*But if thine eye be evil, thy whole body shall be full of **darkness**. If therefore the light that is in thee be **darkness**, how great is that **darkness**! (Matthew_6:23)*

The light of the body is the eye: therefore when thine eye is single, thy whole body also is full of light; but when thine eye is evil, thy body also is full of darkness. Take heed therefore that the light which is in thee be not darkness (Luke_11:34 – 35).

*And the light shineth in **darkness**; and the **darkness** comprehended it not (John_1:5)*

*And this is the condemnation, that light is come into the world, and men loved **darkness** rather than light, because their deeds were evil (John_3:19).*

*Then spake Jesus again unto them, saying, I am the light of the world: he that followeth me shall not walk in **darkness**, but shall have the light of life (John_8:12).*

*To open their eyes, and to turn them from **darkness** to light, and from the power of Satan unto God, that they may receive forgiveness of sins, and inheritance among them which are sanctified by faith that is in me (Act_26:18)*

*For God, who commanded the light to shine out of **darkness**, hath shined in our hearts, to give the light of the knowledge of the glory of God in the face of Jesus Christ (2 Corinthians_4:6).*

It is not in vain that the scriptures used this figure to describe the works of sin. We know darkness, and it is one of the most challenging stumbling blocks to work. Whether used symbolically or otherwise, we understand darkness to be a problem. When the scriptures note that the earth was without form and void in Genesis 1:2, it also informed us that darkness was upon the face of the deep of the earth. But even though God created both heaven and the earth, the same darkness was not upon the face of the heaven. We have come to know that the darkness being referred to was an entity, and not a phenomenon. Reading John 1, we see the Bible indicating that Jesus was the light, the same light of Genesis 1 and that darkness has not comprehended (understood) it. All the words used across board refer to personalities that were obviously clashing with each other. In Genesis 1:4, God divided the light from the darkness, implying that immediately the light surfaced, the first thing was that darkness tried to see if there was a way to overcome, overshadow and snuff it out. But the power of God made manifest in the light was way beyond its comprehension. The darkness led to confusion and emptiness. That is the primary purpose of darkness. When the enemy enticed Eve to eat the forbidden fruit, one would imagine there was an important agenda in his heart, maybe something he would benefit from the whole exercise. But no, his entire aim was to get man on the wrong side of God, take away order from man's life and bring about confusion. His ultimate agenda was death and destruction. He simply wanted to hurt. There was absolutely nothing he would personally gain; no increase to himself on account of Adam's enmity with God except that the man would now be his slave. But it is all about darkness, the end of no destination.

He comes to steal, to kill and to destroy. That does not seem to make sense to rational human beings who are used to constructivism. Yet once in a while, despite our civilization, we still notice an instinct in us to destroy just for the sake of it. Anytime we read the newspapers, it is all about blood and tears. And indeed, we have accustomed our minds to think of news as blood and tears:

- An aircraft that crashed, killing all 296 people on board.
- A flooding or mudslide that claimed the lives of 2500 persons.
- An invasion by a terrorist group that killed more than 8,000 persons.
- A riot that led to a fight between Police and civilians that destroyed 150 houses and left 1,300 dead.
- A clash between two native tribes that left 3500 dead and many more wounded
- A mini war involving three rival drug gangs that left 700 dead.
- A war between government and a rebel group that has lasted for more than 6 months with 420,000 dead and 2.9 million displaced.
- The news of a 'loving' father that killed his own 6 children and confessed that he did not know what came over him
- An outbreak of famine that has claimed the lives of over 135,000 women and children within nine months
- ... And several such 'news'

The list is endless and cuts across the most archaic as well as modern generations. "News" in the media is bad news. Because of the calamities that befall man, many have altogether wondered at the purpose of life. Not even civilization seems to be helping us outgrow calamities. Terrorism does not make sense unless we understand that there is darkness in man that does not answer to education or civilization. Unfortunately, policymakers everywhere, who do not understand the cause or what is at stake, blame everything but the source of the problem. We blame poverty and unemployment; but look the other way when the rich from advanced countries of the world leave their comfort to join terrorist groups and behead people. In such cases, we blame depression. But it is difficult to imagine that the whole of Germany and all the fine officers involved in the heinous crimes of the Holocaust were all depressed.

Each terror unleashed by the carnage of sin usually makes good reading; and news houses crave them because they are the items that guarantee revenue flow. The bad news guarantees revenue because there is a deeper part of man that is in sync with evil. Human nature craves the news. Inwardly, the natural man relishes stories involving violence, disasters, usurpation, denials, betrayals and other negatives. We may hold grandiose meetings and speak eloquently in condemnation of the persons or circumstances behind these 'shocking' events, but the newspaper houses know better than to take us on our word. They know that inwardly, we really do not mind those things for as long as we are not the victims. We easily forget and consign those events to the past and the very next minute, we ask for our food, and life goes on. Sometimes, we may have deep concerns, but they do not last. We also are comforted in knowing that those events are far away from us. For the natural man, news means disaster, sin and all the drama that go with trying to resolve them and keep the society running.

When a man's soul is dark, there is no end to what he can do and within the confines of that darkness, instructions for destruction are given and carried out. No soul can murder without bitterness and hatred, nor can anyone commit adultery without lust. No one can steal without telling lies (at least to himself), nor can a man falsely accuse another without hatred. The preludes (bitterness, hatred, lust, lies, etc) are themselves instruments for bringing forth further iniquities. They are darkness, and within their confines, further darkness is hatched. And here, we again note that many people have no idea what they can do until they have to do them. When wars break out, the people that kill, maim, rape and commit several other forms of atrocities are the same that sit in boardrooms dressed in ties and suits in normal times. No new men are invented during crises than the same who move about at normal times. The difference is not in the men; the difference is in the circumstances that make cruelty needful or desirable. That is why, even in normal times, a believer needs to watch his tendencies towards the more subtle manifestations of sin as they always (involuntarily) lead the man towards the more callous ones if unattended to. Cain had only anger (driven by ego) immediately after the sacrifice of Genesis 4. Thereafter, it snowballed into murder.

CHAPTER 7

THE MANIFESTATIONS OF SIN

There was an argument between the Lord Jesus and the Jews over whose descendants the latter were. The Jews claimed they were children of Abraham and therefore were righteous, but Jesus insisted they were children of the devil (see John 8: 33 – 47). In claiming to be descendants of Abraham as a way of justifying their righteousness, the Jews showed they understood that sin was about who a man is and not just about his acts. They justified the sanctity of their lives and their position with God by tracing their ancestry to Abraham. So they understood that what you are born of counts in whether or not you are a sinner. Of course, as the scriptures say, that which is good cannot bring forth bad fruits. Similarly, that which is bad cannot bring forth good fruits. So there is a very strong link between what a man is and what he does. When sin indwells a man, several things about him point to it, but because sin is very deceptive, a man can live with several signs of sin without knowing it. When Paul listed the characters of sin in Galatians 5: 19 – 21, he indicated that the list was far from being exhaustive. So whereas some sins can be known even by the person in whom they are manifesting, there are others that can remain latent and unknown. Sin is naturally deceptive. But wherever it appears, it shares some common traits that could be identified. It is ever fearful and always wants to hide its nakedness. It seeks its own, takes attention away from God and relies on the community of persons around it for approval, among several others. The shape and degree of manifestations of sin vary from one man to another, but generally it is about self – self-protection, self-promotion, self-belief, self-actualization, self-advancement, self-gratification, among others. In the rest of this chapter, we try to discuss some of these manifestations in turn.

a. Sin and Nakedness – the Fear of Light

In its deepest essence, sin is fearful and lacks courage. When it seems to have the upper hand, it can get tough, bold and cruel, but inwardly, it always grovels. In Psalms 1:5, David summarized the challenge facing sin and sinners: sinners shall not stand in the congregation of the righteous. Sin is unable to stand and look up; it is forever facing down. It is difficult to find anyone living in sin (or caught in it) who is bold. A robber is very cruel when he is armed and dealing with his victims. But he is usually different when caught and paraded. The look on the face, the composure of the person, the attitude towards those around him, all change.

Sin is so cowardly that the Psalmist says "Sinners run when no one is pursuing" (Proverbs 28:1) but the righteous is as bold as lion". Why is this so? Sin is inherently unable to stand the light. It thrives in the cover and would do anything not to get on to where people can see everything. The more it is hidden, the better for it. So at the slightest possibility of exposure, it runs and fights. When a group of sinners see a man with a completely different spirit, who stands out and who cannot be compromised, they usually get violent and want to get rid of him by all means. Whatever extraneous reasons may be given, fact is sinners try to intimidate and run the righteous out of town because they are afraid of him. Where they discover a fault, they use it to assuage their consciences or drag the righteous down to their level. When that fails, the next line of action is to find a means of pushing him away (or even destroying him). This is because of the nature of sin. When lights draws too close, it knows that it is only a matter of time before it gets extinguished. So it fights back. Though sin is weak and fearful, it always wants to be seen as being bold and fearless. This leads to pretense and guile. Internally, he is shivering, but because of the need for good rating, it would do anything to be seen in the best of light. It might even take on apparent works of bravery.

No sinner is confident. This does not mean sin cannot display bravado; it can exhibit significant bravado when it is pushed to the wall and there is no other place to run to. It can also be so when it is in charge and has managed to hold back opposition or when men are captive under it. "As a roaring lion and as a ranging bear; so is a wicked ruler over the poor people"; "... but when the wicked beareth rule, the people mourn" (Proverbs 28:15; 29:1 King James Version). When Sin feels it has taken over the environment and coerced everyone into submission, it usually becomes very bold and tries to intimidate man. It forces people to hail it or incorporates itself into the culture, aiming to make itself acceptable. Where it receives accolades, as is usually the case when it seems to have taken over completely or has managed to make itself acceptable among a people, it pretends to be unafraid. Likewise, when the righteous are overly quiet and do not contend with darkness, it can make a lot of noise. 1 Peter 5: 8 - 9 says, "Be sober, be vigilant; because your adversary the devil, as a roaring lion, walketh about, seeking whom he may devour: whom resist steadfast in the faith, ..." At such times, it might turn towards the light with pretended boldness and roar. But within itself, it has great fear because darkness does not have any lasting foundation or foothold; it is only a matter of time before light appears and the position of sin is compromised. Therefore, wherever sin can, it tries to do away with the possibility of re-entry of light by using force. That is part of the reason why religions and governments that are inherently evil also engage force to subdue people and force them not to consider any other alternatives. We regularly see this in places where communism or religions that resort to force have managed to take full control of the lives of men.

Although in the company of a multitude, sin shows much bravado, it is constantly under some internal threat. The individual in whom there is sin cannot afford peace. He is perpetually afraid that something evil might come upon him suddenly, that his days may be cut short, or that some more powerful person would overcome and outshine him. By its very nature, evil is restless and compels those swimming in it to be so as well. Most evil men that are hailed during the bustle of the day have very troubling times in the loneliness and quietness of the night. A multitude of issues give the wicked no rest. He is either afraid of unseen powers that have the capacity to take him off without warning or he is warring to secure his position from other men and to advance himself, often at someone else's expense. He is constantly and perilously aware of the capacity of others to outwit and take over his position. But in some instances, what he is afraid of is not even the evil from others but the light in a harmless righteous man who may not even be aware he is a threat. Interestingly, while the righteous cannot harm, the light in them makes evil men afraid, often without words, and sometimes without even knowing it. Light does not need to do anything to be a threat to darkness. Whenever an evil man sees a righteous man, he becomes jittery; the light in the righteous becomes a reminder of his personal inadequacies: the evil man knows that sin will not endure forever. Even though he knows that this man is unable to harm him physically, he is uncomfortable to have him around. And severally, he plots to have him shut up or eliminated.

The irony of sin is that it is more concerned about hiding who it is and how it feels than it is about resolving the problem of its inherently insecure position. A man may know that he is dying, but will be more interested in not allowing others know that something is wrong with him than he is concerned about getting life. This is the lifestyle of sin and he uses several instruments to live this way – pretenses, lying, barking when it seems he is cornered, etc. This secrecy is probably the biggest weapon of sin and darkness.

Interestingly, this lifestyle is not manifest in only unbelievers; it is a threat that engulfs many Christians as well. Most believers know the feeling that precedes and accompanies confession and/or restitution to other men. There is this seeming slice of knife that runs through our hearts and spine at the thought of possible leakage of a secret sin or confession to other men. Many of us would rather die than bear that shame. And of course, given that often our lives are more tangible to us than an intangible God, many foolishly ignore or challenge God when He tells us to restitute or confess hidden sins. The fear is that the confession would harm our reputation by bringing shame on us. The believer becomes more concerned about people's perception than he is about God's. In some cases, we use worship and spiritual skills to cover up. Many believers would switch to speaking in tongues when it is time to confess sins in the church. Others would suddenly quit praying, preferring to mutter to themselves. Such hiding is still part of the game by sin to stay under cover and was used by Saul to good effect (I Samuel 15:10 - 34). Following the war with Amalek, Samuel tried to let Saul know that all was not well and that he had sinned. But Saul insisted that he had done what he was told to do. When Samuel eventually assailed Saul's self-righteousness, he also announced to him that God had dethroned him for disobedience, arrogance and deference to men. At this point, one would expect that the young man would be sober, fall on his face and beg God for forgiveness. But not King Saul! In the self-defence that followed, Saul appeared to be saying, "Well I acknowledge my sin to you because you already knew about my disobedience. And I did not obey because I feared the people; I needed to be popular among them. I equally disobeyed the Lord because his instructions to kill off the good and the bad did not seem to make sense. Meanwhile, worship and sacrifice are ongoing and I, King Saul, have to presently lead that procession. I need to appear good before the elders. If I go without you, they will know that something is wrong. They will ask questions and get to know that I sinned. So now, you must honour me and go with me to worship so no one knows that there is anything amiss". Saul was prepared to use force on Samuel if need be than allow his reputation descend to the mud. And he tore Samuel's garment when the latter tried to object! That tendency to hide was what killed Saul's ministry and kingdom. That thinking pattern does not belong to the Light; it is the way of darkness and God hates it. In trying to do away with it, God had to do away with Saul and his kingdom. And indeed, many have been done away with as they tried to surround their acts of sin with further darkness rather than allow light penetrate and expose it.

One would have imagined that with both his life and kingdom at stake, Saul would be less concerned about whether or not his sin became public knowledge and focus on reconciling with God and Samuel. But sin does not think or work that way; it will go to any length, even become irrational, to cover up. In trying to protect the throne, Saul did away with the two persons (God and Samuel) that gave him the throne in the first place, and who had power to take both the throne and his life away. Sin will rather sacrifice everything, including things most essential to its existence, than allow itself to be brought to the light. Men have killed very close friends and relatives rather than allow them expose their secret. Others have sacrificed critical positions, responsibilities and privileges than allow a damaging secret which they fear would humiliate them be exposed. And this will continue for as long as there is man and he is allied to sin. When the scriptures said that Adam and his wife saw they were naked, it was referring to something far deeper than physical nakedness. It is a deep fear of being seen for what one really is. This fear literally takes the better part of a man's initiative, making him act irrationally, as he tries to cover up. Adam and Eve would rather sew fig leaves than fall down before God, and Adam would rather blame Eve than take responsibility for what happened in Eden. Eve also would rather look around for the serpent to blame than admit that she did anything wrong. That nature has continued to run in man since the fall.

The only antidote to this hiding lifestyle is the nature of Christ. Christ takes it away from man. Everyone who is not born of God through Christ would always want to hide. Sometimes, an unbeliever in public office (we see this mostly in developed societies) will publicly take responsibility for something he or others did under his watch. But if you look carefully, you will find out that this usually happens after the event has become public knowledge, in which case, there is really little the person could have done about the exposure. He was not the one who disclosed the misdeed. When cornered, sin may weigh the options and realizing that it stands to gain public applause and respect (which it craves equally by the way), it accepts responsibility. Indeed, that might be the simplest (or only) way to retain any modicum of respect. But the issue at stake here is the ability of a man to stand up, reveal an inglorious act he is guilty of and which no other person is aware of, and take responsibility for it because of God. This is termed restitution and comes when a man possesses the life of Christ and cooperates with Him to grow that life. When a man without Christ does an open confession, it is usually because he is cornered, maybe he has nightmares from the incidence he is hiding or he stands to gain better standing from owning up.

Whenever and wherever sin sees opportunity for critical social capital for exposing itself, it will do so. Pride can lead a man to expose sin in the hope that it will enhance his standing among other men. This is particularly the case with people who live in a Christian community where men elevate righteousness. The desire to be among the honoured can outstrip the shame (especially where the sin in question is considered light) and motivate confession. Such confessions only garner social capital for the one involved. But in reality, he merely exchanged one sin for another – say the sin of lying for the sin of pride. In the bid to be seen as righteous, confessing a sin may be a lesser evil and could be traded off for self-respect. History is replete with brave acts undertaken for the sake of enhancing the individual's profile in the sight of others. It is safe to always remember that pride is one of the grosser manifestations of evil and can permit several other sins to be dispensed with, for as long as it is allowed to have free reign.

b. Sin Seeks Its Own

Another key character of sin is that it seeks its own and rejoices in evil. Many of us can identify with that feeling of satisfaction we get when we hear that harm has befallen a perceived opponent. On several occasions, we are ashamed of what people will think if they should know our true feeling because such feeling will be considered base and anti-social. This does not mean there are no instances where we are genuinely happy for others' success. Often we are happy about the successes of those who are related to us or those who are not our 'competitors'.

By nature, man is not interested in things that do not profit him. That is one of the reasons socialism fails and capitalism thrives. However, we have seen men who seem so selflessly committed to and excelled in things that apparently do not yield them any profit. Indeed, the mantra 'for the sake of humanity' has become so ingrained that an increasing number of people do things, not necessarily for what they get out of it, but for legacies that they could leave behind. But therein is the catch. Just as pride causes a man to confess a lesser sin, desire to make a name for oneself can propel a man to do good for humanity. It might be the fun and satisfaction of seeing other people become grateful or the hope that one's name is immortalized. Whatever it is, it is driven by the natural life, the old man, who is inherently evil but who desperately wants to be portrayed as good.

This is one area where the community is dangerous. God created man to commune with Him first and then use the life he draws from God to interact with others. Under such circumstances, it is the life and pleasure of God that should define what a man does. A man's work should stem from what God wants him to do and he should take pleasure in the fact that God is pleased with what he is doing. But when the life of God was severed from Adam and Eve, the duo were just left to each other and the material environment surrounding them; or what we would today call community. When God's word, thoughts and direction were no longer accessible to them, something else had to replace them in relevance. Each person began to take direction from what the other was doing and would relay back to the other for approval of what he or she has done. Gradually, the opinion of one another became law. Because Adam and Eve ate the fruit of 'knowledge of good and evil' they acquired personal capacity for defining good and evil. Similarly, every community has benchmarks of good and evil, and every member of the community strives to be guided by those benchmarks. Communities now define norms and the people in them strive to attain the set norms. These norms and acts may have nothing to do with God; they usually reflect the biases, level of enlightenment, fears and wishes of opinion moulders and political leaders within each community. Enforcement of the norms is then constrained by the extent to which these leaders are able to bring all others in the community to fall in line.

While humanity is good and important (and usually good deeds initiated by God would always favour humanity), humanity has no eternal value without God. The most important thing in the universe is the will of God, the purpose of God. God's purpose includes humanity, but it is not only about humanity. Spirits and other creatures are also involved. The suffering of Job was not about humanity alone. Initially, the contention did not even involve humanity; it was a contention in the spiritual realm involving God, Angels and forces of darkness led by Satan. Job came into the picture because the outcome of the experiment was going to involve his will. In dealing with the earth, God factors all these and His purpose incorporates all. When He gives instructions, it is in consideration of what is good, not only for the earth but for the entire universe; not only for time but also for eternity; not only for humans, but also for other creatures. Thus, initiating things simply because they are for the good of humanity, when God did not or has not authorize(d) them, is useless. Humanity is not qualified to either initiate or act independently. Man neither created the earth nor is he in charge of managing it. So when an act starts and ends with humanity, no matter how good it is, it may actually be borne of sin and of the knowledge of good and evil. Many (including Christians) have fallen into this trap. No matter how originally well-intended they are, they are not acceptable to God. Besides, in the course of carrying them out, such manifestations of sin as pride, self-will, exclusion and contention would appear to further taint the 'good' acts.

c. ... And Draws Strength from the Community

Community not only sanctions projects that do not have God's seal, it is equally a major obstacle to doing the will of God. God confers with the spirit of man. That spirit then gives strength and assurance to the

CHUKWUMA AGU

soul of man and leads him to dominate. But the same day sin appeared, man's spirit died. As we had tried to explain, this death is different and more profound than the cessation of the physical life. Having lost the source of strength that was within, having lost contact with God, man looked for strength outside himself. So man started coming together to depend on the community. Indeed, seeking comfort, ideas and relevance in community is a major hallmark of those who have left or have been left by God. Saul was one man who thought he could build his kingdom on popularity and the will of the people. Saul received instructions to wait for Samuel for seven days and to offer sacrifices in Michmash and Bethel. But he would not; he proceeded to offer the sacrifices himself. When Samuel confronted him, his defence was, "Because I saw that **the people were scattered from me**, and that thou camest not within the days appointed, and that the **Philistines gathered themselves together** at Michmash ..." (1 Samuel 13:11). Samuel, of course, did not regard any of those excuses but proceeded to sharply rebuke him and announce God's displeasure and rejection of him as well as an appointment of a potential replacement. Saul was not moved; instead he turned around and counted the number of people with him. "And Samuel arose, and gat him up from Gilgal unto Gibeah of Benjamin. And Saul **numbered the people that were with him**, about six hundred men" (1 Samuel 13:15). To him, the kingdom was safe for as long as he had the majority. If God and Samuel decided to be in the minority, that was their business and should have no effect on the kingdom. I guess God gave this initial rebuke to see if Saul would see reason and turn to Him, but that was not to be. Later, Saul was sent to Amalek and he gave a similar excuse for sparing Agag, the Amalekite king and the best of men and animals from there. According to his own confession which came only after a long argument, "I have sinned, for I have transgressed the commandment of the Lord, and thy words, **because I feared the people, and obeyed their voice** (I Samuel 15:24 – 25). Saul was more obsessed about people, his personal standing and image among them than with pleasing God. It took Samuel's refusal to accompany him for the evening sacrifice to unravel his underlying motive.

And Samuel said unto Saul, I will not return with thee ...
and as Samuel turned about to go away, he laid hold upon
the skirt of his mantle, and it rent ... and Samuel said unto
him, The Lord hath rent the kingdom of Israel from thee this
day, and hath given it to a neighbor of thine, that is better
than thou ... Then he (Saul) said, I have sinned, yet honour
me now, I pray thee, before the elders of my people, and before
Israel and turn again with me, that I may worship the Lord
thy God" (I Samuel 15: 26 – 30).

The Lord may have rejected Saul, but Saul did not want to risk the people's rejection of him, just as many of us, knowing that God has rejected us, have turned to the people for acceptance instead of seeking the face of God. He did not even want them to know anything was wrong; else his image among them would suffer. This is typical natural man. God's view matters only in so much as it increases his popularity among the people. Otherwise, God's view will be discarded. People swing with changes in norms and fashion as society defines what constitutes acceptable or unacceptable behaviour. Unfortunately, moods and perceptions of the society vary from time to time and from place to place. As long as man wears the present degraded heart, it is impossible to cut off evil. But the extent to which evil is courted in a society depends on how norms are defined. In places where a particular sin is tolerated, men will boldly indulge in it, but will be more circumspect in places where it is abhorred. The reason is that despite what the sinful nature may push people to do, they would still want to be respected by society. Now, there is nothing wrong with community, especially if the community gets its support and direction from God. But often, the community is not led by God or is altogether antagonistic towards God. Like the constituent members, the community gets its support from independent knowledge of good and evil or from other communities' knowledge. Communities hardly set out in search of God to make Him the centerpiece of their existence.

When man fell, he fell out from God, but fell into a community. When a man is disconnected from God, a void exists. He is lonely. He needs warmth from outside himself because the fire within has been extinguished. He has no Holy Spirit to consult. So he naturally falls back on those around him. Man seeks affirmation, not from God, but from men and judge appropriateness based on the views of those around. In some communities, this has been taken to extreme and it is believed that the voice of the people is the voice of God. In line with this, democracy (using the voice of the people to decide governance) has become globally accepted. How erroneous! God has never handed over His voice to people. In many instances in the scriptures, we find that instead, God chooses and stands by a minority that has opened itself up to know and be known by Him. We see such instances as the Joshua and Caleb minority in the report from Canaan (Numbers 13 & 14), the Macaiah minority standing against 400 prophets of Ahab, insisting that Ahab would die in battle (1 Kings 22), the Elijah minority as he withstood the King of Israel and the prophets of Baal (1 Kings 18), the Jeremiah minority as he battled the establishment of false prophets and insisted that Judah would go into exile (Jeremiah 26: 1–15), the Mordecai minority in Shushan as he refused to bow to Haman (Esther 3:1–5), the Shadrack, Meshach and Abednego minority in Babylon (Daniel 3:12) as they refused to bow to the king's golden image, etc. In these instances, we see God standing by the men that have knowledge of Him while the majority stands without God. In some instances, many perished.

The majority can be, and usually is, wrong. So trouble begins when a man measures himself by the scales set by the majority and judges himself by their views. This was the inevitable outcome of sin as Adam and Eve got disconnected from God. We depend on people to endorse our position on issues, to acknowledge our worth, to tell us how good we are, to spur us into action and challenge us to being the best we can be. These are not bad in themselves. Actually, God created man to be in the community, but it was supposed to be a community guided by God Himself. That way, the way of life and views of the community would cohere with those of God. And God understands the powerful influence community has on us. So He orchestrated and set the nation of Israel apart as a community of people who are under His rule and who would influence one another for good based on God's guidance. In that case, whatever influence the community has on its people would be godly. Every individual would first connect to God and then connect to his community thereby connecting the community to God. But depending on a community that has lost connection with God to provide guidepost for individuals is sinful and deadly. It is sin that makes a man to rely on the judgment of the people around him, particularly when such people are not led by the Spirit of God. Any man that must win the battle against sin must watch out for the hold that community wants to have on every man.

The Church as a community was set up for the purpose of bringing the will and wisdom of God to bear on earth. The church is meant to be an environment of transformation of individual lives and society through Christ. But we often see local churches copying and conforming to the society as they prioritize such matters as individual and community welfare, including care for the poor, building mansions, good governance, among others, over and above the preaching of Jesus. Though all of these are commendable, when they are not initiated by Christ, the wisdom of God, they can at best have temporary effect, and at worst lead men astray to idolatry and perdition.

d. Sin Usurps

By its constitution, sin usurps. It usurps the will, position and materials of man, and indeed whatever else it can. Whenever it can, sin foists itself forcefully on man. Just like any other virus, sin does not seek the permission of the owner to operate; it hijacks whatever it can. It even wanted to do that in heaven, to God, but was not allowed. Isaiah 14:13 said, "For thou hast said in thine heart, I will ascend into heaven, I will exalt my throne above the stars of God, I will sit also upon the mount of the congregation, in the sides of the north. I will ascend above the heights of the clouds; I will be like the Most High…" If it were possible, sin would usurp the place and will of God. According to that scripture, sin was conceived in the heart. Next, God rose up and, war broke out in heaven. Sin and all its accomplices were pushed out of heaven. This is the only reason heaven is still a holy place. But the earth and the seas became plagued, "Therefore rejoice, ye heavens, and ye that dwell in them. Woe to the inhabitants of the earth and of the sea! for the devil is come down unto you, having great wrath, because he knoweth that he hath but a short time" (Revelation 12:12).

When the devil came down to the earth, his first assignment was to usurp the will of man, who, by the way, had been made the de facto ruler of the earth. By usurping man, he usurped every other creature that was put under man. Initially, he needed the cooperation and collaboration of man to change masters. Man needed to deny the authority of God and turn himself over willingly to the devil. The moment the devil got that willing submission, the rest was by force. Whereas under the rulership of God, man had freedom of expression and will, under the devil, those are denied. God inspires man to act, then allows the man to act on the inspiration, the devil possesses man and forces the man to act. He can also act directly through man. Whoever refuses to bring his will under submission to the devil is eliminated or made to suffer. The fear of elimination and the urge for survival therefore become the driving forces for actions in many men. The devil equally usurps position, inheritance, desires, etc. Upon arrival, sin dislodges whoever is in a man; its first law is self. Everyone else must give up his position, desires, and all else to sin; else he is not satisfied and there is no peace. As long as there is an opening to force its way through, it will. Beginning from Eden and later through the history of man, it usurps the place of God in the heart of man and in the society. Sin is noisy and loud; it demands attention and insists that God is kept out of the lives of men. And since the fall in Eden, there is no longer freedom of choice for man, except, of course, when a man first hands over his will to Jesus.

Another major way this usurpation of sin is manifested in man is in the desire to be the only one on stage, at all times. Sin protests vigorously whenever it is ignored. A brother once said to me, "Some people are so badly in want of publicity that they would struggle to be the bride in every wedding as well as the corpse in every burial". This may sound extreme, but it depicts the craving in man for social acceptance, identity and applause. Some men perpetually live in the struggle for relevance. What drives this craving is sin, even where it is not apparent to the culprits. Sin seeks attention at all costs. It can spend and be spent if only that could get attention its way. Take a good look at what goes on in the struggle for power. Often, it has little, if anything, to do with service, even though that is the refrain of those pushing for it. It is usually not also (at least not only) about money or survival because majority of those jostling for power are materially well-off, at least relatively. It is usually about relevance and recognition. Even some who credit themselves with humility do not take it kindly to being ignored.

e. Sin Deals with Man as a Number

Contrary to God's pattern, whenever sin is in charge, it builds institutions and lumps man in as numbers. The world system is built on the foundation of sin; consequently, it has no provision for individual care. God created the world to be populous. But in the population, He still knows and deals with each man as an individual. God's relationship with all his children is on individual basis, no matter the number of persons involved. Even though there were 3,000 converts on the day of Pentecost, God does not count them in numbers. Within the group, Stephen would be filled with the Holy Spirit, but this does not preclude Philip's filling, nor does it preclude Nicanor's. God's arrangement is inclusive and every member of the house has an identity, a discussion table with the Holy Spirit. Each person in the congregation has equal access to God and can discuss with God at the same time and at different rates depending on the need. I always find it delightfully amazing when different children of God come from several parts of a nation or even the world and each is sharing his or her dealings with God. Every one of them is unqiue and depicts a father that not only loves them individually and personally, but has the capacity to attend to them differently and uniquely depending on the needs and peculiar constitution of each man.

Sin and the world system it evolved are not so constituted. They cannot cater for man in this way. First, God is a spirit and created man in a manner that makes man accessible to Him and vice versa. He can relate to all men at the same time and in a manner that is not only coordinated, but that makes each person's actions to positively complement other people's. This was God's intention when He set out to use man to rule the world. But as sin took over, that element of complementation that emanates from a central coordination disappeared. Sin can deal with each man, but it cannot build a structure that makes each person complementary to the other. This is one reason there is so much confusion. To solve this problem, sin uses institutions. Unfortunately, under the institutional structures it set up, each man is made irrelevant. The only way to coordinate things under this world system is by assigning numbers to men. Each of us knows the feeling when we are reduced to numbers. As big institutions are built across every sphere, human beings within them become mere 'numbers'. Every man on earth carries a number in one area of his life or the other. This is a convenient invention that keeps men slaving for sin without having any benefit. In universities, students are identified by numbers. When very large corporations fail, compensations are paid according to numbers. Pensioners are given numbers. Governments give numbers to its citizens and workers. Social security is provided through numbers. It is the rule. Man has no other way of organizing society because he is not equipped with the capacity to deal with each individual uniquely. When leaders of institutions move beyond number to have a closer dealing with any one of their staff, such leaders are surprised at how great and warm a personality the 'number' is. Great relationships have been developed in several instances on account of this.

Every man is unique. God recognizes this hence He identifies every man as a soul. This was why He gave unto each one a white stone containing a name that only He and the bearer would know (Revelation 2:17). Being the omni-Spirit that He is, God is the only one with the capacity to attend to the individuality of each man, satisfy the desires of all flesh (Psalms 145:16) and provide warmth to each person as he desires. He equally maintains the communality and coordination that makes society possible. Just take a look at the personal dealings God had with individuals in the book of Acts and the high level of complementarity and coordination that existed between individual actions and the goal for which the Church was set up. Similarly, when a man breaks free from sin, God enables him to relate with other people as individuals. This does not mean he is now empowered to know and help everyone individually (no man has the capacity for this). The grace reflects in the ability to relate, share and be available to men as they have need.

CHAPTER 8

THE INDWELLING, HARDENING MONSTER

a. How Deep-Seated is Sin?

The corruption that immediately followed the fall of man was captured by Paul in the book of Romans as an 'entry', a break-in.

> *"Therefore, just as sin **entered** the world*
> *through one man … (Romans 5:12)"*

The way the word 'entered' was used in that text almost suggested forceful entry, breaking into or pouring in. We earlier alluded to such aggression when we discussed the invasion of Cain by sin. The sin that entered was something completely different from the man it entered. And of course, before it entered the man, it was a distinct personality from the man God created. Even when it entered man, it remained distinct from the man, but over time the sin that entered and the man it entered have seemed to merge into one entity. In all His dealings with mankind, God continues to recognize the uniqueness, potency and destructiveness of this 'thing' that entered and had remained in man. The scriptures had this to say of the thing that was in man.

> *Now when He was in Jerusalem at the Passover, in the feast day,*
> *many believed in his name, when they saw the miracles which*
> *he did. But Jesus did not commit himself unto them, because he*

knew all men, and needed not that any should testify of man;
*for He knew **what was in man*** *(John 2: 23 – 25).*

The problem was not man; the problem was the 'something' in man. That something in man was a problem, even to Jesus. For simplicity, we describe this entity that entered man as a monster. When the Sin monster entered, it remained. There is no record that it ever came out. What is it doing inside man? First, it possessed and overcame the man, forcing itself upon man. The classic lamentation by Paul in Romans 7:15 – 17 largely reflects this plight of most men:

"For that which I do I allow not: for what I would, that do
I not; but what I hate, that do I. If then I do that which I
would not, I consent unto the law that it is good. Now then
it is no more I that do it, but sin that dwelleth in me.

Now the scriptures say that the life of the flesh is in the blood (Leviticus 17:11). What entered into man permeated the blood, and became his life in the flesh. To be able to take away anything inside the blood, the life of the man in the blood would have to be drained out. And that is the reason why men protect sin with their lives to the point of death. Sin only willingly lets go of a man when it is sure that the man's life is over. So a number of people 'confess' their evils at the point of death. Such confessions are often mere matter-of-fact statements a lot more than they are of repentance. Sin is willing to let out then because the man is already on his way out and there is nothing to hold him again for.

This is also why dealing with sin is such a herculean task. It is a monster that gets born into the man; and remains part of his life all through. This also explains why the only way to deal with it effectively is by pouring out the life, by death. Often, when we read the scriptures and encounter God talking about blood as a requirement for dealing with sin, some imagine God is merely being mean. We quietly wonder, "Is there no easier way of doing away with our small wrongdoings?" I must confess that I have also severally asked this question and thought the same way. Must animals have to be killed so that the sins of the Jews may be covered, and only temporarily at that? Must Jesus die on the cross before sin could be taken away permanently? Was there no other way? I realized that it is only when we understand how deeply ingrained sin is in man that we appreciate why the shedding of blood or killing the entity it occupied are the only ways of dealing with it. The bible validates this argument when it states, "...without shedding of blood there is no remission of sin" (Hebrews 9:22). There is no other way! When we understand this, we also appreciate God's mercy. When Adam and Eve sinned, God had to kill an animal. From there, He brought clothing to the couple. But the animal could not only have been killed for clothing. God could have obtained clothing for them through other means. Even as people with limited knowledge, we do not kill animals everyday so we can clothe ourselves. The God that created cotton could have woven yarn for them, but He chose to kill an animal. In killing the animal, God Himself offered the first sacrifice for sin. The reason was that Adam and Eve had contracted sin; and by that token they should die, not only spiritually as they did, but also physically. But God needed them to continue physically in order to multiply the human race and thereby bring forth the seed that would crush sin. Otherwise, God would have to do away with the present world and create another. To retain their physical lives, another physical life had to be given up. God chose an animal. When God got the people He had chosen to bear the holy Seed, He knew that it was important that sin is continually cleansed for them to be minimally pure till the coming of the perfect one. So He decreed sacrifices aimed at cleansing people when they come in contact with defilement. When the time came to fully crush the devil and redeem man spiritually as well, God sent Jesus. In all these, man has never had to pay with his own blood for his sins. This is mercy. Possibly the reason many never realize or acknowledge the crushing power and magnitude of sin.

Babies are born into sin. On behalf of mankind, David proclaimed that we are conceived and brought forth in sin and iniquity (Psalms 51:5). This is probably one of the greatest evidences of the extent to which human life is interwoven with sin. Sin is natural with us from conception, before we are born. No one ever teaches another how to sin. Instead, all the trainings man receives throughout life is about how to correct some of the cracks in his life and nature emanating from sin. The scriptures declare that foolishness abound in the heart of the child, and only the rod of correction can drive it away (Proverbs 22:15). Foolishness and the fool are alternative words for sin and the sinner in the scriptures. A child abuses a man that has done nothing to him. Many a parent have been thoroughly mortified at the capacity of their children to incubate and hatch all forms of sin. Telling lies comes natural to most children. They need no one to teach them. Children gravitate easily towards negative peers, and for most of their teenage years, the struggle to minimize these negative influences completely occupies many parents, often pitting parents against children. Sin is in man from cradle and grows with man all through his life unto the grave.

b. Sin Hardens the Heart

When I was younger, I used to think that the hold of sin on a person's life weakens as the person grows older. How wrong I was! It is actually the reverse: the older one gets, the stronger the hold of sin over him. The longer a man stays in sin, the more accustomed to it he becomes and the easier he can swim in it without noticing anything wrong. For all men without Christ, the stranglehold of sin remains; the only difference is the capacity of the sinner to cover it. The well-educated and worldly-wise employ civility for cover. The rest have more difficulty. For everyone though, the two extreme ages – infancy and very old age – bear particular difficulty in keeping the manifestation of the self-life in check. A two-year old child has very little capacity to control the manifestations of sin and the flesh. At that age, we see the grosser manifestations of foolishness, raw selfishness and all the tantrums of the natural man. The child needs lots of shouting in order to attain minimum decorum. But as he grows older and learns from others and his environment, he is able to comport himself better, such that the manifestations of sin become more subdued and less obvious to others. As the same individual grows old and the capacity of the faculties begins to weaken, the uncontrolled manifestations of self-life once again reappear. The reason for this is that every man yet to be redeemed from the bond of sin by the Lord Jesus lives with it all life. What the society does is to teach every new member to carry sin in a manner that does not obstruct the movement of others. The moment it defines which sins to abhor and which to accept, it trains (or forces) everyone to imbibe these. Then laws are created with sanctions to deter deviations or incentives to reward those best able to subdue the grosser manifestations. Overall, time is not useful in dealing with sin. I remember when as a boy of about 10, I used to think that it would be easier for me to determine to give my life to Christ by age 12. But throughout teenage, I realized I could do nothing against or about sin till God appeared much later in life to save me. Many are wallowing in that sort of foolishness, thinking there is a miracle age when righteousness becomes second nature to man and when answering God becomes easier. Like most other things, this is the devil's deception. Sin is engraved in man and only cooperation with Jesus can deal with it. And the Lord Jesus says now is the accepted time. There is no better time in the future; now is the time (2 Corinthians 6:2).

Refusing to repent from a sin also strengthens the hold of sin over a man's heart. As a man assuages his conscience instead of expressing godly sorrow over sin, he begins to get more comfortable with the sin. When a man initially falls into sin, he might be uncomfortable in it. But if he does not quickly repent but persists in it, a time comes when he becomes very comfortable in the sin. I once heard the story of a young man, who in a moment of carelessness, slept with his immediate cousin. The little girl did not seem to mind, but the young man rose from the bed and wept his eyes out. However, the girl visited the next time, and they fell into the same sin again. This time, he stood up and felt that something was wrong with all this, and that he should not continue in it. But it was not the same heart-rending tears again. As time went on, the girl kept repeating her visits and not long after, they settled into it as a lifestyle, no more pricks of the conscience, no more questions, no more tears. It became normal. The same way, every robber will tell you of the tension of the first attempt. But over time, the heart hardens and shedding blood becomes normal. Violent persons of all sorts share the same trajectory; everyone begins with trepidation, but ends up hardened. Any sin can become normal if the initial manifestation of that sin is not accompanied by godly sorrow that leads to repentance. Waiting is dangerous.

That was Pharaoh's experience. At initial glance, it appears God deliberately hardened Pharaoh's heart. But could God have deliberately and irreversibly hardened Pharaoh's heart? It is similar to saying that God caused a man to sin. He cannot because it is not his desire that any man should perish. And indeed, God does not need to. Pharaoh's interaction with sin was enough to do that; just as it is for every other man. He was already living in a system of evil established by his fathers, killing little babies that did him no wrong, extracting service from men by violence, worshiping demons and false gods, involving in sorcery and consultation of mediums and spirits, maintaining a legacy of iniquity in Egypt. How much worse can a man get in the pursuit of wickedness? But in addition, the first time he was confronted by Moses concerning God, his response was "I do not know the Lord, neither will I let Israel go" (Exodus 5:2). He never gave God a chance. Moses tried to explain to him that the God in question was the one that created the heavens and the earth, but Pharaoh's heart was already occupied; there was no space for God in it. And God is the only source of light, the only deliverance there can ever be from sin. So Pharaoh's heart became hardened, not because God came against him, but because he stood against God. He was already so steeped in sin that God was kept out for good. Even after seeing all that God set out to do to deliver Israel, Pharaoh was not moved. He would momentarily pretend to repent so a plague is removed, but quickly got back into the dugout the moment he had some respite. He had no qualms playing hide and seek with the God of heaven, telling lies and making promises he had no intention of keeping, thinking to outwit God. For such a man, there was only one possible ending: death. This has nothing to do with God being against him.

Living in sin makes a man to become less sensitive to warning against sin because sin spreads layers of wax and other forms of dangerous covering over a man's heart. Each time a heart contacts sin, a layer of wax akin to film of oil or clay, seems to be laid over that heart. Each layer makes the heart more difficult to reach and therefore less sensitive to sin's damaging effects. Often, it is those around, not the sinner, who perceive the dangers in the evil lifestyle of a man. The more the layers of covering, the more difficult it is for the man to embrace repentance. Some who hear the gospel postpone their repentance. The thinking is that they can repent any time they wish to. This is at best presumptuous. No man can draw near to God or repent by his own volition. None can repent whenever he is ready or feels like doing so, because the man is dead and wrapped up in sin. His heart has been completely wrapped up by several layers of sin-wax. He is completely helpless. Can you imagine Lazarus or any other person, four days in the grave, deciding to come out of his own volition? Whenever we are touched by the power in the gospel, that is Jesus' call and help come for us. Postponing repentance at such time could be eternally fatal. Imagine Lazarus hearing the words of Jesus from the other world, smiling and telling Jesus to please come back some other time, because he is occupied at the moment. All the while Jesus delayed coming to Bethany, Lazarus had no power over either the sickness that overcame him or the death that demobilized and held him bound afterwards. To some, this may seem like a far-fetched analogy, but it is exactly the same. Sin and death are just two sides of the same coin, acting the same way on man. While one kills a man spiritually at the instance, the other kills him at the instance physically. And no man can deal with either of them except it is in response to the resurrection call of the Lord. This is what the Lord Jesus was referring to when He said "No one can come to me except the Father that sent me draws him" (John 6: 44 – NIV). Except God comes to a man with the resurrection power, nothing else can recover and release him from the hold of sin.

However, for every man, God gives a window of opportunity for repentance. It is necessary that a man utilizes that window. At such times, grace is made available to conquer sin and death. Failure to utilize that grace can be dangerous. Without this window, it is impossible for a man to draw close to God. The window of opportunity that God gives for repentance is one reason some think it is God that decides whether or not a man is saved. However, this is an incomplete picture. While God reserves the right to throw open the window of opportunity, man has the responsibility of taking it. And God usually ensures that every man gets at least one of such opportunity in a lifetime. Most people get many opportunities, but refuse to take or even accept them. When a man turns his back on God's opportunity, even God is unable to help him in any other way. In a way then, it is both God's exclusive predestination and man's ultimate choice that define salvation.

Paul made the point about the covering power of sin when he noted that:

> But their minds were blinded: for until this day remaineth the same veil untaken away in the reading of the Old Testament; which veil is done away in Christ. But even unto this day, when Moses is read, the veil is upon their heart. 2 Corinthians 3:14 – 15

This veil does not just cover the eyes; it covers the heart – 'their minds were blinded'. So the individual is not only blocked from sight, he is blocked from life. If a man does not understand that he is totally dead in trespasses and that it is only the pull of God through Christ Jesus that can bring him back to life, there is very little hope for him to get life. Such realization comes as the heart prays and beseeches God to have mercy and take away the veil and remove the layers of clay cake. Then God intervenes, releases light into and softens that heart. That marks the beginning of life.

As the Lord opens a man's eyes, he is able to see both himself and others for what they really are. Among other realizations, the liberated man begins to see how much an illusion the sinner surrounds himself with; how close to danger of destruction and yet how unaware of it he is. This is both frightening and disheartening. Some men may well know and privately admit that all is not well with them, but they are far from appreciating the depth of the threat sin poses to their lives, either here or in eternity. It is because of this ignorance that no one is willing to allow his own failings become a subject of public scrutiny, even if that is the only way to receive help. They know there is sin and this sin is not the best for them, but sin prevents them from seeing how close they are to destruction so they do not shout out to God for help.

c. Sin, the Flesh and the Devil

We come to the interrelationship of sin, flesh and the devil on man. By *flesh* here, we mean what many of us call the 'human nature', the nature every man inherited from Adam after he fell. The bible described it as "And Adam lived an hundred and thirty years, and begat a son in his own likeness, after his image..." (Genesis 5:3). The flesh is not necessarily the human body; the body is the dwelling place for the soul and spirit of man as well as God's dwelling place (1 Cornthians 6:19). The scriptures call the nature of man the sinful nature because it harbours evil: lusts, greed, selfishness, pride, bitterness and every other thing that is anti-God (Galatians 5: 17 – 19). It makes relationship with God difficult, if not impossible. Flesh is in rebellion against God and would want to have everything its own way. It does not mind occasional interventions by God and others, particularly if it is to help it out of some tight situations, but it does not want anyone dictating to it. It wants to take glory for all its achievements and does not like sharing the platform or being made subject to anyone. The flesh wants to get the best of everything; and is sorely afraid of dying. It has the capacity for a lot of good deeds, but whenever it does any such, it wants to take the glory or to get something out of it. It is incapable of doing something for nothing. It seeks gain, sometimes intangible gain, but gain all the same.

It is this entity within man that is responsible for sin. In trying to describe the process of temptation to sin, James (1:13 - 14) had this to say:

*"Let no one say when he is tempted, 'I am tempted by God',
for God cannot be tempted by evil, nor does He Himself tempt
anyone. But each one is tempted when he is drawn away by
his own desires (lusts) and enticed"*

Drawn away by **his own** lusts? Yes. Each man has his own lusts.
They reside inside of him and the container of those lusts is what
the scriptures call the flesh. It has the capacity to drag a man away,
forcefully. Everyday, men are forcefully dragged into drugs, alcohol,
pride, sexual pervasions, bitterness, contention, etc., by their own lusts.
Conmen rely entirely on the lust in their potential victim in order to
succeed. Fraudsters tell bogus stories of potential gains that could
accrue to their victim if he agrees to join them in a particular business.
Then they wait for the juicy offer to evoke a reaction. If a strong lust
resides inside the victim's heart, it will arise and paint a picture of
the good life that is possible with the yet-to-be acquired wealth. This
picture will increase the desire to be part of the business. The victim
then jumps into the business with whatever resources he can lay his
hands on; and then he is hooked. Lust and desire are all part of the
flesh. When the flesh is not dealt with, it carries a man away using lust
and desire. Even men who are involved in what appears to be good
deeds can equally be driven by lusts and desires. No man born of a
woman is free from lusts and desires, except he has been deliberately
delivered of it by the Lord Jesus.

Now, desire is not negative by itself. It serves as a propeller within
to make humanity aspire and to be able to pursue the purpose of God
on earth. However, it was corrupted to now focus and be used, almost
exclusively, for pursuing ephemeral things and for self. Thus it became
lust; poisonous and inimical to the health of man. And understandably,
God detests it. Lust draws away from God. It points man's attention to
pleasures that do not proceed from God. It gives man the impression
that things, both material and psychological, outside of God have the
capacity to satisfy him. So man goes in pursuit of them.

The flesh sits inside and the devil sits outside of mankind. The one
outside needs the cooperation of the one inside to be able to control

man. With the flesh sitting in, the devil often does not need to do much. He does not need to come and tempt everyman every time before the man can sin. The deposit of lust within the man is enough to continue the reproduction of sin. Picture the devil as one with a rope having hook at the end. He throws it at every human being. However, it cannot stick unless there is a hookpin within the individual where the hook can enter and stick to. When he throws it and there is a hookpin, the line will stick to the hookpin through the hook. The devil will then draw the individual using the line and hook. The hookpin within the individual is called lust. The devil searches for it in everyman. Whenever he is able to find it in a man, he throws the hook and line and then the man is drawn towards whatever evil machinations he already has put in place to destroy the man. If he throws the hook and line and there is no hookpin in a man, then the attempt fails. That was what Jesus referred to when He told His disciples, "the prince of this world cometh, but he findeth nothing in me" (John 14:30).

It is the flesh (lust) inside of us that interacts with the world (our external environment), mostly through the senses. In its classic way of economizing words and using spiritual imagery, the scriptures merely told us of the beginning of the sitting of this flesh saying "... and their eyes were opened..." (Genesis 3:7). When that happened, they were introduced into a realm where nakedness reigns. This lust does not only inhabit the man who is not born again, it also enthralls the believer who is worldly. Indeed, the whole process of the formation of Christ in man is to take away this lust and replace it with the pure life that Christ has which is not subject to the control of lusts.

Lust is a jailer. The lust in man sees the world and is attracted to the diverse manifestations of its glory. It then compels man to follow what it has seen and serve the world; even when the man might not like what he is doing. Lust carries him to where he does not want to go and compels him to do things he would not want to do. That is why Paul put the struggle we have with him this way:

> *"For what I will to do, that I do not practice; but what I hate, that I do. If, then, I do what I will not to do, I agree with the*

law that it is good. But now it is no longer I who do it, but
sin that dwells in me"(Romans 7: 19-20).

Lust is very difficult to fight, partly because it is inside the one who wants to fight him. But more importantly because it is extremely subtle; it hardly allows people to know how elusive it is or how impossible it is for man to become lord of both himself and the world. It leads man to pursue independence and control, things God has taken away from man. It then gives man the impression that only a little more effort will enthrone him over the world and other men. It never wants man to understand that he is completely incapacitated and incapable of helping himself. That way, man continues to struggle, hoping to find within him the strength he needs to be lifted out of the stranglehold of the world and of sin.

Every sin usually starts as the desire to be, to do or to get – and this is where the devil comes in. The desire moves on to become enticement; the sort of drama he played with Eve in the garden. A picture is painted in the mind of a man and the devil elaborates the possibilities available when a man follows that path. This is what scripture was referring to when it said "But every man is tempted when he is drawn away of his own lust, and enticed" (James 1:14). In Eve's case, she saw independence, transformation into a god with all the possibilities thereof, healthy food, wisdom all becoming hers by simply stretching her hands to pick up the fruit. At this point, whatever God may have said about the issue looked like an obstacle to her well-being. The devil usually gives the impression that the reason God does not want us to indulge in a certain act is because He wants to restrict our liberty, choices and pleasure. Often then, God is seen as part of the problem, the core enemy and obstacle to this whole range of goodness. Unfortunately, in nearly all cases, the picture being painted is anything but correct. At the point of conception, the act seems not only possible but attractive. But usually, as all sinners will attest, when we eventually get into it, we see that the devil never told us about the death attached to the act. Besides, whatever 'gains' or pleasure we would get is short-lived, if they ever materialize.

CHAPTER 9

SIN AND DEATH –THE ETERNAL PARTNERSHIP

a. The Partnership

Sin and death share contrasting characteristics. While most manifestations of sin appear very attractive and harmless, the manifestation of death is the very opposite: very painful and unattractive. Indeed, the reason sin is patronized and courted by many people is its promise (or actual delivery) of sweetness and fun. Let us take pride for example. For as long as there is something to display, it is extremely gratifying to be the centre of attraction. In fact, training at all stages of the natural life encourages us to show off our best. And we enjoy it when we do it well and people acknowledge it. Fornication and associated vices have a pull, an appeal that appear 'pleasurable.' Exaggeration and lies make us feel good, get us out of trouble or promote our self-image, at least momentarily. Putting other people down behind them often gives those doing it a sense of personal relevance and a feeling of being better than the one spoken about. The pull towards sin often comes with desirable sensations that keep us attracted to them. This good feeling is true for nearly every sin.

But death comes in a different mold. It comes with pain. It comes with incapacitation and sickness; it comes with degeneration and consignment to irrelevance. While many sins are means of expressing oneself and becoming visible, death consigns a man to oblivion. It seals the fate of a man and completely removes the probability of self-expression forever. Nobody likes death; just about everybody dreads death. With its stillness, irreversibility, coldness, dampness and clamp finality, there is nothing flashy, friendly or attractive about death. All the attractions of sin are absent in death. If men could, they would stop themselves from lying in state at death because then, there is nothing to see. Death takes away all the beauty and expressive qualities people hold dear, leaving emptiness and ugliness.

But herein lies the challenge. Men often do not perceive that the two entities – sin and death – are two sides of the same coin. Sin is death-in-progress while death is sin-completed. Death is the destination of sin and sin is the pathway to death. The main reason sin exists is that it might call forth death just as the only framework upon which death hangs is sin. Death is powerless without sin just as sin does not have the power to harm except by leading to death. This seems to be taken for granted in the scriptures as shown by many passages. But men hardly see it.

> *"O death, where is thy sting? O grave, where is thy victory?*
> *The sting of death is sin; and the strength of sin is the law.*
> *But thanks be to God, which giveth us the victory through*
> *our Lord Jesus Christ (1 Corinthians 15:55 – 57).*

O death, where is thy sting? Death has **no** other sting apart from sin. A snake is not dangerous and indeed has no power if not the power resident in its sting. The only reason people do not go clasping scorpions in their hands is because of the sting. The sting is the power of the stinger and in many cases animals that sting do not have any power except that of injecting stings. For many of such animals, if the sting could be removed, one can play about with them. So is it with death. Its power over man is held by sin and without sin, death is completely powerless. For as long as a man does not contact sin, he cannot be contacted or overcome by (spiritual) death. That is the reason death had no power over the Lord Jesus Christ – He had no sin. When a man jostles around sin, he is meddling with the potency of death. Any man therefore who does not want to have anything to do with death simply has to avoid sin.

For I was alive without the law once: but when the
commandment came, sin revived, and I died" (Romans 7:9)

Sin revived … and I died. Paul, who made this statement, was still alive when he penned down the words. So the death he was referring to could not have been the sort many of us are familiar with, and are afraid of. It is therefore important at this point to differentiate between two kinds of death – spiritual and physical. Spiritual death is the death God told Adam of 'on the day that ye eat of it, ye shall surely die' (Genesis 2:17). That is the death Paul referred to here as sharing in. And indeed that is the death which everyman has died. And that death came when sin revived.

But spiritual death must first be before physical death can be. Spiritual death makes possible physical death. The physical death, which most men identify with, begins at the point of spiritual death and so cannot also come except by sin. The revival of sin is the beginning of death, again affirming a very potent relationship in which sin is the forerunner (or ancestor) of all deaths. No man dies without reviving sin and it is impossible to revive sin without death following. The decay in the body of man comes because man is wearing the human nature which has been corrupted by sin. The life to come is not tainted by sin; that is why it is potent and eternal; and cannot be overcome by death.

*Wherefore, as by one man **sin** entered into the world, **and***
***death** by **sin**; and so **death** passed upon all men, for that all*
have sinned (Romans 5:12)

The above passage shows the sin-death relationship very clearly. Sin entered by (one) man and death entered by sin. It would be impossible for death to enter if sin did not first create the road. Death cannot (does not have the power to) chart its own course. Whatever death any man can experience can only come because such a man has been tainted by sin. As we all know, sin takes away strength and boldness from a man and makes him bow to the power of death. Death does not dare confront any man who has not sinned. It is too shy and weak to do that. The scriptures say the wages of (payment or reward given for) sin is death (Romans 6:23).

> *For the law of the Spirit of life in Christ Jesus hath made me free from the law of sin and death (Romans 8:2)*

Sin and death share the same law. There are no two laws, one for sin and the other for death. Just as the law of the Spirit is of life in Christ Jesus, so is the law of sin also of death. Once the law of sin has been contacted or breached, nothing else needs be done before death naturally follows. Sometimes, there could be temporal (time) difference and men therefore fail to make the connection, but the law is certain and the interpretation sure. Time means nothing in eternity and the connection does not fail because of time. The law of sowing and reaping is so universal that unbelievers know it as well. And so when we see a man sowing wickedness, we know that it is a matter of time before death catches up with him. The above scripture indicates that there is only one hope for anyone entangled with the law of sin and death; that hope is the law of life in Christ Jesus. And the law of life in Christ Jesus does not relieve a man of death without dealing with sin in him. The power of the law of life in Christ Jesus to annul death is in its capacity to deal with sin. As long as sin hangs around, death retains a potent claim on a man's life. This is the reason it is dangerous to cast out a demon or bring healing to a man without instructing him to go home and sin no more or teaching him how to stay without sin.

We referred to the assertion by the Holy Spirit in James 1: 15 that 'when lust hath conceived, it bringeth forth sin: and sin, when it is finished, bringeth forth death'. This might give the impression that the relationship between sin and death is like that between a father and a son where one gives birth to the other after attaining a certain age of maturity. But this could be quite misleading. Both actually co-exist and are inseparable. Sin and death exist side by side and for every sin, there is death. Death is the flipside of sin … and indeed though sin might seemingly endure for a while without physical death appearing, the spiritual death is instantaneous. And the coin could flip any moment to bring about physical death. It needs no further notice and the timing of the flip is completely unpredictable, outside the control of man. It is only a matter of divine mercy that physical death does not show up every moment sin is contracted. In the timeless world of eternity, both co-exist and concurrently manifest. But in the temporal world, God's mercy permits the separation in occurrence so as to allow human beings time to repent and be forgiven (2 Peter 3:9). In putting this discourse this way, we are deliberately separating spiritual from physical death. But such separation is only notional and completely arbitrary. Just as spiritual death is instantaneous with sin, the sentence of physical death is also instantaneous. However, the mercy of God often holds off manifestation of physical death so as to give time for man to repent. Unfortunately for many people, this grace is hardly utilized. Instead, the gap in time of appearance between the two makes it difficult for them to mentally link sin to death. There are instances where after extending the rope for too long for a man and seeing that man persistently refuse to hold it, God would be left with no option but to allow instantaneous manifestation of death.

We see a few instances of such cases in the book of Acts. Acts 12 tells the story of Herod, the powerful governor of Judea, who not only knew the privileges and powers of the political office he held, but reveled in and regularly abused them. He ruled with a combination of threat, oppression, and violence and got so power-drunk that he began to stray into and stand in God's paths, using his office to prevent the spread of the gospel of salvation in Christ, initiated and backed by God. So Herod killed James, the brother of John and one of the pillars of the early Church, ostensibly without trial. This gave a much needed boost to his popularity rating among the Jews. It was a perfect coincidence of wants: the Jews hated the truth of the gospel the same way he did and killing those behind it would not only help scuttle the spread of this virus, it also yielded much political capital. So he proceeded to arrest Peter also, another pillar. But as the brethren prayed ahead of the date set for Peter's judgement and possible execution, God sent an Angel to release him. Herod was very infuriated and ordered the execution of all the soldiers into whose hands Peter was committed. God was very patient with the man, hoping that one day, he might see the light. But like many in his shoes, he got from bad to worse. The people of Tyre and Sidon relied heavily on him for supplies, but maybe he was not getting the sort of political support he believed he deserved from them. So he decided to teach them a little lesson on political loyalty; he cut their supplies and refused to grant them further audience. As is usually the case, the people were forced to their knees and had to look for someone who had access to Herod to help them. They got Blastus, the king's chamberlain, whom they induced to facilitate a meeting so they could come to appease the king. On the said day, the people came out in their numbers to hail and show their loyalty to this all-powerful king. It mattered little if they had to do this with much hypocricy; they needed the supplies to survive and this man had it. Both sides knew what the issue was; they had not really offended the governor, it was just that the governor needed to remind them that someone was in charge. There were no cases to answer, no appeals and no panels. The governor went straight to his speech, reminding them of the history of his family in the power equations of the region, how much weight he pulled even in Rome, how all resources in the entire area is concentrated in his hands and why it is futile for anyone to ever imagine that they could undercut him. He lectured them on the importance of loyalty and what they stand to lose by not fully supporting him. He also reminded them of how he mercilessly dealt with previous oppositions. The people had been through very difficult time and knew how much it cost them to even get this audience with the man. So they would not miss this opportunity of giving him the larger-than-life image of himself that his ego so badly needed. So they shouted, "It is the voice of a god, and not of a man". Though many of them could not have meant it literally, it was good for Herod's ears. This was the very thing he has been longing for. Now men appreciate that he was no ordinary man; he was a god and should be immortalized. At that point, God had to come in and terminate Herod. This sin had to carry instantaneous death.

The relationship of sin and death holds even when the person involved is a believer. The scripture says that 'the soul that sinneth, it shall die ..." (Ezekiel 18: 4, 20). Often, when God is punishing sin, as in the example of old testament wars, punishing nations, the impression left in the untutored heart is that of a God of retribution and vengeance. There is the thinking that a God of love should not be mean on people. But the fact is, it is not the men but sin that is under judgment. Men get involved because they are instruments of sin. Again, it is not really God standing up to say, "I am going to have my pound of flesh from these people because of what they have done or are doing to me". Just as the opposite of light is darkness, so also the opposite of righteousness is sin and sin is equal to death. Touch anything with sin and you have inflicted it with death. So even if God says or does nothing, because those things are sin-stained, they shall also be death-stained. It is an immutable law of nature that the soul that sinneth shall die; just the same way the law of gravity demands that when a physical object is thrown up, it must be drawn down. In this, God does not have to move around to seek out who has sinned to punish him. The laws of life and death, working without intrusion from any other entity, will naturally bring death to the person who has sinned. This understanding helps a man not to accuse God foolishly when he is faced with the consequences of who he is or what he has done. Of course, the devil would always want to point us away from him when we suffer for sin and give us the impression that God is against us because He is a hard man. But how useful it would be if we are to know that this is not about God; it is about the law upon which all creation and the relationship among them is founded. If God permits any sin to go unpunished, then He might as well have to apologize to the devil and to numerous others throughout creation whose sins have been punished. Indeed, the people who get punished the most for sin are the children of God. God has almost zero tolerance for sin from those who are supposed to know better. The Israelites have been more frequently punished for sin in history than any other nation on earth. While God will bear with Nineveh and send them Jonah the prophet to avert the punishment of sin, Israel is regularly sold to their enemies in response to sin. Individual Christians can also attest from their experiences that God deals with them the same way as well.

God showed His distaste for sin with believers in the story of Ananias and Saphira (Acts 5). Unlike Herod, this husband and wife were part of the new move of God. They had repented and had been part of the sharing and communality that had fast become a way of life with the brethren. They also noticed that this sharing lifestyle was sustained by members' giving. But after one particular meeting, they noticed that the Apostles were quite excited about one man, Joses who sold his land and delivered the proceeds to be distributed. In fact, Joses even acquired a new name 'Barnabas', meaning Son of Consolation, given to him by no less a person than Peter. He later noticed how everybody else talked about the same man; his humility, his generosity, his commitment and the power of the Holy Spirit in him. Ananias became agitated hearing all this; he figured that if nothing happened, he would be relegated to the background by men like this. And that would be very fatal given that this new faith was fast gaining momentum and gathering followership, including the high and mighty. Joses just came back from Cyprus and joined this movement about the same time as Ananias. How come he was overtaking everybody in popularity? Well, Ananias reasoned that if it was just about selling land and handing over the money, he was not going to allow this man outdo him. Afterall, he had many properties and could relinquish one to improve his standing among the brethren. So he put it up for sale, got a buyer and sold it. But there was a problem: did he really believe that all this giving and sharing was beneficial and not making people lazier? He had always had questions about the way things are run here. He had never been one to give away so much money, especially when it is to feed people who were neither sick nor disabled, but who "chose" not to work. All these people that gather daily could do better for themselves than waiting to be fed and provided for from a common purse. These apostles were not really teaching people to use their time and talents well. Instead, everyone waits for the next person that would sell his things and bring the money. Of course he knew this was not sustainable. If not for people like him who had made money before joining, where would the resources for sustaining this come from? A time would come when everyone had sold all they had and they too would become dependent. Who would provide the money then? But he had to solve the popularity problem first. If all went well and he became popular, he could be promoted through the ranks and become a council member. Then he would change the way things were run.

There was a second challenge. He was not sure in his mind that he needed to give out all that he got from the land to achieve his aim. The price he got from the sale was pretty generous and though he did not know how much Joses gave, he was pretty sure it was not that much. Besides, there would be the rainy day and he needed to remember that. After much thought, he felt he needed his wife's input into this. So he conferred with her. Interestingly, she had shared these same sentiments for long, but had not been very sure of what he would make of them seeing his zeal for the new found faith. Did she not go into this whole thing following him? It was quite a relief. So they agreed on how much to give and how much to keep back. They had unattended needs in the house and it would be foolish to simply hand in all they had on their hands to these men. They agreed that they would just hand in the money, but if the leaders became too inquisitive, they would tell them it was all the money they got for the land. It was a win-win; Peter and his cohorts would get much needed money for sustaining the bazaar while he and his wife get much-needed popularity and become more relevant in the scheme of things. In fact, given the amount they planned to give, he was sure Peter would heap praises on them as he did Joses. After all, he did not know how much the land was sold for. But coming from a background of Judaism where hypocricy and lies were a way of life and where both leaders and subjects pretended to one another, this husband and wife underrated God's hatred for double living. Fellowship time came and the husband needed to go and hand in the money but the wife had a few personal things to sort out in the house. So he left first. He gave Peter the money but the latter looked at him. Instead of expressing happiness, Peter seemed to frown, looking troubled. He seemed to guess what he and his wife had done. Before even Ananias could say anything, Peter started off, reminding Ananias that both the sale of the land and the handing over of the money to the brethren were his choices. But he had chosen to taint these choices with lies and dare the Holy Spirit with a life of hypocrisy. Ananias was still in shock, looking at the man and wondering how he came to know all this when he swooned and fell. He breathed his last; end of life for Ananias. Three hours later, Saphira came in. But by the time she came, the buzz and flurry of activities that followed her husband's death and interment had quietened down. She greeted the brethren cheerfully, some answered, but others just looked at her as though they were no longer so sure who she was. She did not like the empty stares that they gave her, but she decided to ignore them. After all, many of these people could act weird sometimes; good enough, they do not all count in the overall scheme of things. She could afford to ignore them when they come up with these unfriendly moods. But she had to go up and greet the apostles; it was important to do so. Peter and the rest answered warmly, as usual, and for that she was grateful. Then Peter calmly asked her about the money she had agreed with her husband to give the Church. "Tell me whether ye sold the land for so much?" Her mind raced; maybe this was it. But was there any reason anyone should suspect what they did? Her husband was not the flippant type and could not have snitched on her. He could not have told anyone a secret held between the two of them. So, why the question? Well, if they expected her to contradict her husband, then they got it wrong. She had to steady her voice as she replied, "Yea, for so much". Then Peter's demeanour changed and the last she heard, he was talking about tempting the Holy Spirit and her husband being dead and buried. Then she passed out.

Scripture says "For the wages of sin *is* death; but the gift of God *is* eternal life through Jesus Christ our Lord" (Romans 6:23). Assuming we put the text mathematically, using standard notations where 'of' stands for multiplication and 'is' stands for 'equals to', we will have the equation:

Wages *multiplied by* sin *equals to* death
Or simply
Wages x sin = death

This implies that whatever a man may have, which is looking like payment or wages, if touched by sin, yields death. Whenever wages are of sin, the product is death. We need not wait for God on this matter, except if waiting for mercy, He neither needs to add or subtract from the relationship; it is an equation. The only intervention God can make in the matter of the relationship between sin and death is to take advantage of the gap in time between the manifestation of sin and that of physical death to employ mercy for the salvation of the sinner. However, because it is sin, it still has to be judged. So God will judge sin, but can set the sinner free. But that is only on the condition that the sinner cooperates with God through repentance (1 John 1: 9). This principle is applicable to specific acts of sins in our lives. If there is a sin you are guilty of, you have to pick it up as an entity and confess it. Deal with it and do not assume that it will go away. Sin does not stop on the way or just go away of its own accord; it stops only when it has arrived at death, usually taking the sinner along. Let no man be in any illusion over this matter; all sins must be judged. That is why trifling with it is such a terrible risk.

Proverbs (14:12) and (16:25) note the relationship between sin and death as that between a road and its destination. Hear the word of God "There is a **way** which seemeth right unto a man, but the **end thereof** are the **ways** of death". The way (or road) being referred to is sin and the scriptures say the end of that road is death. Sin is a road, not the destination; and that is the reason many often trifle with it. Everyone is afraid of the destination of sin, but then while the road leads to the destination, it physically does not look like the destination. James made the same point in a slightly different way as follows:

> "Then when lust hath conceived, it bringeth forth sin: and
> sin, when it is finished, bringeth forth death (James 1:15)

Sin cannot yield any other thing except death. The pathway of (and from) sin leads straight to death. ... *And sin, when it is finished, bringeth forth death* is an eternal declaration of an unalterable relationship.

b. When Sin is Completed ...

Let us dwell a little bit more on the second part of that James 1:15, "...and sin, when it is finished, bringeth forth death".

When a being conceives, it brings forth its kind. It is impossible for an eagle to be hatched from the egg laid by a lizard or for a woman to put to bed a slithering viper. At the point of birth, the difference between the mother and the baby is merely the age, not the nature. A small calf looks weaker and smaller than the cow that bore it just like a baby eagle looks smaller and weaker than the adult eagle. But there are species that bring forth things that do not initially look like them. For example, a hen lays an egg which does not initially look like it. Insects go even further. The egg of an insect usually hatches into larva and even transmutes into a pupa before the insect emerges. None of the egg, larva and pupa looks like the insect into which they would eventually transmute. But the transmutations do not in any way affect the ultimate outcome. However, when viewing initial products of species that give birth to things that do not look like them as in the insect and larva, it is easy to miss the connection between the product and the producer. In fact, as a child, until I was taught the connection between larva and the insect in biology class, I never made the connection. But the fact that I did not make the connection did not in any way stop larvae from transmuting into adult insects. Strikingly, the form and content of the younger species is in no way inferior to that of the adult species. So is sin not inferior in any way to death. All the genes that form death and which make it so potent are found in sin.

As people, we will prefer to interpret the finishing in the sentence *'and sin, when it is finished'* in terms of space and time, because space and time are all we know. But such linear rendering could raise problems. The fact that sin finishes before death comes to fruition does not necessarily mean that it takes a while after sin has started before death could arrive. Always, as in the case of Adam and Eve, spiritual death is instantaneous with sin. "And the eyes of both of them were opened" immediately upon eating the fruit that God told them not to eat; that did not wait. They died the same day, they saw they were naked; they became afraid and started hiding the same day. There was something that left them the day they ate of the fruit of the tree of knowledge of good and evil; the very essence of God that gave them dominion over all creation... and they died. They were overcome by sin ... and then they died that same day.

But physical death arrived later. The fact that they lived another 900 years plus afterwards makes many people wonder if God really meant that they would die the same day or that the sentence was merely figurative. It is anything but figurative. In fact, the death associated with 'eyes being opened' is a far deeper and more impactful phenomenon than the death of 'they slept with their fathers'. This will be quite difficult to understand for the key reason that none of us ever were Adam; so we never enjoyed the two worlds, first of being alive in God and later being dead. So we will never know what the comparison between the death of eyes being opened and the death of sleeping with our fathers is like. Only Adam and Eve could appreciate the blanket of thick darkness that fell over them, closing them up from all spiritual sight. They are the only ones that can explain how it felt realizing that all they could see was the physical and immediate world around them and their own nakedness and exposure to the very hostile elements around them. They understood immediately what it meant to be a condemned criminal and that the fearsome entity, (physical) death, could pick any of them anytime that it wanted. They understood the immediate loss of strength and energy, the transformation that empowered ordinary beasts of the field to overpower the one whom they all used to take instructions from. Only Adam and Eve could explain these. We never lived in that world. The already darkened world of limitations which we inherited is the one we know and is the only one we can explain. The challenge is that because it is the only one we know, we have also come to imagine it

is the only one that exists. So when we are told that we will die, we only know the death that everyone fears, the physical stillness of the body. And because that happened to Adam many years later, we have difficulty understanding what God was referring to when He insisted that **'on the day'** ye take of the fruit, ye shall die' (Genesis 2:17). It is not strange that we cannot understand nor difficult to understand why we cannot understand. Assuming you were to live in the third century, when wars were fought on horseback, but God gave you insight into the technology of the 21st Century, would you not sound incredulous explaining that 300 men could fly together inside an equipment for 12 hours non-stop at 900km per hour. The men of that age could picture the how and why of birds flying, but definitely would have problems understanding the how and why of a flying machine, carrying several men and moving at such terrific speed across seas and lands. The details of precision engineering and the practical experience of flying itself were definitely beyond them, not because they are intellectually less endowed, but because they never lived it. A weak analogy you may say, but simply aimed at making the point that Adam's first world (the world before sinning) was Adam's world. We never lived in it and so cannot understand it; but we inherited and now live in Adam's second world. That is the only one we know and can explain.

For many people, the inability to link the death associated with 'their eyes were opened', with the death where 'they slept with their fathers' poses a challenge. How many times have we expected that something big and evil will happen to someone whom we think has been extremely wicked and how many times have we been left in wonder because despite our expectations, nothing of sort happened? If there is a God somewhere and He really is God, we reason, He should take care of iniquity quickly. But He does not. It is usually the case that the manifest expression of death could trail the dominance of sin, sometimes by many years. While this is very useful tool in the hands of God unto salvation, it is a big snare for man. Most of the first generation sinners lived for nearly a thousand years after they sinned or were born in sin. That can give a man a false sense of security. Besides, many righteous men have been tempted to forsake the Lord

on account of the seeming prosperity of the wicked. David observed this in Psalms (73: 2 – 9) and lamented:

> *But as for me, my feet were almost gone; my steps had well-nigh slipped, for I was envious at the foolish, when I saw the prosperity of the wicked. For there are no bands in their death: but their strength is firm. They are not in trouble as other men; neither are they plagued like other men. Therefore pride compasseth them about as a chain; violence covereth them as a garment. Their eyes stand out with fatness: they have more than heart could wish. They are corrupt, and speak wickedly concerning oppression: they speak loftily. They set their mouth against the heavens, and their tongue walketh through the earth ...*

There is hardly any righteous man that has not come to that point. Often, it becomes a basis for arguing that the whole sin-to-death relationship does not often hold, at least not in the short run. And this 'short run' can sometimes translate to nearly all of one's lifetime. But all this is simply because sin is the pathway to death, and the difference in the timing of physical manifestation can be quite immense going by human perception, particularly for a man whom God is deliberate about showing mercy to. But how regularly this is misread! For many, it is a sign of weakness on the part of God and an indication that sin really has no lasting consequences; that men can escape the effects of sin.

If we all physically die the same way we die spiritually at the point of contacting sin, then none can be saved. So the Lord relies on that difference in time to plead with the sinner and try to show him the way of righteousness. Hear the Apostle Peter on that matter:

> *The Lord is not slack concerning his promise, as some men count slackness; but is longsuffering to us-ward, not willing that any should perish, but that all should come to repentance (2 Peter 3:9)*

God has the whole of eternity and is not bound to fit into the tiny timeframe we carve. The 'slackness' in physical outpouring of God's wrath is His own way of helping those that will accept His salvation, coming in between the time a man has contacted sin and the time (physical) death is manifested. But I have heard so many who think God has problems making good His promise to deal with sin decisively or bringing elements of the earth into compliance simply because of this tendency on the part of God to wait and show mercy. Such would not listen to God when He calls in between sin and death. Therefore, many perish. But even those that think God has problems dealing with sin have no questions that sin leads to death. Evidently, every man has this inner witness of sin-to-death link. Even in godless cultures and through many generations, men associate evil behaviours with evil consequences and often attribute calamities to iniquities committed by men. In Romans 1:20, Paul asserted that 'the invisible things of (God) from the creation of the world are clearly seen, being understood by the things that are made ...' Oftentimes, people who are guilty are not bold because they quietly anticipate the whips of God and do not know when it might come. There is an invisible thing of God within each of us that tells us that evil is evil and is recompensed using evil.

The matter of sin finishing its course before the manifestation of death is often more pronounced when God is dealing with nations. Proverbs 14:34 says "righteousness exalts a nation but sin is a reproach to a people". God spoke to Abraham concerning his future generation and the sins of the Amorites in Genesis 15:16 saying "But in the fourth generation they shall come hither again: for the iniquity of the Amorites is not yet full". In the fourth generation, the Israelites would return to the same land of the Amorites where Abraham was dwelling and wipe them off. Why would the Amorites not be annihilated now? They would not be annihilated yet because, in God's calculations, their sin (iniquity) was not yet full, was not yet completed. Of course, neither Abraham nor the Amorites, nor even anyone of us, knew or knows the basis used by God for the calculations of fullness of sin. While God was willing to extend the rope for the Amorites for another 400 years, He was on His way to destroy Sodom and Gomorrah. And then

He told Abraham "Because the cry of Sodom and Gomorrah is great, and because their sin is very grievous; I will go down now, and see whether they have done altogether according to the cry of it, which is come unto me; and if not, I will know" (Genesis 18: 19 – 21). He was weighing the sins of Sodom and Gomorrah and trying to evaluate whether it had reached the brim. The Northern Kingdom of Israel was scrapped nearly 150 years before the Southern Kingdom. The captivity of the South was for 70 years, after which Jerusalem was rebuilt. But the North never recovered. Several nations in modern history have moved from glory to shame and many have been completely wiped out from the face of the earth, all on account of sin. The problem is that it does not often appear that it was because of sin that nations are punished. We simply know that there were civilizations of the past that are no more; possibly their people were annihilated. We see nations overturned, diminished or altogether wiped out. The scriptures seem to suggest that it is because such nations have reached tipping (or finishing) point. As it is with nations, so is it with individuals. Therefore, trotting around as though I have a hand in deciding how long before the carrying out of the sin-induced death sentence hanging on me is possibly the worst form of self-deception.

People mock at the message of salvation and some who still live in sin ask, 'When will this day of the Lord, the so-called second coming of Jesus come? Being deceptive, sin eclipses the truth that sinners are spiritually dead or will physically die as well if they do not repent. But we are all like condemned criminals because we touched sin, and a condemned criminal sits within the jail not knowing which day the hangman comes. Literally speaking, such a man is dead. It is only a matter of when the application of the death will come on his body.

Dear reader, it might be useful to pause at this point and ask if there is any sin in you which is yet to manifest in death. For anyone that would believe, God has made great provisions for cleansing in the blood of Jesus. Appropriating the blood at this moment when it seems as though God is yet slack concerning you does not only have the power to withhold the consequences, but also cleanses you from all unrighteousness. Jesus can neutralize and annihilate the power of

sin over you. Do not let death envelop you before you relinquish the sins that are attracting it. Appropriate Christ as propitiation for your sins, even now! Otherwise, after sin has finished eating up your spirit, it will also eat up your flesh. Because we know not when physical death comes, we have to turn to Christ NOW.

c. Sin and Fear of Death

One of the greatest paradoxes of life is that man is thoroughly horrified by death, even while he trifles with, is fascinated by and excited about sin. The fear of death is the most potent force driving many to what they do and what they become. Hebrews 2:15 confirms that all humanity are held bound by the fear of death. The problem is not so much about death as it is about the fear of death. Death occurs once, but the fear of death is with us all through life. It is that fear of death that holds us from the liberty to live life to the full and inhibits us from walking with God. There are a number of things we cannot do because we are afraid to die. The devil uses this fear of death to compel us to follow his desires. We know by experience that our worst fears often do not come to pass. Often, death does not come because God is in control and is able to shield us. He always does so in mercy. But in order to withhold us from the mercies of God, the devil gives an impression that death is around the corner, he rouses fear in us thereby taking us away from the grace and provisions of God.

> *"Forasmuch then as the children are partakers of flesh and blood, he also himself likewise took part of the same; that through death he might destroy him that had the power of death, that is, the devil; And deliver them who through fear of death were all their lifetime subject to bondage"* (Hebrews 12: 14).

Being a partaker of flesh and blood automatically puts a man in subjection to the fear of death. In saying this, we acknowledge that there are men who neither have Jesus nor are apparently afraid of threat, pain or death. They appear brave, take risks, and make successes of the risks. The existence of such persons does not invalidate the assertion of scripture that all men (for whom Jesus died) are subject to the fear of death. In earlier discussion about the nature of sin, we noted its capacity for bravado. Besides the bravado that emanates from societal acceptance, there is one that comes from self-will. And when self is in charge, it can go to great lengths and take unimaginable risks to prove its point. We have seen men who would rather die than give in even when they have nothing to lose by giving in. That is one of the major hallmarks of the self-life. In some cases, such bravado can even come from delusion resulting in deadly fatalism that allows a man bear the pains of physical death without the benefits of eternal life that should accompany it. Some are deluded to believe that death is mere annihilation while others are so overrun by the desire for worldly glory that the fear of death is almost completely subdued. There is the story of young people from Africa that carry cocaine to some Asian countries where such crimes carry the death penalty. Many are caught and killed, yet many more continue to dare. Someone told me that he ran into one of the young men and asked him why they continue to take the risk. His answer was that the alternative is to die in poverty, ignominy and irrelevance. Money is the only hope that they would amount to anything and this is the only route they can think of to make good money as young men. So it only makes sense that they try, and if they fail and die, so be it. But if any of them succeeds, then they celebrate. And to buttress this, whenever any of them succeeds, they gorge themselves with food and drink, holding parties for weeks on end. There are many others who take similar risks in other endeavours and are prepared to die anytime. Yet such fatalism is not accompanied by the hope of resurrection and eternal life, making it ultimately meaningless and self-injuring.

In addition, when the scriptures speak of the fear of death, it is not necessarily referring to the 'fear of dying'. Sometimes the object of fear may not appear to be directly linked to death. In the instance given above, the object of fear is poverty and suffering. Poverty and suffering may appear unrelated to death, but here, death means every form of incapacitation and has several manifestations – fear of failure, poverty, fear of putting the wrong foot forward, fear of tomorrow, fear of going against the grain, fear of being mocked, fear of obscurity, etc. The issue is that that fear is a handle for the enemy to begin to manipulate the life of the individual in question. In fact, the fear of death can lead a person to act bravely. The Holy Spirit could not have been leading the young men into drug peddling against the law of the land. That means their daring is not of God. What is driving them is the fear of poverty, physical suffering and social irrelevance. This fear has become so intense as to obscure (if not altogether substitute for) the fear of dying. All the while, whether through the fear of dying or the fear of poverty, the person remains a victim of Satan who drives him in whatever way he thinks best for his agenda. The manifestation of the fear of death may vary from one individual to another. Some apparently fearless persons regularly jerk up from nightmares drenched in sweat; a witness by the subconscious mind that they are not altogether immune to the fear of death. All men are subject to the fear of death; otherwise, Jesus would not have come to die for all men. He could have died for only those who are subject to it.

Strangely, almost universally, this fear of death co-exists with the love of sin. Many men do not love their fear; they wish they could stand up against those things they fear. But fear is a driver; and like any other thing from the devil, it just pushes the man to do what it wants him to do. The grip of the fear of death on a man is made potent by the presence (or sometimes the love) of sin. Scripture says, "The wicked flee though no one pursueth:, but the righteous are bold as a lion" (Proverbs 28:1). What makes a man to flee is wickedness; sin makes it possible for a man to even be afraid of 'nothing' in particular. It is impossible for a man to simultaneously harbor wickedness and boldness or courage. And this does not refer only to the sort of men we call the wicked because they are very deeply involved in acts of wickedness. It refers to any man who has not been regenerated in Christ Jesus. The old nature in man is cowardly, always in search of a hideout (like Adam). As a universal rule, it cannot stand in the presence of God, and has difficulty standing in the presence of men, especially the congregation of the righteous (Psalms 1: 5). Internally, those who work unrighteousness are empty and continuously need the cover of darkness, both to commit evil and to veil their true nature. Some try to overcome this fear of death by deadening their consciences. But this does not guarantee immunity from the harassment that comes from being a partaker of the nature of sin. It is not uncommon to see hardened criminals break down in regret at the point of being brought to justice; an indication that the hardening only worked while the criminal was seemingly in charge.

Many men recognize this fear of death in their lives, yet are incapable of standing against it, principally because they do not recognize its source or cure. Sometimes, we fail to make a link between our tiny commissions, negligible omissions, small denials, and other failures on the one hand and the tyranny of fear over our lives on the other. Not recognizing it does not change its potency though; the source of fear remains sin. Like Adam, the moment a man runs foul of the righteousness of God, it is inevitable but that he would run behind trees and be afraid, even if he would not admit it publicly. "He (Adam) answered, 'I heard you in the garden, and I was afraid because I was naked; so I hid'" (Genesis 3:10, New International Version). Throughout generations, men tend to react to fear and sin in the same way Adam did – run behind excuses and try to cover up. But not only is this unsustainable, it leads to further captivity, fear and finally death. Dealing with sin requires confession, renouncement, taking responsibility for its possible outcome(s) and pleading to God for mercy.

PART II

OBTAINING LIBERTY FROM SIN

CHAPTER 10

MAN'S APPROACH TO DEALING WITH SIN

Nobody likes sin. Even as all men are bound in sin, the struggle to live without sin is a universal one. People do enjoy the plunder from sin for a little season, but such 'enjoyment' is most short-lived. Those who seemingly enjoy indulgence in sin scarcely find fulfillment in it. And definitely, no one enjoys being at the receiving end of sin or being a victim of sin from others. We all sympathize with victims of such sins as rape, robbery, kidnapping, false witness or even those hurt by others' exhibition of arrogance. Sin hurts everyone - the giver and receiver alike. The bible puts humanity's relationship with sin very simply but profoundly, insisting, 'There is no peace, saith the Lord, unto the wicked' (Isaiah 48:22). It is impossible to be in sin and have peace. Consequently, nearly all men strive to be free from sin.

But the challenge is that human beings aim to be free from sin by their own works. That has never worked and can never work. When God met Adam and Eve after the Eden rebellion, He told them what they should expect as servants of sin, that He (God) would send the 'Seed of the woman' to crush the head of the serpent. He never recommended anything that they should do to be free from the power of sin, as some of us would have expected Him to. God knows that what has come to Adam and Eve was far more powerful than they and that it was futile expecting them to undo anything that they had done. The capacity to resolve the matter of sin does not exist within Adam and Eve, or within any man that ever walked the earth. Help can only come to man from elsewhere. Had man not become a victim of sin's deception, this should not have been difficult for him to understand. When one has fallen into a very deep pit without footholds, he relies on the efforts of those outside the pit to pull him out. His job while in the pit is to cry out, draw attention to his plight and raise his hands to receive help.

God is outside the pit; He did not fall in with Adam and Eve. And He is the only one outside the pit capable of and prepared to undertake the difficult job of pulling man out of sin. Angels may sympathize with man, but they did not create man and do not have the wherewithal to pull man out of sin. As we see in the death and resurrection of Jesus, the requirement for dealing with sin is grievous. The scriptures say, "Without the shedding of blood, there is no remission of sin" (Hebrews 9:22b). Whoever must deal with sin must shed (possibly his) blood. He must die. But it is not even enough to die as not all deaths can release a man from the consequences of sin; else all dead men would have been released. If the one who dies is also sinful, he then lacks the legal basis and power to give life back to himself. In that case, his death simply would mean he has also been swallowed up by sin and death and therefore cannot release himself from their hold. So the person willing to die must also have the capacity to give life back to himself, even while dead, in order to be able to deal with sin. Anything short of that would eat up the one trying to save man as well as the man he is trying to save. So neither Angels nor other creature is capable of helping man. That is how grave the matter is.

This perspective of the sin challenge eludes people. Man finds it hard to understand that he has absolutely no remedy for sin within or around himself. Consequently, it is common place for man to want to pay for his sins or give up something in exchange for his sin. It just comes naturally to us to want to pay for our sin, partly because we want self-justification and self-glory. It is still the same sinful nature manifesting as pride and wanting to show God that we are capable of taking care of ourselves. Humanity does not want the help of anyone and definitely not God's. So, when we feel we have gone against the laws of the universe, we also want to pay the price and be able to thump our chest and boast that we have taken care of that which was made wrong. This is not only abhorred in the sight of God, it is futile. The only thing that can take care of sin is blood (death). But even if man were to die or give anything of himself for his sin, it is neither acceptable nor capable of freeing him from sin. This is because the blood containing that self-sacrifice is in itself corrupted and that which is corrupt cannot be used to pay for corruption. What is needed to pay for corruption is a completely clean sacrifice; and that was what Jesus provided for our cleansing. For a while, the blood of animals was used to provide temporary atonement (not eradication) for sin while God prepared the people through whom the Messiah would come. And when Jesus came, that which is temporary and weak had to give way to the perfect.

Yet, with God's provision in Christ, many perish in sin owing to a combination of ignorance and arrogance. Many do not know Jesus. They hear about Him and His ways from very far off. But they have their notions about Him and do not intend to change them. Many have their ways fixed and know that accepting Jesus would alter things dramatically, and they do not want that to happen. Sometime in the past, I preached to a young Belgian undergraduate. Like many young Europeans, she had the notion there is no God, so our discussion kicked off with a long debate as to the existence or otherwise of God. Proving my point about God from the bible was not allowed since she did not believe the bible. God helped as I relied on logic, history, current affairs and anything else to make the case. Steadily, but surely, her arguments were dismantled. At the point she admitted that her position lacked merit, I moved in with the gospel and the scriptures. But she gave a snappy and troubling conclusion, 'well I have lived my whole life without God and your Jesus, I have family and friends who I rely on and who add value to me, I do not want to bring God in now to complicate matters for myself!" With that she shut out any further discussion and all through that evening, I could not find a way to re-start the discussion. So I left town and she would continue with her life outside of Jesus unless something different takes place in her.

Some get pretty close, but never really get to know Him. Yet there are some who do not like what they see in Him or are not willing to go the way He requires of them. In His days on earth, multitudes followed Him. At some point as in the account of John 6, they exhibited highly commendable zeal. They had left Him the evening before back to their homes after the day's ministration. On coming back the following morning, He was not there. They then realized He must have gone to the other side of the sea. The men took ship and made their way to look for Him at the other side of the Sea of Galilee, paying their own fares. Besides the cost, this was no risk-free exercise; the disciples of Jesus met a storm while making the same journey the night before. Yet, when the men found Jesus, He neither commended them nor seemed even the least impressed. He was quite confrontational, accusing them of seeking for Him because of the free meal He gave them the day before. He insisted they did not care about Him or His doctrine and started charging them to seek for food that endures and not that which perishes. One would imagine Jesus was too hard on them. But a discussion ensued, leading to deeper explanation from Jesus about the implications of following Him. By the time the discussion got deep, many of those that paid their way to come realized that what He had was not what they were looking for. First, there was a murmuring. There was also an open confrontation and finally, they deserted Him. They paid their way back to where they came from, determined not to have anything further to do with Him. The exit from Jesus was so massive that He had to turn to the Twelve to find out if they still intended to continue with Him or not. The day before, those same men had wanted to crown Jesus king by all means. It took His disappearing from the scene to quell that attempt. They spoke so well about Him as they went home. The next morning, they had all arisen early, left off all they had to do and went in search of this new phenomenon in town. But now they were angrily walking away, cursing Him and His ways and determined not to come again. What changed in between? Nothing really! It was just that Jesus actions did not fit into their pre-conceived idea of what salvation should be about and how it should be given and obtained. He was giving too much attention to Himself and much less to them. He was demanding so much from them and not giving much promise of what He would give them in return. His language suggested He was not even going to organize the kind of feast He did the day before. He was not interested in saving them from the hold of Rome, which was a pressing political issue and He was not interested in being crowned king so that He may have a viable platform for continuing His miracles of provision. He was speaking long term, eternity and life afterwards, and did not really seem very interested in the now. He even had the guts to question Moses, the relevance of Manna and the Law – things they inherited and had become accustomed to for many years. And His alternative was that He would give them His flesh to eat and His blood to drink! The men were not willing to have any more of this talk about flesh and blood nor were they willing to have anyone talk down on what they have been used to for generations.

There were also the Pharisees, who knew there was something about this man, but were deeply engrossed everyday trying to kill Him and snuff out that good thing they knew and acknowledged. Nicodemus, one of their own, echoed the thinking among many of them when he visited, "Rabbi, **we know** that thou art a teacher come from God: for no man can do these miracles that thou doest, except God be with him" (John 3:2). They knew. Later, towards the close of His ministry, they came to tempt Him with payment of taxes to Caesar, intending to catch Him in His words. They prefixed their temptation with "Master, **we know** that thou sayest and teachest rightly, neither acceptest thou the person *of any*, but teachest the way of God truly" (Luke 20:21). They knew and they were right that this Man was of God. Yet they continued in their own ways, trying instead to see how they might condemn and do away with that which they knew to be of God. That is man.

God has His way, but many of us would not have it. We know that God is in Christ reconciling Himself to the world, but we are not very keen to know more about that or to align our lives with it. Over the years, we have instead invented several means of dealing with sin our own way. And such inventions traverse cultures. They are mostly driven and sustained by the human nature and most ineffective in handling the complicated matter of sin. We will examine some of these ways and why they do not work before we examine some of God's provisions for man's salvation.

a. Penance: Many men want to impress God by their ability to restore what they have destroyed. Several people over many generations have gone to great lengths to undo sin in their lives. Some have even killed themselves on account of guilt and the inability to face the consequences of what they have done (or who they are) as such consequences stare them in the face. Some men striving for perfection have seen the contradictions of who they are coming stark before them and have gone to extremes to wipe off that image. Martin Luther, the German reformist, tells the story of how he struggled with sin and went on to starve, cane and punish himself, using many untold sufferings in a bid to deal with sin and its consequences on him. Unfortunately, while that may seem just and fair, it is actually part of the problem. We say again that humanity does not have the capacity to pay for sin. What a man gives - self penance, self-sacrifice and self-denial or any other work rendered by man to restore life to him amounts to nothing. They are completely ineffective against sin. So self-penance is not useful. No matter how much a man puts in to substitute for his iniquities; no man has the capacity to deliver himself. It is foolish for a man trapped inside a 100-feet deep well of water, with no means of escape, to pinch or beat himself as a way of getting out. My wife once met a young lady and noticed her legs had fresh wounds. She had deep cuts across her two legs. Upon enquiry, the lady told her that she moved up a rocky mountain with sharp stones all night on her knees, deliberately placing the stones along the way to drive home the pain. She was seeking release from her sin and wanted to punish herself as a way of letting God know that she is serious. Very many people are like her, starving and denying themselves of some good in the bid to pay for sin and earn eternal life. But grace speaks otherwise, declaring, "...But the free gift of God is eternal life in Christ Jesus" (Romans 6:23b). *The free gift of God ...!* That is God's own declaration; and that declaration lies side by side the scripture that says, "The wages of sin is death". If you cannot get it free, then you cannot have it. In the struggle against sin, whatever a man pays for does not have the power to blot away sin.

b. Confessions: Millions around the world have been schooled to believe that regular confession of sin to an ecclesiastical authority saves them from the consequences of those sins. This is another fallacy. Not all confessions are useful in delivering a man from sin. The scriptures support confession, but it must be a productive confession that is preceded by godly sorrow that leads to repentance. Repentance demands change in direction. Therefore true repentance must be followed by the forsaking of sin. Just as confession can come from godly sorrow, so can it also come from worldly sorrow. In some instances, confession can even come with no sorrow at all. Worldly sorrow is more concerned about doing away with the consequences of sin than it is about doing away with the sin itself. We have known of men in history who sinned, but were not as interested in having the sin cleansed and forgiven as they were in preserving themselves from the consequences. People do not like the negative outcomes associated with sin like sickness, accidents, poverty or suffering. They also do not want to severe their relationship with God and are afraid not to have God become displeased if that would deter material or other gains getting to them. A number of examples abound in scriptures of people who, despite sinning and having judgement over them, would not want to taste what they meted out to others, or even to suffer any form of inconvenience.

Cain did not want to be killed by another as he killed his brother. God obliged him and announced that He would put a mark on him so that no one would kill him. But his selfishness showed again when God told him he would be a vagabond on earth. He complained that his punishment was greater than he could bear. He never showed any remorse about his brother's life that he had wasted and never even referred to it again. To him it was a non-issue, but he needed to preserve his own life. Saul did not wish to have his image dented despite having disobeyed God and would want to force Samuel to go worshipping with him. Eli did not seem to care about what his boys were doing despite repeated warnings, yet he wanted to remain priest in Shiloh and wanted the ark of God to remain effectual in his days. Judah and his brothers sold their younger brother, but feared greatly when it appeared they ran into trouble in Egypt. They clearly made the connection between their past and their ordeals in Egypt as they came to buy food, but would want God to show them mercy. When their father died and it seemed as though Joseph might come for retribution, they cooked up a story about their father instructing him to forgive his brothers before he died. Aaron and Miriam freely criticized Moses and his ministry. When God appeared to deal with the gossiping, they had to beg the same Moses to use his ministry and relationship with God to beg for Miriam's healing from leprosy. In nearly all these instances, we see men confessing and pleading for mercy, but we note that those confessions were not based on heartfelt convictions about the evil-ness of their actions; it was mostly to curry favour and escape the punishment that goes with sin. Saul told Samuel in effect, "I have sinned, yet you must go with me to worship so I do not lose face before the elders". Judah and his brothers went and fell before Joseph saying, "Forgive, I pray thee now, the trespass of thy brethren, and their sin; for they did unto thee evil: and now we pray thee, forgive the trespass of the servants of the God of thy father" (Genesis 50:17). Aaron told Moses, "Alas my Lord, I beseech thee, lay not the sin upon us, wherein we have done foolishly, and wherein we have sinned. Let her not be as one dead, of whom the flesh is half consumed when he cometh out of his mother's womb" (Numbers 12:11). In these instances, there was confession, but the confession targeted relief from the trouble caused by sin.

Because confession is regularly misapplied, it is important that the context and content of every confession be examined, even by the person who is making the confession. People make confessions for various reasons. The sinful nature, selfish and personal gains, worldly sorrow and a number of other factors can motivate confession. For example, when a dishonest man finds himself in a community or circle of acquaintances that consider honesty and confession an acceptable behaviour, he can use confession to raise his standing before them. Worldly sorrow does not come with remorse. Where it does, such remorse is only skin-deep or focused on obtaining relief. Confession can be used for plea or to bargain for exemption from punishment. And some people do confess under physical, psychological or sociological duress. Whatever the circumstance though, confessions under duress are hardly useful as they are not borne out of the free volition of the person that has sinned, nor are they based on proper appreciation of the dangers of sin or a decision to abandon it for good.

These instances all point to the fact that confession is not an end in itself; and if misapplied, can fail to be a means to justification. Consequently, it is important that in thinking of the confession that brings life, a man queries the motive of his confession. The confession that helps a man can only be one borne out of deep realization of what sin is, how it affects God and man and the ruin it aims to bring a man. Such confession should then immediately be followed by a decision, based on grace, never to be entangled by the sin again. Any confession that does not emanate from godly sorrow cannot help a man overcome sin. Godly sorrow arises from the conviction of the Holy Spirit, and leads to a strong desire to keep away from the sin by all means. At this point God comes in to present the finished work of Jesus on the cross to the sinner. This finished work of redemption positions him on the path of hope again and sets him free from the burden of sin in his soul.

In some religious circles, confession is regularly demanded, and sometimes made a requirement for such privileges as taking Holy Communion or receiving other entitlements. Such confessions are sometimes made to be accompanied by restitution. In such institutional structure, confession for many can become routine, while accompanying penance and restitution are farcical in the minds of the worshippers. Specifically, restitution can, and does follow salvation but it does not precede it. For this reason, the sinner does not need to first undo all that he had done before he can be saved. It is the sheer weight of gratitude for the forgiveness that a man has received that propels him to publicly identify with God's salvation through restitution; not the other way round. Confession and penance can be dangerous when they become man-made substitutes for godly sorrow. When that happens, a man goes for confession week after week, but does not receive the power to overcome the sin he confesses. Godly sorrow that comes from Jesus builds into a man the will and power to overcome sin. This is what Titus 2:11 – 12 suggests, "For the grace of God that brings salvation has appeared to all men. It **teaches** us to **say no** to ungodliness and worldly passions, and to live self-controlled, upright and godly lives in this present age". The grace of God teaches and instructs. Thus, any confession or penance that does not empower a man to say no to ungodliness and live righteously in **this present age** is inadequate to deal with sin.

c. Gifts and Good Works: Another approach pervasively adopted by people to settle the matter of sin and the guilt of conscience is giving more to or doing more for God or man. There are two implicit assumptions to this. The first is that there is a balance between good and evil, where a man can offset the evil he does with some good. The second is that God is in need and like man, we can hurt Him in one way and appease him in another way just as one can offend his child and afterwards appease him with a gift. Both are very simplistic views of what dealing with sin is all about. Sin is not just an offence to God; it is also an affront and a violation of the processes of and all parties in creation. Many of us are familiar with the fact that one action (of good or evil) generates a chain that touches many people and other segments of nature. For example, one illicit sex can give birth to a bastard, who, because of neglect, becomes frustrated and leads a criminal life. Many unconnected lives and property may, in future, be terminated or destroyed by this criminal; other girls may be raped while other bastards may be born. Whenever a man starts a chain of evil or good, he has absolutely no control over what else it can generate or how far and deep it will go. It is difficult to stretch our imaginations to cover all possibilities that could emanate from our actions. But there is an even deeper angle that we hardly think about. Many of us are not familiar with the fact that there are non-terrestrial, non-human entities touched by our actions and inactions. Hebrews 11 shows a list of men who lived by faith and are mostly long dead. Then Hebrews 12 called them the cloud of witnesses of the things that those presently alive do. Likewise in Job chapters 1 and 2, we see God discussing with the devil about Job, with the entire hosts of heaven listening. Later, when David sinned by taking Uriah's wife, God sent Nathan who told David, "For thou didst it secretly: but I will do this thing before all Israel, and before the sun...the Lord also hath put away thy sin; thou shalt not die. Howbeit, because by this deed thou hast given great occasion to the enemies of the Lord to blaspheme, the child also that is born unto thee shall surely die" (2 Samuel 12: 12 – 14). Nathan admitted that this thing was done secretly. So who were these enemies of the Lord that were given great occasion to blaspheme? They were obviously not human as people did not yet know that David killed Uriah and it was not out of place for Uriah's wife to remarry if her husband died. They were part of the cloud of witnesses that watch all we do here and are affected by the outcomes. Depending on which side they are on, they either rejoice or mourn when we do well. These instances indicate that we are not the only ones affected by our thoughts and actions. There are witnesses and affected parties both on earth and outside it. Indeed, every single sin sets into motion ripple effects that run through time and space, through the lives of thousands (if not generations) of people, and reinforces the hand of evil in the eternal space. There was a reason God allowed the devil free space on Job and later on Jesus. Something much bigger than our tiny interests is under contest in our deeds and attitudes.

The challenge therefore with one good work that aims to 'compensate' for an evil is that it is impossible for it to get back and repair all the people, beings and things that were originally affected by the evil. How can a robber's good gifts compensate for all the people he made orphans? Many of us know that the moment a word is spoken, it cannot be taken back. So how can a man who has told a lie against another take back what he has spoken. Sometimes, he may even go to confess the truth, but by that time someone has already been physically hurt, incarcerated or psychologically damaged. When the processes of creation are violated, giving gifts to God cannot undo the violation.

As in Job's case, it is not only God that takes note of what we do, the devil also does. The devil himself has been the worst hit by the course of justice. When he sinned, he received neither mercy nor an opening for 'undoing' his own evil. So he is very interested in having justice meted out to all sinners to ensure he is not ultimately shortchanged. The Bible gives a classical case in Zechariah chapter 3 of Joshua, the High Priest, who came to sacrifice with a sin-stained garment. Satan was right beside him, and according to the bible, it was specifically to resist him. How would a man wearing a garment of sin be allowed to 'sacrifice'? The devil would make sure that never happens. You cannot touch sin and stand before God as well; the devil has assigned to himself the job of a whistle-blower on this matter and it is nearly impossible for God to ignore him. Neither will the devil ignore any man's sins, no matter how minor it may seem. In the Zechariah story above, God, in the abundance of His grace, provided for atonement to be made for Joshua first before he could proceed. But the devil would not have that. So the Lord standing by had to directly address Satan saying, "The Lord rebuke thee O Satan, even the Lord that hath chosen Jerusalem rebuke thee: is not this a brand plucked out of the fire?" Thereafter God turned to address the very item that makes Joshua culpable in the matter "...And He answered and spake unto those that stood before him, saying, Take away the filthy garments from him. And unto him He said, Behold I have caused thine iniquity to pass from thee, and I will clothe thee with change of raiment" (Zechariah 3: 1 – 4). It was only at that point that Joshua could proceed with the priestly sacrifice and offering for which he was appointed.

These matters are no trifles. When a man wants to use good works to take care of sin, he should realize that it is not enough to appease God and man, he must also find a way of closing the devil's mouth. And the devil has no regard for good works. He insists that the course of justice be duly followed and God does not deny him that. God may intervene with forgiving grace, but that requires cooperation of the sinner to have God's clothing of righteousness and not the sinner's righteousness. Joshua did not find alternative garments for himself; it was God that provided him the garments that the devil could not controvert. In effect, sin has to do with a lot more than what a man can give God. This is why it is unwise for a man who ostensibly lives in sin to spend huge resources supporting godly projects, such as charity or church buildings. Wasting such resources is unnecessary. Besides the childish thinking that building a church meeting hall or giving alms to about anyone translates to God's work, it must always be borne in mind that giving to God or man does not wipe away sin. A man cannot undo the poison he put into another man's cup by offering him (or someone else) a bottle of soft drink. One carton of soft drinks cannot neutralize a drop of cyanide already administered to a man. When a man is killed, no amount of gift restores his life. And sin kills; only that it sometimes happens imperceptibly. It is worse when we give the carton of soft drinks to another person whom we did not even give the poison while the person who was given the poison is irrecoverable. The only way of dealing with sin is by completely exhuming it, bringing it before God and laying it at the feet of Jesus. There the blood of Jesus which has been shed for that purpose will cleanse and take away the sin. His is the only pure blood that has the capacity to cleanse.

Jesus confirms the inadequacy of good works to tackle sin when he said: we prophesied in your name, healed in your name, and performed miracles in Your Name. But He said He will tell them to get away from Him because they are workers of iniquity. A particular Nigerian local (Igbo) language translation of that verse puts it thus: "get thee away from me, ye that work and also perform iniquity" (Matthew 7:23). The impression given here is that of one who works with one hand and commits iniquity with another; builds with one hand and tears down with the other. Interestingly, I have seen many who think that when they arrive in Heaven, God would compare their works of iniquity with their works of righteousness in order to find out which is greater. Then they would be rewarded on the strength of the outcome. This view shows little understanding of why God hates sin with such passion and why the blood of Jesus had to be shed before sin could be handled. When one mixes poison inside water, the potency of the poison has little to do with whether the poison is larger than the water or otherwise. None of us will agree to drink water knowing that some toxic materials were poured into it, even if it is a finger-drop of the toxin in a bucket of water. We do not ask the quantity of the poison; we are only interested in the presence of poison because every poison is dangerous. Likewise, every drop of iniquity cancels out all that is good. Similarly, in mathematics, when a positive number is multiplied with a negative number (even if it is only minus one), the result is negative, the size of the positive number notwithstanding. Whatever touches sin gets corrupted and the moment that which we look upon as a good work is corrupted by even the slightest taint of sin, it is made sinful.

But even more fundamental is the question of what good works or good gifts are. If the sinful nature of man is corrupt and unacceptable, can that which proceeds from him be otherwise? The Lord Jesus said that an evil tree cannot bear good fruit (Matthew 7:18). Therefore things which appear good may not necessarily be good. Often when we classify works as good or evil, it is merely because we are unable to see the motives; unable to see the corruption in the nature that gave birth to the 'good work'. It is unlikely that one who shudders at the sight of a serpent will cuddle what is born of a serpent. But he may sit on top of a coiled serpent if he does not know that it is one. Whatever is born of the sinful nature remains sin, even when it appears as good work. A cash gift to orphans does not make the giver acceptable to God. The money could have helped solve someone's problems, but if the gift is not prompted by the Spirit of God, then whatever else that gave birth to it is of sin. Whatever does not proceed from faith is sin. Baptizing it in Church does not change its nature.

Cain attempted to impress God with gifts and sacrifices. It appears his relationship with God was already frayed when the idea of a sacrifice occurred to him. Like many of us, he possibly thought whatever grouse God may have had with him would be taken care of when He sees his offering. So Cain set out and met the shock of his life. And thank God he could at least recognize that God did not accept his sacrifice; many today do not know or recognize God rejecting their offerings and do not have means of knowing. With Cain, God kept harping on his heart, telling him that sin was crouching at the door of his heart; that it was important that he overcame sin. God never for once made reference to his sacrifice; He was interested in his life. In fact the Bible said "And the Lord had respect unto Abel **and** to his offering: but unto Cain **and** to his offering he had no respect" (Genesis 4: 4 – 5). It was to each man first and then to his offering. God's respect was for Abel before his offering; just as His disrespect was **unto Cain** first before it was to his offering. Without respect unto the man, there is no way God would have respect unto his offering. Afterall, what is an offering without the person offering it? God looks at the person of a giver before knowing what to do with his gifts. And that emphasis has not changed.

d. Frustration and Despair – Frustration and despair often accompany sin. It cuts across culture, race and creed. It is most manifest when a man tries to keep away from sin and stick to righteousness. Most right thinking men admit to themselves (and sometimes to those around them) that there are certain things about them that they do not quite like, and which they wish were different, but which have obstinately refused to go away. And this is a source of frustration for many. Some mock and make jest of theirs while others try to ignore theirs after some attempts to change them failed. Most men try to 'do something' about their weakness because of their conviction that if only they could try hard enough, they can get rid of or at least atone for sin. But this is wrong thinking about sin and keeps man in the bondage of trying.

In 'trying hard enough', we make resolutions. And almost universally, resolutions appeal to the natural man. People make resolutions at the beginning of the year, quarter, month or week. They make resolutions at periods when they feel threatened, when they are sober, when they want to get something new from God or from other men, and when confronted with new challenges. There is of course nothing wrong with resolutions except that when they are not backed with grace to do, they are ineffective in bringing about the righteousness of God. They render absolutely no help in dealing with sin. Unfortunately, they remain the major (if not the only) method known and frequently used by many. But as nearly all adults can attest to, resolutions are hardly, if ever, kept. Sin knows how to apply pressure and wear the most resolute man down; and most men capitulate under that pressure after a while. But even when kept, resolutions do not solve the sin problem. Some have the capacity to keep certain resolutions, but they draw the power to do so from the soul life. They keep their resolutions to prove a point, maintain relevance, to teach someone a lesson or to convince themselves that they are not failures. They rely on something 'within' or 'about' themselves to be able to keep their resolutions. That in itself is using sin to reinforce sin. The power that enables a man to produce the righteousness that is pleasing to God must be that of grace. David was one of the most righteous men of the Old Testament; and it is easy to attribute his exploits in righteousness to a strong and capable personality. But as one listens to him sing in the Psalms about the grace of God and its role in keeping him, it becomes easy to appreciate that David was no different from any one of us. He merely recognized that God did not give laws and abandon us to find a way to keep them, but is interested in working through us to keep it Himself. So he relied exclusively on the power of God to please God; and God approved of him. David's life is evidence that anyone who wishes to can have God's unlimited power for righteousness available to him. It is usually awkward to hear someone discussing personal capacity for righteousness and prefixing it with 'the kind of person I am', or such other talks as 'what I like', 'what I can do' and 'why I act the way I do', etc. Such talks simply show the person does not really understand the source of true righteousness or the negative capacity of that same seemingly righteous person within. Resolutions based on 'my kind of person likes to keep my word' are borne of the self life and even if they are kept, remain part of the sin problem. They reinforce a life that God had already passed a sentence of death on.

When some persons fail to keep their resolutions, they despair and quit trying. Some have even gone further to question why God should hold man accountable for his sins when He (God) knows that man is naturally sinful. Others ask, 'Since we cannot help but sin, why try to avoid it? If sin is really as strong and as pervasive as we have outlined, why do we have to bear the responsibility of its works, given that we are 'mere victims'? All these may sound reasonable and logical, but fact is, man entered into sin of his own accord. And with salvation already provided in our Lord Jesus Christ, anyone who remains in sin remains of his own freewill. In Christ, God has provided all that is required to deal with sin permanently. He has also told us that the challenge is not about what we can do, it is about to what extent we are willing to abandon ourselves to God and rely on what He can do, and has done, to be our righteousness. "For Christ is the end of the law for righteousness to everyone that believeth" (Romans 10:4). That requires absolute humility and self-abandonment. To the natural man, this is many times more difficult than keeping resolutions. For many, this way is completely unknown. Yet for as long as we are unable to find this way, the potency of sin remains and we reinforce its hold upon us.

Despair often brings along with it abandonment to fate or throwing caution to the wind. Some men have been known to turn to drinking and fun as part of the escape from the reality of their weaknesses. Some try to convince themselves that there is no punishment for sin while others simply throw caution to the wind and decide to do as much evil as they can and face the consequences (if any) when the time comes. The more I think of it, the more I am convinced that the idea that there is no God was birthed from fear of what holds if there is really some eternal punishment for sin. Following the inability to overcome personal sinful habits, it seemed convenient to simply wish God away altogether as part of the struggle to quieten the conscience from the turbulence of sin. Many who have taken up alcohol and substance abuse are merely trying to escape from the stillness associated with staying sober, when their conscience would not let them rest. Some are hardened because they tried being righteous by their own strength and failed. So they turned to pursue the way of sin with vigour. Sometimes, this is done to spite God and life. Nevertheless, none of these is an appropriate response to sin. There is a better way. The same scriptures that declared that "There is no peace for the wicked" (Isaiah 48:22), also showed Jesus saying, "Come unto me all ye that labour and are heavy laden, and I will give you rest ..." (Matthew 11:32). If any man would come, he would realize that the Lord is not making an empty promise; whoever comes wholeheartedly gets peace and rest.

e. Reclassifying Sin

A lot of people simply excuse their sins and tell themselves that the matter of sin could not be as bad as it is portrayed. So they give varying, comfortable and inoffensive names to the manifestations of sin in their lives. The story of the unjust steward as written in Luke 16: 1 – 8 shows how this works.

> And he said also unto his disciples, There was a certain rich man, which had a steward; and the same was accused unto him that he had wasted his goods. And he called him, and said unto him, How is it that I hear this of thee? Give an account of thy stewardship; for thou mayest be no longer steward. Then the steward said within himself, what shall I do? for my lord taketh away from me the stewardship: I cannot dig; to beg I am ashamed. I am resolved what to do, that, when I am put out of the stewardship, they may receive me into their houses. So he called every one of his lord's debtors unto him, and said unto the first, how much owest thou unto my lord? And he said an hundred measures of oil. And he said unto him, take thy bill, and sit down quickly, and write fifty. Then said he to another, And how much owest thou? And he said an hundred measures of wheat. And he said unto him, take thy bill, and write fourscore. And the lord commended the unjust steward, because he had done wisely: for the children of this world are in their generation wiser than the children of light.

When this brother in the scripture above was accused, he had at least three options – a) to dig out the issues, appreciate them for what they are and lay them before the master in all honesty; b) to acknowledge his errors and beg the master for his life and his job; or c) to ignore the master and connive with men with the hope that they will receive him into their houses when he becomes jobless. He chose the third. And that's quite a choice! Consider the actions the third option he chose required of him: lots of hiding, lying and dissimulation. He not only had to change figures, he made others to partake in that sin as well. He renamed things and gave them new impressions they originally did not carry. Consider the outcomes he would have reaped had he chosen the first or second options. Everything would have returned to normalcy. He would have had peace and would have had no need to further complicate his life.

When men are accused of sin before heaven, many of them do exactly what the steward in this story did. Every one of us carries a conscience, which either accuses and condemns, or praises and acquits us. When the conscience (as well as the Spirit that bears witness in the case of the believer) convicts us of wrongdoing, many of us insist we cannot dig or beg. The sin is sometimes considered too small to warrant efforts of soul searching, introspection or confession. We are often too lazy or careless or we imagine the matter does not warrant the noise our conscience is making about it. So we wave it away. Pride, which is the bane of the perishing servant as in the case above, sets in. We know we are supposed to confess to someone, but we feel it may be too demeaning to do so. The position we occupy or our sense of self-worth makes us to wave off the option of confession. Sometimes, in our light estimation of the issue, we even forget to ask God to forgive us.

A number of sins have metamorphosed through the years, going from being abominations to becoming socially acceptable behaviour. Indeed, only very few items of iniquity (like robbery) still make it to the 'unacceptable' list. Many others have transmuted. For example, fornication and adultery used to be social no-no, but now, they are celebrated in many societies with such new names as 'mutual consent' and 'flirting'. Many persons justify these on the basis of experiences with their spouses. Even homosexuality is rationalized as a matter of 'sexual orientation'. These are all indications of man's determination not to dig or beg God, but to re-define what is acceptable and unacceptable behaviour based on convenience.

The result of all this is that there is now a generation of women who cannot dress modestly because it is old-fashioned to do so. There is now a generation of young men who cannot do a job without gratification because 'nothing goes for nothing'. There is now a generation of men and women who must sleep with people of the same sex because they have been told they were made so by nature. There is now a generation of young men and women who would not take up any demand on themselves, but must get what they want because it is their right to get them. We now have a generation of bigots, murderers, gossipers, pen-robbers, looters of public treasury. And we respect them all for what they do because the society has redefined sin and made what they do acceptable. We have come to think that because they are doing the things they do well and make fortunes out of them, they are acceptable.

f. Excusing Self and Blaming Others

The beginning of man's trouble with sin is with Adam and Eve's refusal to admit anything wrong with their actions even when confronted by God. Each had a good reason. Adam reasoned that if God did not come up with this idea of a helpmeet, the temptation to eat the fruit would not have arisen in the first place. He forgot the deep sigh of relief, satisfaction and approval when Eve was presented to him and his exciting exclamation of gratitude to God, 'this is now the flesh of my flesh and the bone of my bones' (Genesis 2:23). Eve, on her part, forgot that she took time to consider how good the fruit was for food and for wisdom and that she desired to be like God. She conveniently forgot that she, of her own accord, went to pick and eat the fruit by herself. She summarized her situation as 'the serpent gave me and I ate'. Since then, excusing self and blaming others for sin have been the most pervasive, yet the most deceptive, means of dealing with sin.

While the sinful nature will want to take credit for any good done anywhere, it is quick to point fingers in the direction of the next man for its failures. Nearly all unregenerate men fall victim to this force that compels them to look for the cause of failure in others. Sometimes, the blame is not on a person, but on circumstance(s). And sometimes, the blame game is taken to very irrational extremes. The example Adam and Eve set was copied by their son. Cain's sacrifice was rejected because his heart was in terrible shape, and God told him so. But instead of looking after his thoughts, he probably reasoned, "had Abel not brought a sacrifice that was comparatively better, all would have been well". So he murdered Abel and left the matter of his heart unattended to. When Esau lost the inheritance, he comforted himself in the fact that his father would soon die; so he would murder Jacob. He was sure that would sort things out. As far as he was concerned, his role in the pottage saga, including swearing away his birthright had no role in the outcomes he faced. It took many years and intense prayer on Jacob's part for the bitterness in Esau against his brother to go away. After an all-night intense prayer for Saul, Samuel confronted him. After initially denying that anything was amiss, the young king eventually shifted the blame for everything that happened to his soldiers. They were the ones that wanted something to be sacrificed, they were the ones that refused to allow him do the will of God; they were the ones that desired the fat animals and mounted pressure on him to allow them. His arguments seemed to indicate that if he had gone to war without the soldiers, he would have been very successful in doing the will of God. A few years later, David appeared with the glory of God and was the exact opposite of Saul. Saul began to think that eliminating David, who appeared every inch the key obstacle to the stability and longevity of his government, was crucial if his kingdom was to last. The state of his heart, about which God had confronted him a number of times in the past, could not have been the issue here. To him that was of no consequence.

The list is endless, and many of us have taken similar position about things that go wrong in our lives. But, as we have come to know, this is self-deception of the highest order. Indeed, blaming others is one way to know we are wrong. It does not matter the circumstances of an issue, the right place to look for the reason for failure is in me. And

I should be honest in the search, trusting in the promise of the Holy Spirit to help me. Trying to do this of one's own accord and without the help of God will fail. Sin is very potent in its ability to hide within our hearts, while directing us to look elsewhere. In 2 Corinthians 3:14 – 15, Paul discussed a particular veil that spreads over the heart of people, "But their minds were blinded ... but even to this day, when Moses is read, a veil lies on their heart". This veil prevents a person from having the right perception and positioning of things around him, making them look like the obstacles to his progress with God and with man. For this reason, many are not able to come to God, blaming even God Himself for their circumstances. When God asked Adam a direct question, 'Have you eaten from the tree of which I commanded you not to eat?' One would expect a simple 'yes' or 'no' but the foreign nature which Adam had acquired would not let him handle matters that way. He rather blurted out "the woman whom You gave to be with me, she gave me from the tree and I ate' (Genesis 3:12). So did he eat it? Yes. Was it important who gave him? No. But the sinful nature in man tells him that part of the solution is to transfer the blame to someone else for things that go wrong. And so he would rather tell about the one that gave him than simply admit and repent before God that he (Adam) deliberately went against an instruction passed on to him first-hand. The devil knows that were the man to simply admit, confess and repent, God would show him mercy. So he ensures that man never comes to the point where he falls down, admits to God's uprightness and justice and sees his rebellion and rejection of God as the root cause of the wreck he has made of things and equally become himself. The Eden scenario between God and Adam has been repeated a million times over across several generations, with the same result. And till date, denial and blame game are still the most important meters with which any man (including you the reader) can measure how ingrained the sinful nature is in him. How quick am I to accept that the buck stops with me and there is no one else to blame? Not God, not the devil, not angels, not government, not economy, not circumstances of birth, not education, not my employer, not my friends, not my parents, and definitely not other men, are to blame for my position on matters or the consequences that arise on account of my decisions. How quickly am I to recognize a wrong for what it is and be bold to call it a wrong and commit myself to changing it, instead of looking for a way to justify it?

But to the glory of God, verse 16 of the same passage has good news for all, "Nevertheless, when one turns to the Lord, the veil is taken away. Now the Lord is the Spirit; and where the Spirit of the Lord is, there is liberty". It is equally interesting that whenever a man turns to the Lord to pray, the Lord first starts dealing with the one offering the prayer. When we go to God to complain about a circumstance we do not like, we think He would hurry to take away the obstacle and make right the wrong. Not so. The Lord rather starts off with issues in our personal lives. Why does He do that? Because getting us to have the right perspective is more important than taking away the obstacle that is facing us. The main challenge facing man's dominion is that sin thwarted the way he sees things. We no longer see things as God does. As long as this is so, we can never agree with God on anything, let alone joining hands with Him to address issues in the interest of the kingdom. The Lord Jesus insists that whoever does not remove the log in his eyes cannot remove the speck in his brother's (Matthew 7:5). But is it really possible for me to see what is in my eyes as a log and see what is in my brother's eyes as a speck? Yes, it is. But I do not have the capacity to do that on my own; I must have to turn to the Lord for grace.

Other range of self-sins (self-defence, self-justification, self-pity, self-consciousness, self-determination, among others), mockery, denial, decisions, resolutions, as well as attention to demons are a few of other self-induced initiatives that work together with excuses to perpetuate sin in a man. Many struggle but never achieve freedom from sin in their entire lives. They die with fear and uncertainty about eternity despite having done their best to be good. This is so because there is a way that seemeth right unto a man, but the end thereof is the way of death (Proverbs 14:12). Employing the wisdom and way of man, like any of those listed above, to overcome sin may seem right, but they lead to death. They are ineffectual.

CHAPTER 11

GOD'S PROVISIONS FOR OVERCOMING SIN

Just as man cannot overcome sin alone, so God cannot deal with sin alone. Because man has freedom of choice, God needs his collaboration to deal with sin. God took the lead in effectively fusing Himself into man in the person of the Lord Jesus. In God is the power to overcome sin which is lacking in man. But God requires the will of man to engage that power. Most men do not render their wills to God, so the power to overcome sin is not made available to them. Jesus came as both God and man rolled into one. With that joint personality, take-off was made possible. Yet Jesus did not take things for granted. He made it clear that He did not take a step without first watching out for what his Father was doing and then taking a cue from that. For believers, God also tried to make that agreement easy by giving us Himself in the person of the Holy Spirit. So a believer does not just have the privilege of cancelled sins, he also has the opportunity to minimize struggle against sin by ensuring agreement with the Holy Spirit, on a daily basis. For any man wishing to overcome sin, it is important to bear in mind that God needs man's active collaboration before victory can come.

a. God's Commitment to Man's Deliverance from Sin

One of the most exciting facts of scripture is God's commitment to the deliverance of man from his self-inflicted slavery to sin. When

Adam and his wife went against God's clear instruction not to eat the fruit of knowledge of good and evil, they least anticipated the severity of the consequences and must have been very surprised at the change in themselves. The serenity they enjoyed up to that moment deserted them sharply and in its place was a terrifying fear of their environment and of God. They realized they needed to cover themselves against the elements of life, the wind, the sun, and even against animals, which they had up till now controlled. They even needed to protect themselves against themselves and against each other. In the company of thieves (and indeed all sinners), everyone is a suspect; each of them knew then that the other was capable of evil. Adam realized that Eve could be treacherous and disobedient, evil hearted and dangerous; and vice versa. The very creatures that had been at their command suddenly went wild, threatening to eat them up. They suddenly found that foxes were hostile and lions were so deadly they had to run for cover. They had been driven from Eden and no place was safe any longer. They needed cover and hiding at all times. Unfortunately, the best available to them were leaves and trees. So they made covering of leaves and hid behind trees. We all know how useless such coverings and hiding places were and still are. Yet we still use them.

When God came down, He first went to the erring parties and showed them what they had brought on themselves by virtue of toying with sin. God cursed the serpent, but He could not do the same to Adam and Eve; He merely alerted them about the natural consequences of their actions. But He also did something else. He declared their deliverance from the bondage of sin the same day that they got themselves into it. And He set in motion the process of actualizing it immediately thereafter. In the same Genesis 3:15, God announced that the 'Seed of the woman' shall bruise the serpent's head.

As always, it is man that gets himself into the hole of bondage; but God committs to bringing him out. For as long as a man is willing to cooperate with God and be delivered, God is committed to working out his deliverance. The devil wrapped man up in a terrifying bondage following the latter's consent to his suggestions in Eden. But throughout the pages of the scriptures, we see God working assiduously to rescue him. The first major step towards structured salvation following the 'Seed of the Woman' promise was the call of Abraham. For nearly fifty years, God worked to get the life and priorities of His man right. Abraham was a model in leaving his city and country to the land which he did not know by name or location as at the time God called him. But there were other distractions in his life. He could not reconcile God's proclaimed intent for him with his childlessness and at some point was willing to take a short cut towards the dream of having a child. But God held on. Finally, God knew He had a man He could trust, not only to keep His commandments, but also to teach his children to do the same. Then followed many more years of shaping his children into vessels, first with the more pliable and quiet Isaac and later with the very stubborn and self-confident Jacob. But through it all, God won. He won each man to His side, and won over the influences that kept them away from Him, thereby securing the base for a long-lasting recovery of man from the devil.

God's dealings and struggles with the children of Israel were not small either. Beginning with the jealousy, moral laxity and violence of the sons of Jacob, God shepherded the people into Egypt to translate them from a small family into a mighty nation. They showed resistance and unbelief to God as He worked to get them out of Egypt. Severally, they would murmur, cry, doubt, curse and resist God, but God held on. With Moses, a man whose mind was working in the direction of salvation as God's, the job seemed doable. The history of the Israelites is strewn with straying. But all through, God kept fighting to restore the people. He would regularly draw them into repentance, yet they would always resist Him. God would try to overcome their doubts with mighty miracles, words of assurances and other measures aimed at settling the question of God's personality and intent. God bent over severally to show the Israelites that He meant well for them and for all humanity. The reason it took God as long as it did to send the Lord Jesus was because He had to work through man. The job of rescue can only be done by a man, and it needed to be a man who had the nature of holiness. So God had to work long preparing a people that He could communicate holiness to. In the midst of a terribly corrupted race, this was a herculean task. And as we see from the history of the Israelites, God labored hard to overcome their doubts, waywardness and plain rebellion for hundreds of years.

Till date, the question of God's intent remains unsettled in the hearts of many. The first person man blames for the confusion and emptiness of his life is usually God. We seem perennially incapable of seeing in what ways we could have contributed to the difficulties we face. The devil works well with this attitude. In fact, for the enmity between God and man to be strengthened, it is important that man sees God as the architect of his problems. As long as man sees God from this light, it becomes impossible for him to see or accept that God is good. And for as long as man perceives God as being unkind and unreliable, he will reject whatever offer God makes to him. It is a perfect set up to make man continuously suspicious of God.

Mankind got itself into a hole; but God is committed to redeem him. However, the big problem is that man has been made to see God as part of the problem. Individually and collectively, we blame God for every negative thing happening around us even when we are aware of the wrong choices that may have caused those things to happen to us. Part of the nature we inherited from the fall is that of trading blame.

But God persists with man, and thank God He does. Were it not for His persistence, our consistent taking sides and agreeing with the thoughts and suggestions of the enemy would have brought us to complete ruin. We hear Him almost pleading with man, *"Come, let us reason together. Though your sins be as crimson, they shall be white as snow* (Isaiah 1:18). Somewhere else He would declare, *"The hand of the Lord is not too short that He cannot save, nor His ears too heavy that they would not hear, but our sins doth separate between us and our God"* (Isaiah 59:1). And then later, *"I have held out my hand to a people that desired me not"* (Isaiah 65:2)

The Priest, Zechariah outlined God's intent with man thus,

> *"That we should be saved from our enemies; and from the hand of all that hate us; to perform the mercy promised to our fathers; and to remember his holy covenant, the oath which*

He sware to our father Abraham, that He would grant unto us, that we being delivered out of the hand of our enemies might serve Him without fear, in holiness and righteousness before Him, all the days of our life" (Luke 1:71 – 75).

God's position on the matter of deliverance is unequivocal. God's most important commitment is the salvation of man from the ruins of his personal straying. God is committed to saving man from the hand of the strong man, sin. But like a drowning person, we always resist God and treat Him as the aggressor. Yet for any man that must be saved, the first help God grants him is the knowledge that God is for him. A man must be able to see that God is working for him and therefore be willing to work with God to secure his own salvation. "For he that cometh unto God must believe that He is and that He is a rewarder of those that diligently seek Him" (Hebrews 11:6). Without believing that God is, faith cannot build in the heart, and without faith in the heart, salvation cannot occur. The sinful nature in us likes to shift blames. And who else is it most convenient to shift man's blame to than the greatest enemy of the sinful nature, which is God?

b. The Blood of Jesus

When Adam sinned, God killed an animal. What was recorded in the book of Genesis was that He used the skin to clothe Adam and Eve. But God could have clothed them with anything else. For example, He that made cotton could have woven some yarn to provide clothing for them. But why did He kill an animal? It was because He had to. Sin had entered, and blood had to be spilt for 'without the shedding of blood, there is no remission of sin' (Hebrews 9:22). So the animal that was slain served two purposes. Its blood atoned for the sins of Adam and Eve. Its skin was then used to provide clothing for them. In the rest of the Old Testament, as God found Abraham, we see God often requiring Abraham to make sacrifices of animals. Afterwards, the children of Israel received extensive instructions on sacrifices of different forms to atone for different kinds of sins and bring peace between God and man. Reading the account of the establishment of Isreal and the rules and regulations, one almost gets the sense of a bloody God, one who loves to have animals slaughtered for any and every reason.

What was God really after in those sacrifices? Was it that He loved the bloods that were shed? Not quite! Sin is a stranger on earth and scriptures say that the wages of sin is death (Romans 6:23). Sin must always go with death, implying that whatever sin touches or wherever sin goes, it takes a life away, usually the life that is involved in it. However, if God should allow all men on earth (or even the nation of Israel) to die for their sins, then there cannot be any salvation. The devil would have succeeded in the plan of destroying mankind and all the works of God he is supposed to supervise. So someone or something else with blood has to be given any time a man (since it is only man that) sins. Animals do not commit sin since they know not good or evil, so their blood can be used. But man is a superior being and cannot be sustainably cleansed by the blood of animals. Besides, even when the blood of animals has taken away some sin produced, the producer of the sins, which is within man (remember our fruits and trees analogy) would still produce more sins. Now, having found His own nation, God gave them a set of laws that define the limits of acceptable behaviour, helping them have a clue as to what righteousness looks like. This was particularly important given that the Israelites were coming from Egypt where idolatory was the norm. But God knows that the old nature in man would always rear its head and cause them to violate those laws, the people's good intentions notwithstanding. There was something in man that is lawless and would make guidance by laws impossible. Meanwhile, God cannot behold or dwell with sin. Given that He intended to continue to fellowship with the Israelites, His presence being the singular most important distinguishing factor in their lives (Exodus 33: 13 -17), He needed to make room for temporary reconciliation. The sins of the children of Israel had to be atoned for to make it possible that God continues to fellowship with them. So He had to provide for the sacrifices of blood; the blood of bulls and oxen.

But even as God made these arrangements of sacrifices with the Israelites, He made it clear to them that they were temporary. Moses, at the time of his death, told the Israelites that the Lord your God shall raise a prophet among you, who is like me, Him shall you hear (Deuteronomy 18:15). Several prophets followed after him and many of them indicated that there is perfection on the way. The perfection would be in the form of a man, generally referred to as 'the Messiah'. He would reign as King, but as Isaiah also showed, He would first suffer and afterwards reign in glory. In the days of Herod, Jesus came. Unfortunately, Israel has had a set of teachers who portrayed the Messiah as a super hero. Add this to the grievous deprivation and humiliation that the Roman Empire meted out to the people, expectations were high that the coming Messiah would lead the revolt and subsequent liberation from Rome. But the person that eventually came claiming to be the Messiah could not have been more disappointing. He came from a poor and struggling home, born of insipid parents and the most unlikely of circumstances befitting a king. As they supposed, He even came from the north, from a town people acknowledged was no good in producing prophets, when the real Messaiah was supposed to be from David's home town. There was nothing attractive about His personality. He turned out a quiet and non-violent man, gathered 12 illiterates and semi-illiterates around Him and went about on foot speaking of a kingdom that was close by. Yes, He performed miracles and healed people, but He also appeared arrogant and disrespectful of customs. Worse, He taught strange doctrines, appearing to raise the bars of holiness and the requirements of God from the people. He seemed to associate more with irrelevant and nondescript people than with the high and mighty who could help Him make things happen. In fact, even the already weak people that were with Him would grow weaker with His kind of doctrines. He seemed to delight in turning men to women and making everyone around Him even feebler than they already were, all in the name of God. He seemed to make bogus claims about Himself and regularly challenged the leaders of the nation, openly confronting them with their sins, and this irked them in no small measure. He never challenged the Romans for one day; instead He directed His rebukes to the leadership of His own people, who clearly appeared the lesser evil than the godless Romans.

From day one, the leadership of Isreal could not hide their disdain for this man. Occasion after occasion, as He dared them, their rage against Him and all He stands for grew. They made several attempts to silence Him but failed. The challenge was that the man was popular and was becoming increasingly magnified among the commoners. Thus, attempting to take Him in the public would be suicidal. Yet He was hardly, if ever, alone. Then one day, one of His close associates came by and offered to take them to a private place where they could get the man without the crowd. Providence seemed to have finally smiled on them. They went there and truly there He was. They caught Him and arranged a mock trial. Of course, He was guilty even before being charged, so they sought and got the permission of the Roman leadership to do away with Him. They nailed Him to a cross after much torture and humiliation.

But who would have known that this weak-looking, apparently poor man, whose holiness not even his worst detractors could deny, was God Himself. No man, not even angels and demons, knew of the mystery that God kept close to His chest over many centuries. He had programmed to appear in flesh and blood so as to knock the enemy of mankind away from within. The book of Hebrews described the event thus *"Forasmuch then as the children are partakers of flesh and blood, He also Himself likewise took part of the same; that through death he might destroy him that had the power of death, that is, the devil"* (Hebrews 2:14). God had arranged that the days of blood of bulls and rams be over. Therefore, a perfect blood, which was highly superior to man's blood and altogether sinless, could be shed once and for all to take care of all conceivable sins. This blood can cleanse **all** men **everywhere** from **all** unrighteousness. *"But if we walk in the light, as he is in the light, we have fellowship one with another, and the blood of Jesus Christ His son cleanseth us from ALL sin"* (1 John 1: 7).

The plan of God was that in shedding no less than His own blood, Jesus might once and for all put paid to the matter of atonement for sin. He was God's permanent reconciliation of man to Himself. Every enmity between God and man could be dealt with the moment God looks down at man through the medium of the blood of Jesus. Though He came from Israel, He was not only for the Israelites. He would reconcile the whole world to God, fulfilling God's declaration to Abraham that in him shall all nations of the earth be blessed.

c. The Two Natures – Adam and Christ

To understand why Jesus had to go to the cross, we again need to go back to Eden. When the trio of Adam, Eve and the serpent transgressed against God, He specifically said to the serpent, "I will put enmity between you and the woman and between her seed and your seed; He shall bruise your head, and you shall bruise His heel". All Christians believe that this pronouncement in Eden was God's promise to Satan that He would destroy sin and all its bye-products using the seed of the woman, a 'He' that shall bruise (crush, overcome, annihilate) the head (power, source, life) of the devil. Paul later referred to the work of Jesus as "having disarmed principalities and powers, He made a public spectacle of them, triumphing over them in it (the cross)" (Colossians 2:15).

Adam gave away the liberty of men and made them subject to the devil, the world and to sin. It therefore behoves another Adam to crush him that deceived man, get the liberty back and liberate man unto the original purpose for which he was created. So the Bible said, "The first man Adam was made a living soul, the last Adam was made a quickening spirit" (1 Corinthians 15:45). Jesus is God's answer to sin and to all that sin can infect a man with, the savior of the world now and in the life to come, the complete package of salvation from God. We cannot effectively appreciate our relationship with the Lord Jesus and the life He brings if we do not appreciate our past relationship with sin, the troubles and pains we passed through while in sin, the contradictions our lives were made of and the certain destruction we knew we were headed for but were incapable of stopping.

When God told Adam not to eat the fruit of the knowledge of good and evil, you will notice that He told him that he may eat of every other fruit of the garden (Genesis 2:17). Now the scriptures particularly noted that the tree of life was also in the midst of the garden, meaning man was free to eat it. *"And out of the ground made the Lord God to grow every tree that is pleasant to the sight, and good for food; the tree of life also in the midst of the garden, and the tree of knowledge of good and evil"* (Genesis 2:9). Now that fruit of life contained eternal life and had man eaten it, he would have had eternal life. Indeed, the potency of eternal life contained in the tree was such that if man had eaten it after he ate the fruit of the tree of knowledge of good and evil and sinned, he would still have lived forever. But man did not eat it. By permitting man to eat of every fruit in the garden except that of the knowledge of good and evil, the purpose of God was for man to eat of the tree of life and then acquire everlasting life that exists in God. But eating it must be by choice.

What was at stake here was choice, Adam's choice. Adam had to deliberately choose dependence on God and the life that goes with it or independence from God and death. Eating the fruit of life was to be Adam's deliberate choice on the understanding that God wanted the best for him. That would have brought Adam to a level of life higher than what he already had. Many Christians believe that Adam had eternal life in Eden and lost it and Christ came to restore it. It was not so. Adam never ate the fruit of the tree of life and so never had eternal life. In fact, the main reason God had to put Adam out of Eden was so as not to allow him eat of the fruit of the tree of life. *"So He drove out the man, and He placed on the east of the garden of Eden Cherubims, and a flaming sword, which turned every way, to keep the way of the tree of life"* (Genesis 3:24). That was also the reason Jesus came to bring much more than Eden to us. No doubt Adam had a glorious life in Eden, a life that had the capacity of naming all the animals without having to go hunting them down; a life that was surely in charge of all creation. But Adam did not have eternal life. That was for him to choose by obeying God in eating the fruit of the tree of life. Or he could descend further (to what the natural man now carries as life) by eating the fruit of knowledge of good and evil, which promises him a life independent of God. He chose the latter and we know the rest by experience.

So the scriptures say that the first man never went beyond being a living soul that he was when God breathed into his nostrils. But the soul life was destructible and what man needed was an incorruptible, indestructible life. And so we see Jesus, as He went about His Ministry, was always talking of a certain water (river, spring or well) of life, which He would give to anyone that comes to Him. When He came back in the book of Revelation to re-introduce Himself to a visibly overwhelmed John, He insisted that "To him that overcometh will I give to eat of the tree of life, which is in the midst of the paradise of God" (Revelation 2:7). Could it be the same tree of life? Could it be the same paradise of God? Eden and all its contents have become completely out of the reach of man as God stationed Cherubim and flaming sword to keep out the fallen man, but Jesus came, not to show man where he could pick the most important things of Eden, but to be those most important things of Eden to man. They are embodied in Him. He said of Himself, "I am the Way, the Truth and the LIFE; no man cometh unto the Father, except by me" (John 14:6). He is the way to life and the destination of life; He is the Life; the life in the tree of life.

What does this mean to us? Man in Eden needed to eat the fruit of the tree of life, but because he did not understand what it would give him, he turned and rather took the fruit of the tree of the knowledge of good and evil. Now, that tree of life is back and accessible. But it appeared in the form of a person; in the person of the last Adam, the conclusion of the old race and the beginning of a new species. Jesus has the life that overcomes sin; and it is eternal. In accepting and allowing Jesus as the driver of one's life, one acquires the life that is in Christ. The life that Adam had before the fall was structurally different from the life that the fallen Adam has and both are still very distinct from the life that the last Adam (Jesus) has. The life in the first one was a transitional life; it was to be made either eternal or terrestrial depending on the choice Adam made. It was uncorrupted, but it was not eternal. Adam chose corruption and therefore had to take on mortality. The latter life, the mortal, sin-ridden life that man currently carries, is in itself very corrupt.

The difference between the Adamic nature and the Jesus nature is not in training; it is in nature. We know there is a kind of life in fowls that makes them fly, chirp and do other things that we know them for. There is also a life in cows that makes them eat grass and move together in flocks. There is yet another life in lions that makes them predators and carnivorous. None of these animals need to be taught what they do. As it is often said, it is 'in their nature'. They just grow into it. No amount of training will equip a goat to bounce on other animals and eat them up for breakfast because it is not in its nature. In the same way, no amount of training will equip the natural life (in the image of Adam) to accomplish the things of eternal life or righteousness because it is not in its nature. Paul put it simply in his letter to the Romans "Because the carnal mind is in enmity against God; for it is not subject to the law of God, **neither indeed can be**". The point is it cannot. It cannot be subject to God even if it wanted to. A pigeon cannot bark even if it wants to; it can make its own kind of sound, the one given to its nature to make, but it cannot bark. It has to be a dog in order to bark.

Jesus did not just come with that new nature; He is the new nature; "He is the Way, the truth and the Life" (John 14:6). He does not have the way, the truth and the life; He **is** the Way, the Truth and the Life. This distinction is so fundamental that even for Christians, if this revelation does not dawn on us, we are in trouble. No man can come to God without passing through Jesus. The understanding of who (or what) Jesus is and what He means when He says that anyone who does not eat His flesh and drink His blood does not have life in him is at the very centre of what it means to be a Christian. Among unregenerate men, there are various images of Jesus - John the Baptist raised from the dead or a great religious leader in the class of Buddha, Confucius, and Mohammed. Some look at Him and ask, "Is not this Jesus, the son of Joseph? How come He claims to be the bread of life?" Even among believers, the biggest challenge is the revelation of the Man Jesus. Many like Nicodemus know Jesus, the great teacher who came from God (John 3:1); others know the great prophet that came in the spirit of Elijah, while others see a noble man that should be emulated. Unfortunately, none of these represents the Lamb of God that taketh away the sins of the world. And frankly, many of such images obscure the real Jesus from men. But except a man gets to know Him by way of revelation, he cannot access the blessing that comes from following the Lord *"Blessed art thou Simon bar Jonah, ... for flesh and blood hath not revealed this to you ..." (Matthew 16:17).*

The natural man is proud of himself. But when a man sees Jesus, he repudiates himself, falls in complete abhorrence of all he has cherished and stood for. He then accepts what he has seen of Jesus as the complete truth and chooses to allow the same things to be transplanted in him. Knowing he is not able to tranform himself into the image he has seen, he then prays for God to help him. We call this repentance and it is the beginning of transformation. We are incapable of translating ourselves to the image we see. But our part is to hate what we know of ourselves: the selfishness, pride, ambitions and all that excited us in the past must come to be seen for what they really are. We desire to become the things we have seen of Christ. This awareness sends us to our knees. We cry out for help in the place of prayer and we study to know more about the person and life of this Jesus. While we thus hunger and search, God begins to change our nature from the inside into the image of his son, Jesus. This is the miracle of transformation; and it is God's responsibility. But we must hunger for it before it can come. That is the beginning of the process of eating Jesus and it is not a one-off affair for the man that has come to believe. God has so much to teach and transform us into. And he does it precept upon precept, line upon line, here a little, there a little (Isaiah 28:10). But repentance will always be the beginning point.

CHAPTER 12

THE POWER TO BECOME

a. The Power to Become

We often do not appreciate why it was important that after Jesus had fulfilled all the requirements of the law, He still had to go to the cross. People often think that if only a man can keep the commandments, including the Sermon on the Mount, then he should be acceptable to God. But this is not only objectionable; it is far from God's way of helping man. Indeed, the entire law, including the Sermon on the Mount, was not made to be kept and/or fulfilled by man. They were given to show man that he does not have the capacity to meet the requirements of righteousness. And had Jesus ended with the sermon on the mount, or with any other requirements of righteousness as outlined in the new testament, He would have been no better than Buddha, Mohammed, Socrates, Ghandi or any of the many noble men who have commanded significant followership across nations for the good guide they provided. This is because the challenge with mankind is not lack of guidance; it is the power to implement what is outlined in the guide. There is no nation where the righteousness, justice as well as the awesomeness and judgment of God have not been spoken of, if not by men, then definitely by other creations of God (Romans 1:19 – 20). There is no nation where men do not acknowledge, and extensively preach, the necessity of fair play in dealings with others, of love and peace, of selflessness and moral rectitude. Yet meanness and disorder are the norm in human existence. There is no nation on earth where lies and cheating are promoted and respected, yet trust is a very rare commodity and trustworthiness extremely scarce. There is nowhere where cowardice and betrayal are celebrated. Yet across the world, these vices continue to plague man mightily. Indeed, what have restrained men from displaying their vilest nature are the numerous laws made to ensure social stability. These laws have merely kept men in check, mainly through fear of punishment or rejection by the society. They have absolutely no power to remove or reduce the hate, irritation, bitterness, selfishness, greed and lust which each man carries within; they merely ameliorate their exhibition.

Why is this so? It is because there is a huge difference between knowledge of what to do and the power to do it. There is probably no man that has not come to appreciate this difference as he struggles to reconcile the discrepancy between what he knows to be right and what he does. Every man born of woman who makes the feeblest attempt towards living a righteous life immediately identifies with Paul's cry of desperation in Romans (7:15) "that which I do, I allow not, for what I would, that do I not, but that which I hate, that do I". What is needed is not just knowledge, but power, the power to do.

Throughout the pages of the scripture, this necessity of acquiring the power to do is emphasized. The bible makes it very clear that in his fallen nature, man does not have the power to do anything that endures. 'Without me ye can do nothing (John 15:5). Man may know, but his knowledge becomes grossly limited as he is not able to do that which he knows. This can lead to frustration.

In finding a way out, let us consider John (1:10 – 13), which talked about this power (or what some versions of the bible rendered as 'right').

> He was in the world, and the world was made by him, and the world knew Him not. He came unto his own, and his own received Him not. But as many as received Him, **to them gave He power to become the sons of God**, even to them that believe on His Name: which were born, not of blood, nor of the will of the flesh, nor of the will of man, but of God.

In Christianity, the power to **become** (to become son(s) of God) is crucial. Severally, the Bible describes what God is like and what therefore the sons of God should be like – holy, faithful, righteous, pure, just, true, full of power, etc. Such expressions as "Holy, holy, holy is the Lord (Isaiah 6:3); He is faithful and just (1 John 1:9); Jesus Christ the righteous (1 John 2:3); "even as He is pure" (1 John 3: 3); all point to the nature of God. In other instances, men who have experienced his presence declare "God is light, and in Him is no darkness at all" (I John 1:5). Many of us have no problem with this nature; we (seemingly) understand and appreciate what God is. We worship Him for what and who He is. We rever those attributes of God and sing them in praise. But the challenge begins when we note that the scriptures insist that we also have **to be** as God is. "Be holy for I am holy (1 Peter 1:16)". And then John boldly declared "As He is, so are we in this world" (1 John 4:17). Now this should be true, but usually we do not have the experience. The reason is simple: while a critical first step towards overcoming sin is knowledge (my people perish for lack of knowledge – (Hosea 4:6), knowledge without the **power to be** avails nothing. Knowledge must be matched with capacity before righteousness comes forth as life and not remain mere thought in the heart or word in the mouth.

It is instructive to note that in discussing **the power to be**, John 1 mentions three kinds of people. The first group are called "the world", *He was in the world and the world was made through Him, and the world did not know Him"* (John 1:10). The second group are called "His own", *He came to His own, and His own did not receive Him* (John 1:11). The third group are "Those who receive Him", *But as many as received Him, to them He gave the right to become" (John 1: 12).*

For the group of 'the world', the challenge was that they did not know Him; they had no idea who He is. They may be vaguely aware that there is someone out there, but that is all; they do not know Him. They may claim to know Him but in reality, they have no idea how He works, what He wants and why He wants them. They do not have the power to be of God; they may claim to be close to God because they pray or read the word of God or go to church services, but these do not have the power of life. Their lives and thoughts are not consistent with God's Word or life. They are oblivious of the demands of God upon their lives. Such people may have testimonies of the provisions and protection of God, but they do not understand that none of these makes one a child of God. God is around them, but they do not know Him. They receive several mercies from Him, but fail to realize that those mercies are the same as He graciously gives to all who are alive and so they imagine that those mercies make them children of God. God manifests in their circumstances, but they really do not know the personality, the dictates, demands, likes and dislikes of God. They may even think that it is about generically staying away from sin that makes a man a child of God and would not understand how someone who does not kill, does not tell lies, does not cheat and does not engage in any of the evils of ordinary men can be excluded from the family of God. They constitute the world and do not know God.

The group of 'His own' consists of those who have touched the Lord at some point. They may have acquired the unique identity as 'born again'; as God's children at some point. But they have not made up their minds to receive God's way in its entirety. While the problem of the world is that they do not know God, these people in the 'His own' group know Him, but they have not received what they know. For such men, what they know is strikingly different from what they do. They hear much and teach much, but they are not doing much. Sometimes, they like and teach what they know, but they are not wholly committed to allowing what they know to become real in their lives. They seem to have seen the ways of God, but are not sure that is how they want to live their lives.

A classic example is found in John 6, which we had referred to in chapter 10 – Man's approach to dealing with sin. These men had given impression that they were sold out to Jesus. They appeared zealous and made great sacrifices to attend meetings. They heard Jesus speak about heavenly things and nodded their heads as He did. When His apostles requested that they sat in groups of fifties so they could receive the free lunch, they obeyed without questions. They were neither unruly nor tumultuous. They appeared every inch the perfect congregation. But they lacked something. Their hearts were not wholly on Him to the extent that they could go any mile to retain and remain with Him.

They were yet to receive Him but it would take only hard and extreme sermons as in the quoted scripture to unravel this lack.

The third group consists of 'those who received Him...that believed on His Name'. They did not only receive His word, they received Him. They received His ways. They are willing to be whatever He is and to do whatever He wants. His ways may be queer and unattractive to the world, but these ones embrace Him that way. He does not retaliate and they choose not to retaliate simply because He wants it that way. Their hairdo, clothing pattern, talking and thinking are all subjected to His choices and decisions. In totality, they receive Him. They equally believe on His name and are not afraid to take risks on their beliefs. They defy men on the Master's wish. Their hearts are so disposed as to allow Him about anything and would not do anything except He authorizes such. Scriptures say it is to this group of people that Jesus gives power to become. He gives them power to become because first and foremost, they want to become. They are not ashamed of becoming nor do they fear the consequences of becoming, which things hinder people in the two earlier groups. If becoming takes them to life, all well and good, but if it takes them to death, they receive it also with thanksgiving. Men are free to mock them and give them names for not conforming, but they are not moved by any of those. They simply live to please the one who has called them. With this sort of heart, they do not also need to shop for power; Jesus gives them the needed power. God finds willingness in them and then takes on the responsibility of giving them ability.

The power to become comes as grace upon a man; it is a gift from God; it is not something a man acquires of his own self. It is embedded in the knowledge of the Word of God - a revelation that does not just make a man see the light of the Word of God, but also able to take a decision and firmly follow it through. That is why it can only be obtained through prayer and study of the Word of God. Education, enlightenment or training can not fetch a man any divine grace or gift. Only the Word of God received with meekness can save a man's soul (James 1: 21).

The power to become is inherited, not acquired. In the story of

Haman and Mordecai that we referred to in Chapter 6, Haman's friends declared, "**If** Mordecai be of the seed of the Jews, before whom thou hast begun to fall, thou shalt not prevail against him, but shall surely fall before him" (Esther 6:13). One wonders why the 'if' in that statement. Haman has always known that Mordecai was a Jew. Neither Mordecai nor the Jewish race was new to either him or his friends. It was even the knowledge of who Mordecai was that made him spurn the idea of killing only Mordecai and instead resorted to looking for all Jews in the Kingdom. So how come the 'if' at this point? It is one thing to claim to be a Jew, and a different thing altogether to really be a Jew. Sin is not afraid of those who claim to be Jews, it is afraid of those who are. And how do we know who is? The friends of Haman said, 'if Mordecai be of the **seed** of the Jews...' There is something about seeds, implants, genes, blood inheritance, and other transferred capabilities that is important in the Christian race. We have talked about the promise of God to give His nature to any man who comes to Christ. That nature was described as "seed" by Apostle John, "Whosoever is born of God doth not commit sin, for His seed remaineth in him, and he cannot sin, because he is born of God" (I John 3:9). He **cannot** sin? Yes, he cannot sin! And he cannot sin, not because he does not dwell among sinners or because he cannot be tempted by sin, but there is something inside of him that cannot permit sin in his life. He inherited that thing at the point of the new birth. It is a capability, enduement, strength that makes standing against sin possible. That seed within has given him the same kind of heart that Jesus carried which helped him to see the emptiness of the world without, see his own fickleness and continually depended on God for grace to overcome. He thinks with the mind of Christ (1 Corinthians 2:16) and lives under grace, coated with power from on high. So he is able to say no to sin, unlike most other men. He does not only know that sin is destructive, he is able to stand against the suggestion to be part of that destructive nature. Beyond these, he is inspired unto righteousness. He can innovate in righteousness. He hears God and is able to respond to His command in the spiritual. He is able to get inspiration from heaven and live it out here on earth. When a man genuinely gets born again, God puts this something, this power inside of him. For as long as he nourishes and does not despise this grace, God will continue to work out victory over sin in him.

If the seed is not there in a man, there is very little that even God can do for him in fighting sin. He will always be defeated. Whatever is not born of God does not overcome the world, even if it acts valiantly, roars mightily and does big things. When a man comes to the devil challenging him on the matter of sin with scriptures, the question the devil asks is 'is he really a Jew?' If the man is indeed a Jew, there is no hope for the enemy. But do not be deceived, the devil will raise this challenge concerning every man even when such a man prays well, preaches well, gives bounteous alms and is committed to the church. The validity of each man's standing would have to be tested. But if the seed is there, the man will overcome. Sometimes, he may feel overwhelmed depending on the extent to which that seed is nurtured, has grown or has matured. But ultimately, the seed overcomes the world – "for whatsoever is born of God overcometh the world (I John 5:4). That is the verdict. The seed is a gift; it is not acquired by practice. Just like every man on earth picks up physiological and character features from his parents, so does each believer pick up the nature of God at the point of giving his life to Christ. It is the most important equipment that God gives a man in the fight against sin. Hanging around churches, being religious, gentle and giving to good causes do not bequeath that nature (seed) to a man. It is a gift of God at the new birth, a part of the power to be and the empowerment to overcome.

b. Liberty from Sin and Fear to Serve God

God knows the debilitating power of sin, the death that comes from it and accompanying fear associated with death. Sin and guilt rarely coexist with courage. Almost invariably, anyone who is guilty is also afraid. Adam and Eve's first realization after sinning was that they were afraid of the presence and judgement of God and of their environment. God knows that no man can truly and fully serve Him unless such a man is delivered from his sins, guilt and fears. So He provided that in Christ Jesus, we should be delivered from the power of our enemies, including fear of any kind. Jesus died on the cross because it is important that He directly faces death and conquers it. Only then would he be able to disarm death and empower those who follow Him (Hebrews 2:14). In fact, the scriptures go on further to say that He did not just defeat death; but He made an open show of the defeat. "And having spoiled principalities and powers, he made a shew of them openly, triumphing over them in it" (Colosians 2:15). This was to give a very strong, undeniable and unshakable basis for those who follow Him to directly confront death as well.

As earlier noted, it is impossible for any man to fully follow God without being delivered from fear. If a man is not liberated from the fear to which all mortals are subject, following God becomes tedious, if not altogether impossible. The fear of the future makes it difficult to take God by His word. It keeps men so busy that they can neither answer the call of God in their lives nor work to fulfill the purpose of God. Rather, they are engrossed on how to take care of and support themselves and their dependants. The fear of man leads to denying God before men. A believer who is afraid of men would not be able to truly follow Jesus because His ways are not wholly acceptable to men. The fear of hurt is the reason many cringe before those they believe can hurt them. Trying to escape hurt can make a man vulnerable to being used against God. Every fear is an inhibition. Fear destabilizes the will of God in the life of a man and makes him inaccessible to God. That is the reason it is absolutely important that God delivers any man that would follow Him from fear. And that is the reason Luke 1: 73 and 74 says that the promise God gave to us through Abraham is "that he would grant unto us, that we being delivered out of the hand of our enemies might serve him without fear, in holiness and righteousness before him, all the days of our life". For Solomon to undertake the very critical assignment of building the temple for God, he had to first receive rest from God. He told Hiram "You know how my father David could not build a house for the name of the Lord his God because of the wars which were fought against him on every side, until the Lord put his foes under the soles of his feet. But now, the Lord my God has given me rest on every side; there is neither adversary nor evil occurrence" (1 Kings 5: 3-4). David fought wars; so he could not build a house for God. For his son now to build the house, God had to give him rest. Solomon was a man of peace, not because he could not fight wars but because for him to concentrate on the important task of building for God, he had to be delivered from wars and fears. He had to focus on the building.

The enemy knows our susceptibility to fear and usually capitalizes on it. Many men would have been great in the hands of God but for fear. Fear of the opinion of men, for example, keeps us from preaching the Word of God; fear of failing keeps us from ministering to the sick, from commanding demons and from liberating other men. How many times have believers been unable to speak out the Word of prophecy even though they know that it is the Word of God? Some fear that what they say may not come to pass or may not be pleasant to their audience. In such circumstances, God's command and will are made to take the second place to man's opinion. This is also the reason God invariably prefixes instructions to men whom He would use with 'Fear not'. It was important that Joshua feared neither the Canaanites who were huge and fearsome nor even the Israelites who might be opposed to certain instructions from God which they considered irrational. It was important that Jeremiah feared not the authorities of his day as He delivered what was obviously very unpalatable news of the impending captivity and God's purposes for a reprobate Israel. Saul was a man accustomed to excuses and as he was accosted by Samuel following his failure to destroy Amalek, he tried to re-write his terms of reference and assured Samuel that the work was completely done. When Samuel managed to eventually pin him down, he admitted "For I was afraid of the people ... "(1 Samuel 15:24). Saul's tragic end began because he was afraid of the people. It was then consolidated by his fear of losing the kingdom for which reason he spent so much time hunting down David who looked every inch his inevitable successor. Next there was a war and he was afraid of the outcome, so he went to a witch. That sealed his fate.

A strange occurrence in the lives of many believers is that giving their lives to Christ is often not accompanied by deliverance from fear. This may not be unconnected with the fact that in many of such circumstances, the individual is not even very sure that he has been delivered from sin. This is an agonizing situation. Severally, we believe that Christ has saved us from our past sins, but it is not always experientially so. We also understand that we are delivered from our present sins and the power that sin wields over men. But when we flounder and find ourselves unstable, the devil reminds us that no man can be perfect. And sometimes indeed, it seems as though even God has abandoned us. At such points, we do not 'feel' delivered. Then, living with a conscience smeared with offence and sin, we are not able to stand fearless before the enemy or before the throne of mercy. Being unable to stand means we cannot achieve anything for God. For this reason, understanding the far-reaching consequences of the finished work of Christ on the cross, the liberation we have obtained in Him and the possibilities available to us is a pre-requisite for being able to enter into the fullness of our inheritance in Him. That understanding helps us enter into our deliverance from sin. Christ did not only deliver us from past sins, He also delivered us from the power that sin presently holds over our life. He delivered us from death and from the fear of death, fears of man and circumstances and liberated us unto Himself. It is not God's will that any believer should cower before anything. No one can confront the lies or threats of the world without the boldness of Christ. The world does not only tell lies and demand that a man accepts the lies; it also intimidates anyone who tries to swim against the tide. So it is important for us, for God and for His purpose over our lives that He (God) is the only One whom we fear. Someone has said that if we fear God, we have nothing else to fear. That is the only guarantee for fruitfulness.

Indeed, if there is anyone that should invoke fear in men apart from God, it is the man who is born of God. In the biography of John Knox, it is reported that the then King of Scotland admitted that he did not fear the whole armies of Scotland as much as he did the prayers of Mr. Knox. Throughout the scriptures, we see men that trusted in God also standing up to circumstances and authorities, boldly and fearlessly. For this reason, men of God have faced death as though it meant nothing. We would have had nothing to learn from the three Hebrew boys if they had come before Nebuchadnezzar, apologizing for not bowing to his image when others did. If in the name of wisdom, in the name of becoming all things to all men and other forms of rationalizations that present day believers give when under duress, they had decided that it was not needful taking things to the extreme, they would not have had the life changing intervention from God. The complete absence of the fear of death is very conspicuous in the manner they responded to the King "Oh Nebuchadnezzar, we are **not careful** to answer you in this matter, we know the God we serve is able to save us, but in case He chooses not to do so, it makes no difference. We will neither serve your god nor bow down to it" (Daniel 3:16). When Daniel learnt that the decree not to call upon any other god had been passed, he went into his room, **opened** the windows and **prayed three times** a day **as he used to**. Being liberated from the fear of death by fire or death by the mouth of lion was important for the men in the above stories to be free enough to serve God. The testimonies of these men confirm the truth of the word of God that says, "And they overcame him by the blood of the lamb.......they did not love their lives unto death (Revelation 12:11).

This liberation comes from understanding that Jesus conquered death, sickness, sin, and all that are associated with them. Death and his cohorts may bark, but they have no power over the life of the believer. And this is not because a believer has learnt seven keys to liberation. The reason is that we have received Jesus' sacrifice for our sins, God has mercifully accepted us as His children and given unto us His Spirit: the Spirit of love and a sound mind, which has no space for fear. Apostle John described this relationship in the following words, *"There is no fear in love; but perfect love casteth out fear: because fear hath torment. He that feareth is not made perfect in love"* (1John 4:18). Paul, writing to Timothy, also insists that neither love nor soundness of mind can co-exist with fear and that the Spirit we have received is antithetical to fear, *"For God hath not given us the spirit of fear; but of power, and of love, and of a sound mind"* (2 Timothy 1:7). Therefore fear is from the devil and should be resisted in the place of prayer and confession of scriptures. When we operate in this atmosphere devoid of fear, we can safely say,

"O death, where is thy sting? O grave, where is thy victory? ...
but thanks be to God, which giveth us the victory through our
Lord Jesus Christ" (I Corinthians 15:55, 57)

Such understanding liberates a man from fear of sin and death and releases him to a life of fruitfulness. God is never willing to use any man meaningfully except that man is first released from fear – fear of death, of man, of sin, of shame, of poverty, of hurt, of debasement, of the devil, of the unknown, of the future, of the past, of failure, of principalities, of demons, of enemies, and of anything else except God. This understanding that liberates from fear does not come by determination or lecturing. It is received – "for God hath not given us the Spirit of fear ..." (2 Timothy 1:7). Knowing that he should not fear does not free a man from being afraid; he can consistently shrivel in fear even while knowing that he ought not to fear. When a man fears God and bears His nature, the fearless nature comes naturally to him on account of the nature of God in him. That explains why many frail-looking fellows (among whom were even little children) who ordinarily should cower at the voice of army Generals, stood firm and bravely bore some of the worst forms of torture that could be imagined by man. In the presence of kings these ones declared their willingness to face death for the sake of Jesus. History is full of shining examples of many that fearlessly laid down their lives in honour of the glory of God rather than bend to the will of man or the push of sin. This nature can be acquired through prayer and by allowing the word of God take root in our hearts. As we beseech God, He will give unto us His nature, which is devoid of fear. As we chew His word, we constantly sink it into our inner man. The Holy Spirit knows when and how to call up that word in us as circumstances arise.

c. The New Birth Imperative

In our natural state, it is impossible for one to do anything that can please God. The attempt to please God with our human nature is like a dog trying to be of good behavior in order to become a son. No matter how well behaved a dog is or how long a dog has spent in a house, it can never transform into a son. This is the problem of using the human nature to live as a child of God. In the scripture, we are plainly told that the issue is about being born of something, whether one is born of the flesh or of the Spirit. It is about the nature and the origin of whatever acts and thoughts we have. So in John (3:6), the Lord Jesus told us "That which is born of the flesh is flesh; and that which is born of the Spirit is spirit". We were all born of the flesh, born of natural parents and born into sin and our acts and thoughts were born into us. Many people (including born again Christians) try to convert acts and thoughts which originated from the flesh and arrogate them to the Spirit. They do this by either ensuring that those acts are performed within spiritual/religious circles or by spiritualizing what originated from themselves or from the devil. But this is absolute futility; there is no baptism that will change a monkey to a human being. Whatever is born of the flesh will remain flesh until it dies. That is the reason the salvation of Christ for us works towards the crucifixion and death of the flesh.

Many preachers stress the point that we need to be careful what we do so that we can please God. While this is true, fact is our attempts at not displeasing God makes sense after (and only after) we are born of God and the Spirit. It is futile trying not to displease God while we are still born of the flesh, while the source of our inspiration and goal of our aspirations remain the flesh and while the contents of our living consist of the desires and egos deposited in us by Adam. God's way of dealing with the sinful nature is by killing, burying, taking it completely out of the way and replacing it with the life and nature of Christ. A river can never be different from its source. James told us that both salt and fresh water cannot flow from the same source (James 3:1). The same way, God can never complete what the devil started.

The first need is to be re-born. So whoever reads this but is not born again should start from the reasonable kick off point – get born again. Genuinely feel remorse for your sinful nature, acknowledge that it can ruin you; do not excuse your thoughts and actions even if they seemingly hurt no one. Move into your closet and cry to God! Ask Jesus to come and be Lord over your life. Ask Him to release the Holy Spirit into your life to become the guide that will lead you through life. He will listen, hear you and give you a new life.

Having been born again, we must go a step further. Walking with God demands that we engage this new nature in our thoughts and acts. In John (3:6 – Amplified Version), the Bible says "What is born of (from) the flesh is flesh (of the physical is physical); and what is born of the Spirit is spirit". Note that this scripture did not say "whoever is born of the flesh … (or) of the Spirit". It says "what (ever) is born of the flesh … (or) of the Spirit…" So the birth is not limited to living things and man. It goes much further to include acts and intentions, thoughts and desires, worship and sacrifices, words and relationships, among others. Whatever is born of the flesh is flesh and whatever is born of the spirit is spirit. Several spiritual acts we get busy with (e.g. fastings, giving, prayers, etc.) could be born of flesh when they are not directed by the Spirit. Our motives for engaging in good deeds are also viewed, accepted or rejected based on who parented them – the flesh or the Spirit. Whatever is born of the flesh is flesh. It does not have to work to become flesh and there is no other baptism that it needs to be flesh. It is, by definition and constitution, flesh. Likewise, whatever is born of the Spirit can only be spirit. By contrast, when God initiates a programme, for example, in the place of prayer, the Lord impresses it in the heart of brethren to organize a meeting, and they follow up on that, the meeting is born of the Spirit. It has its source in the spirit and so watered by prayer and obedience, it will bear fruit that remains. Likewise, when God quickens a person to give, the giving is rooted in the Spirit and so is spiritual. The intention is not show-off but obedience to divine directive.

The book of I John (3:9) says, "Whosoever is born of God doth not commit sin; for His seed remaineth in him and he cannot sin, because he is born of God". Meanwhile, the same book of 1 John (5:4) says "for whatever is born of God overcometh the world; and this is the victory that overcometh the world, even our faith". There are two related, but distinct items here. The first is the birth of the person; the second is the birth of all the 'whatever' associated with the person. Countless times, very sincere brethren get born again and then stop at that, in part because they are made to believe that once they are born again, all is well. This is right only to the point that it does not counter the instruction in Romans (12:2), "...but be ye transformed by the renewing of your mind ..." Why do we need to renew our minds when we are already born again? J.M. Boice, in his book *"Renewing your mind in a mindless world"*, makes a case for developing a distinctively different view of the world and everyday life. He suggests stepping away from the trends of a mainstream culture, and following a narrow but rewarding path to the transformation of our minds and lives. Even after a man is born again, the pressures from the world can force his mind and action to be patterned after the system of the world. The world system has a way of trying to force everyone in it to conform. It develops norms and compels people to abide by those norms or risk being mocked, ostracized or persecuted for being different. If a young man does not have indicators of material success around a particular age or a young woman does not marry around a particular age, eyebrows are raised. The world system sets a standard for just about everything – from school to work, from family to society, even giving and receiving. There are expectations about how a man at a particular income level should behave, what he is allowed to do and what he is not expected to do. There are expectations about civility and self management, and whenever any of us fails on any of these expectations, trouble ensues. Such a person is vilified and made to look odd, if not altogether punished. In many instances, people, even Christians, especially the young ones, use carnal strategies to meet these expectations. This leads to failure.

One of the first requirements for living an overcoming life is to know that we do not have to meet the expectations of the world system. Indeed, except one is extricated from living to the dictates of the web of expectations from different groups and people surrounding him, he cannot be free to live for God. When scriptures spoke about liberating us from the hands of all them that hate us, it is not just about sin and evil; it is also about liberation from such apparently harmless issues as expectations of the environment around us. Men will always will us against God and it is nearly impossible to freely walk with God while trying to make men happy. God needs to liberate us from the expectations of friends, well-wishers, neighbours, colleagues, bosses, parents and other leaders, to be able to get our unalloyed allegiance. He will use them to mould us, but that is after He has secured our loyalty to Him alone. Jesus made the same point differently, "no one can come after me except he hates his mother and father, and wife and children, yea, even his own life" (Luke 14:26).

Practically, how do we go about being extricated from the world system? We have to get it deeply settled within us that we do not owe anything to the world system or to the flesh. Scriptures said "Therefore brethren, we are debtors, not to the flesh, to live after the flesh" (Romans 8:12). Indeed, we are debtors, but none of what we owe is to the flesh. The issue is that Satan and the world come to us as though we are indebted to them, as though we must pay something to them. They compel us to live and act according to set dictates. Even people around us come upon us as though we owe them, to live according to norms and beliefs they hold. The first measure then is to realize that we do not have to. What we owe, we owe to God. Jesus is the one that paid the price for our redemption from the slavery of sin and the tyranny of the flesh. He is the One to whom we owe our lives. We must use our lives to please Him and it is our responsibility to find out how. Societal expectations make this difficult, but until a man frees his mind from believing that he must live according to some norms around him, he remains tied. That is the reason we are exhorted to renew our minds.

And be not conformed to this world: but be ye transformed by the renewing of your mind, that ye may prove what is that good, and acceptable, and perfect, will of God (Romans 12:2).

We must be released from the sense of obligation to the world system. Our minds must appreciate that we are indebted to God because of what Jesus has done for us and we owe nothing to anyone else. That way, it will be easy to make ourselves the servants of Jesus. That non-conformation to the world will be followed by a transformation which comes as our minds begin to get acquainted with God's expectations on us through His word. Our actions would then follow the revelations we get from the Word of God as our final authority on all matters. For example, while Jesus may send us to serve men, service to men (and God) is not the initial priority. God expects us to sit with Him till we have obtained life before we can serve men with the life we have obtained from Him. So prioritizing service to men at the expense of time for knowing God puts the cart before the horse. Deciding to do the will of God opens the door for further knowledge of the mind of God. From small matters, God begins to make His will known to such a man on bigger matters.

Indeed, walking with God is an exciting lifelong journey. And like all other journeys, it begins with a step. The very first step comes as one seeks to obtain grace through Jesus by acknowledging ones sins, appreciating God's righteousness and accepting His Lordship over one and right to be worshipped. As the first grace comes, it springs up subsequent graces for the rest of the journey, including the wisdom and strength to say no to ungodliness, live purely and hope for the appearing of the Lord Jesus (Titus 2:11 – 13).

God wants to lead us and He has given us His Spirit to provide this leading. The Spirit gives instructions and approval for the things we ought to do. When we identify and follow these, then our actions are spiritual. We can identify this through the Word of God or through the still small voice, through counsels of experienced brethren or through other means that receive confirmation within us as children of God. When a man has given himself to obeying God, he will also know (that he knows) the voice of God. When that voice comes, we follow and act. But when a man introduces a matter himself and then wants to force the Spirit to accept it, he errs and acts in the flesh. Part of the reason the Bible encourages us to be sober is so we might correctly pick up the signals of the Spirit. We need to listen intently and hear the voice of the Spirit before we take off. When we move on our own impulse, we risk taking up activities because they catch our fancy. And because such activities are not born of God ... we sin.

Growth of the life of Christ in us is the mark of true and consistent followership. At the point of new birth, we received the nature of God that was meant to be nurtured unto growth and maturity. When a newborn is left for days without care, it will naturally die. It must receive attention to live. The type of food it is fed, the environment it is placed in, the amount of love it is showered with, will all go a long way in determining how fast and well it grows. Like the newborn baby, the newly born Christian has a part to play. Though it is the work of those around to make the baby grow, the baby itself must desire food and care. It must cry when it does not have the things it requires. Likewise, the baby Christian has to desire spiritual milk (I Peter 2:2). He will be fed by both the brethren and the Spirit of God, but it is his job to desire to be fed with the right mix of the substance of the word of God for proper growth and stability in the faith. This principle is both natural and spiritual. It is not practical for a child born a year ago to become an adult today, yet many Christians are impatient with spiritual growth. They want microwave Christianity where everything is 'with immediate effect' and have come to think that being in a jet age can also deliver jet Christianity. This is incorrect.

d. Salvation through Grace in Christ Jesus

Grace underscores everything we do as believers. We are saved and sustained by grace. One of the greatest challenges to living for God is the heart, which is prone to believe that good things come our way because of any goodness on our part. Yet God is not indebted to any man. Scriptures have said and we repeat it here that our righteousness is like a filthy rag before God. God responds to us because of love not as an obligation. Romans 5: 7-8 says, "... But God commendeth his love toward us, in that, while we were yet sinners, Christ died for us".

To illustrate grace, we look at the story of the woman caught in adultery in the book of John 8: 3 – 11. It was early in the morning and Jesus had just stepped down from the Mount of Olives, intending to continue ministering to the crowds gathered to hear Him. The Scribes and Pharisees suddenly appeared, dragging a woman who looked forlorn. They would have proceeded to stone her to death as is demanded by custom, but this opportunity to trap Jesus was too tempting to let pass. Jesus had defied every wisdom they manufactured to hook Him. Now, it was easy to handle. They knew Him to be lenient on sinners, in fact, sometimes dinning with them and giving all manner of excuses for His 'indulgence'. So it was possible He would ask them to let this woman go, in which case it would become clear that He was against Moses, against the Law and against God. They would consider stoning Him alongside the woman, for supporting evil. If He should ask them to proceed to kill her, then they would know that He was no different from them at all. All those seemingly righteous condemnation that He had visited on them over time amounted to no more than self-imposition. The leader spoke, *"Master, this woman was taken in adultery, in the very act. Now Moses in the law commanded us, that such should be stoned: but what sayest thou"?*

The record in heaven was that "this they said, tempting Him, that they might have to accuse Him". They called Him "Master", but that appellation had nothing to do with the intent of their hearts. They would gladly descend on Him and anyone with Him as well if need be. The Law was the law and whoever stood in the way of the law had to be crushed.

Appropriate answer to their question should have been either a 'yes' or a 'no'. It may not have changed anything among those men; they already had stones in their hands and would execute her anyway, Jesus' views notwithstanding. Afterall, Jesus was not the custodian of the Law. Instead all His tendencies had been to disdain and break the Law. This was merely to rope Him into the whole scenario and find a way of increasing the number of condemned culprits. And this was too tight a scenario for Him to smartly escape from as He had done previous ones.

Just consider yourself for a moment in the shoes of this woman. Death, of the most painful sort, was staring her straight in the face. By reason of the law, she was guilty and she knew it. She deserved this death and it was impossible for anyone to save her. She got herself into it, fully aware of the consequences. She probably did not bargain for things to turn out this way, but here she was, caught and firmly in the hands of a fierce multitude. She knew there was no escape. She had been slapped in the face till there was blackness all around her; individuals had dissolved into black masses in her head. She heard rumbling noises, mostly of curses and abuses, all around her. People, mostly men, pushed and struck her from all sides. She had pains all over, but she knew the worst was yet on the way. She was counting the seconds, waiting for the stones to land any moment. Then suddenly, she heard someone mention something about being on the way **to see Jesus.** Was Jesus not the new man in town whom she had heard preaches righteousness with power, cast out demons with ease and healed people of all forms of ailment? She had heard so much about this man, but had never cared to go see Him. She never really wanted to have much to do with very religious people or people who make others feel inferior with self-righteousness. She did not understand what purpose this visit would ever serve. She was neither sick, nor possessed and she was very sure the unfriendly arms gripping her did not intend to bring her to someone who would preach for her conversion. Maybe they wanted to fulfill all righteousness by having Jesus preach to her before they finally kill her. Otherwise, this visit to Jesus did not seem to make sense. She had heard that Jesus was a very kind man, but even if He would want to help her, what can one man do to extricate her from these ferocious beasts, thirsty for blood? But would Jesus even have any reason to look her way? She could not imagine any reason He would. Afterall, she never liked what she heard about His messages and His ability to sniff out sinners. Getting near Him might just bring unwarranted embarrassment and she would not take that from anybody in the name of religion. She had snubbed Him and His ways because of this same adulterous lifestyle that is bringing judgement upon her now. So why would the Man care about someone who never cared about Him while she had the opportunity? There was no chance. She knew she was facing a certain death and there was nothing anyone could do for her. By this time, they were standing before the man and the heavily bearded leader of the mob had just finished addressing Jesus. She listened as the man spoke directly to Jesus about her being caught in the act, what Moses said and demanding to know what Jesus would say. Everyone waited with bated breath for the response from heaven.

God can never be held to ransom by the wisdom of principalities. The biggest mistake the murderous crowd made was to carry the woman to Jesus. They expected a simple resolution that would licence them to go on with the murder and possibly also rope God into a legal tango. They expected a yes or no, but Jesus does not have a yes or no answer for people or issues. After what seemed like eternity to the woman as Jesus wrote on the sand, He lifted up His voice and declared, "Let him that is without sin be the first to throw a stone at her" (John 8:7). There was silence, again for a long time. A stone fell to the ground with a thud, and there was shuffling of feet behind her. A little while later, another stone fell, followed by yet another shuffling of feet. She imagined that someone, maybe two, were leaving, but she dared not look up or look back. It did not take much time before her suspicion was confirmed, the men were actually leaving. Who knows whether it was to regroup, but why would they leave only to regroup? She did not quite understand, and dared not move. Somehow, she did not even seem to feel the urge to run again. The man before her seemed solid security. She dared to dream; it is actually possible they were responding to the question the Man asked them by leaving. How grateful she would be if this be real!

Before long, she was only left with the Man. The men that brought her had disappeared. As she looked at Him, the sort of love she had never seen seemed to flow from Him. This was not the sort of amorous look she had seen among men who wanted her body. It was a look that had compassion, hope and love mingled together. This One was different. She could not understand the Man. Who was He? Why did He choose to have mercy on her, someone He had never met? What did He stand to gain by delivering her from the hands of those men? And to think she had despised this man so much in the past! What if the man gets to understand what she used to think about Him? She had heard He had some psychic powers and could read minds. Yet, in her many questions she felt such sense of security and purity in the presence of this stranger. Then He spoke "Woman, where are thine accusers? Hath no one condemned you?" She stuttered but quickly found her voice, "No one Lord!" Then He came back "Neither do I, go home and sin no more". With that and a wave of hand, He started another story to the crowd before him, a story seemingly unrelated to the event that just took place. She could not understand. Just like that? She has just been given a brand new life in a stunning manner. But the Man through whom it came seems to behave as though this was what He has been doing all His life. She was pleasantly surprised at the turn of events, but one could not tell from the Man's face that He was part of the process that gave her back life. No airs, no sense of indebtedness and no probing questions. No queries about who she was or why she was living that kind of life. No reprimands for being useless and a shame to God and man. No moral instructions for someone like her who obviously had need for mending her life. No illustrations to the crowd before Him about the dangers of immorality and no attempt to put her on the spot. He started teaching about something different, as though the event that just took place never happened. She stood rooted in utter disbelief and looking into the man's face to see if she could read anyting. But nothing came. Then it struck her, she was now once again a part of the living, and she was free! God had made great providence for her through this Man.

Thought of home came to her. But which home? Home to those men? How could she ever look anyone of them in the eye again or have anyone of them come across her path. But as she looked inwards to her heart, she could not see the sort of deep seated hatred she had felt for those men when she saw they laid hold on her but ostensibly left off the man she was with. Is this connected to the love that this man had shown her? All the same, it did not seem to make much sense to go back home, she needed to find out more about this Man. She really had nowhere else to go. Her mind was made up; she would join the people following the man, and she was not going to ever go back.

We are all like the woman in this story. Every person on earth was at some point (and the majority still are even now) in the grip of a murderous crowd of bloodthirsty demons, led by the devil himself. We are all objects of wrath (Ephesians 2: 3), destined to die, and justifiably so. The principalities that hold us captive are themselves even worse offenders, but that means nothing. They know judgement is hanging over their heads, but they would not go down alone. For now, they would not allow any human who deserves to die to escape. And they know that all men deserve to die, for all men have been offenders of the law, some ignorantly, others deliberately. None is free (Romans 3:23). They all clamour for the head of men. People can raise all manner of arguments over the correctness or otherwise of the intentions of the men behind this story, and by extension over the entire process of judgement and repercussions on earth. Did this woman commit adultery alone? If not, where is the man with whom she committed the adultery? Was she the first and only one to have ever committed adultery in the town? Just transpose this to yourself and you hear the sort of questions many of us have asked severally. Am I the only sinner on earth? It is important to pray that God rather shows us the utter uselessness of arguments in this matter. If the demons cannot get all the adulterers, they would not spare the ones they have laid hands on. Here, we are dealing with beings whose hearts are extremely vile, far more than they are reasonable. In Luke 13, some persons came to the Lord Jesus to report their repugnance and horror at what Herod did to people that came to worship, mingling their blood with their sacrifices. Jesus' seemingly failed to address the justice of the whole situation and instead pointed them to their own dangers. He not only went on to tell them more about some upon whom the wall of Siloam fell and crushed to death, but also insisted that for those listening, arguing over the reasonability or otherwise of Herod's actions was no use, they all potentially faced the same cruel treatment unless they repent. "Except ye repent, ye shall all likewise perish" (Luke 13:5).

Were Jesus to make this statement in any of the world's major capitals, the press would be falling over themselves to show how insensitive He was to the plight of these sufferers and how He failed to openly condemn what was obviously a horrible genocide. But such reasoning is concerned with only the cosmetic; the sort regularly handed down by political leaders who have no clue about what is wrong with the world and have no heart to seek for genuine solution. Condemning terror and abuses does not change the hearts or lives of men, nor does it prevent the perishing of victims. Jesus would rather get to the root. He knows there is only one way of taking the sting off the sin that is behind all the errors and terrors of life – and that is repentance! 'Except you repent, you shall all likewise perish'. Yet, even as He says it, He is writhing in pain and His heart is crushed with the burden of the sins of man and the sufferings it has brought upon him. No one can be more sensitive about the plight of mankind than the One who gave His own life just so that the ills of the corrupt nature could be dealt with. 'Greater love hath no man than this, that a man would give his life for his friends', He declared (John 15:3). And He is right.

The Law came through Moses but grace and truth came through Jesus (John 1:17). Grace came in the person of Jesus. Because the woman had been brought to Him, she must be saved. When we come to Jesus, He does for us what He did for the condemned woman. But we can only come if we repent, if we want out from sin and seek to be saved. Jesus never drags a man, nor does He save a man against His will. Repentance humbles the soul and creates space to usher in Jesus, the custodian of grace. The devil and his crowd have each of us in their grip. Many are spiritually blind and therefore unaware of this. But that does not reduce the potency of the force against us or the danger each man faces as eternity draws near. But the big mistake the demonic crowd often make is to take us to Jesus in a bid to trap Him as well. They have to use us to tempt Him. But in doing so, they have brought many of us to obtain grace. Just like the woman, eternal death stares us in the face, and there is no escape. By reason of the law, we are guilty and deserved to die. We got ourselves into it and have had so much buffeting in the flesh already. Many of us can no longer see well on account of the troubles we have faced on earth; our reasoning has been marred by the shoving of circumstances as well as curses and abuses from men. Yet the worst is yet to come. We are afraid of death, but have no answer to it. We know it can come any moment, yet we are helpless. Sometimes we close our eyes and it seems as though it has come upon us. Then suddenly, one from the crowd muted that they were on the way to see Jesus, with us in their grip. We hear a message on the radio or get spoken to by a neighbor. We watch a Christian who challenges us with his lifestyle or we get to Church, whatever! Something happens and we get in touch with Christ and He immediately silences all our accusers and presents us with a chance for a new life through grace.

Reactions of men when facing Jesus vary greatly. Some would look at Him and wonder what His motive in trying to save them is. They do not understand this whole story of grace and are not sure Jesus is unselfish. So they turn away. Others would remember all the disdain wherein they have held Jesus and think themselves unworthy to receive His mercy, and they turn back. Yet there are those who are unable to see any problem with their lifestyles and are convinced they have no need for a saviour. These believe they can handle their lives and have no need that anyone else, not even God, should direct them. They walk away. Whatever the reason though, walking away from Jesus means walking away from grace, it means deciding to go face death all alone. Those that believe they can manage their lives through laws, principles and personal discipline fail to realize that which is written 'for the law maketh men high priests who have infirmities, but the Son... (Hebrews 7:28).

CHAPTER 13

MAN'S RESPONSE AND RESPONSIBILITY

a. The Place of Man's Choice

Though God is committed to saving man, men still die from sin and get eternally separated from God. Someone would wonder why God allowed man to fall into sin in the first place only to 'start struggling' to redeem him. Well, that question has been answered by many in the past and we can only repeat some of the high points we got from the scriptures. It is in the nature of free moral agents to be free. If the liberty to choose is absent, then there is no freedom in morality; and it is impossible to hold the agent accountable. Other creatures (both animals and plants) are not held accountable (definitely not in the sense of putting them on the dock) for their actions or omissions, positive or negative. God did not create a man He would manipulate, but one that has the choice to either come to Him or walk away. That is one of the most important features of being created 'in the image of God'. Even for God Himself, being righteous and hating iniquity is a choice, "Thou hast **loved** righteousness and hated iniquity" (Hebrews 1:9). The serpent, in his deception captured this point as he talked with Eve, 'For God doth know that in the day you eat of the fruit, you shall **be like Him, knowing good and evil**. It is this knowing and choosing that makes man what he is and what God created him to be.

In Adam, mankind rejected God and His good and embraced the devil and his evil. The repercussion is that man as a race should perish, for the wages of sin is death (Romans 3:23). As a result, a lot of us throw up our hands in despair, blaming Adam for the sufferings of mankind. But God never intended that Adam's choice would automatically become everyone's permanent choice. Being the first man, Adam's choice admittedly complicated things for the rest of mankind, because it endowed everyman with the sinful nature. But having the sinful nature merely makes sticking to the choice for God more difficult; it is itself neither the choice nor does it obliterate the choice. History is full of the stories of men like Abel, Enoch, Noah, Abraham, Moses, Joshua, David, Daniel and very many others who chose to walk with God notwithstanding the fact that they carried the same sinful nature imposed on all mankind, and which many of us use as excuse. They may have floundered, like many of us do flounder, but they made a choice. Enoch did it for 300 years, the longest by any man, and God had to set him aside from death. The same history gives us the story of many who chose against God and not only walked in the sinful nature, but showed us what it can do beyond what we ever imagined. Ahab and his wife showed that it is possible to extend the frontiers of evil, even in a nation founded on righteousness. That was a choice. In modern day, Hitler showed what the devil can achieve through a man that has yielded himself to him as an instrument of hate.

Everyman must exercise his choice, either accepting God or walking in his own way. Choice is exclusively the responsibility of man. Being faithful to that choice is a different matter, and that is where God comes in to help. It is useless to blame Adam in this issue. Adam will not be sentenced for any other man. He made his choice and whatever choice any other man makes will be treated as independent of Adam's; the same way the choices of a man's father or his children are judged independent of his own choices. It is only after a man has deliberately chosen God that He comes to him with the power to be and to do. Many wait for God to show them evidence of His ability and willingness to help them before they commit themselves to God. But God is not an intruder, He is a gentleman, willing and able to wait. God would rather wait, even allow a man walk away (Mark 10: 22), than intrude into the man's right of choice. But the moment a man makes his choice, God appears on the scene. Jesus put the matter this way *"If any man will do His will, he shall know ..."* (John 7:17). It is only when a man **will** (is willing to) do God's will, that God permits him to know what His will is. Knowledge and ability can never be given to a man precedent to the exercise of his will or choice to follow God. This is the stumbling block (and puzzle) that many men face. They want God to demonstrate another willingness to help. God has already done that by sending his son, Jesus to pay the full penalty for our sins. Many cannot understand that God does not make special efforts to make Himself visible or known to man. We worry that God does not go the extra mile to put up additional proof to man in order to give man a basis to follow Him more committedly. And really, He would not do it. God does not ever compromise on the matter of allowing man liberty to choose first. This is because choice is a matter of the heart and the heart is the very essence of man. The choice to follow God must come first and fully rendered; God must know where the man has channeled his choice first before He approaches to help or hinder.

Whenever a man makes that choice, no matter how feeble, God steps in. Several scriptures prove this. It is written, "For the eyes of the Lord run to and fro throughout the whole earth, to show Himself strong in the behalf of them whose heart is perfect toward him" (2 Chronicles 16:9). In effect, God scans the whole face of the earth to see if there are people who have come to this point of surrender, whose hearts are perfectly set on Him. Whenever and wherever He finds any such person, He shows Himself strong; He proves His strength, equips the individual with divine capacity to do what he ordinarily would not have been able to do. Did the scripture not say, "To those that believe on his name gave he power to become sons of God" (John 1:12). We do not only read about this; many of us have seen many successful Christians whose only qualification was their willingness to follow God, their choice. They chose God and we watched as God transformed their lives and gave them unimaginable strength against evil and the world. Until a man comes to the point of choice, God is helpless.

Paul's conversion has raised seeming contradictions in the hearts of many people. I have heard some refer to it as an example of God pursuing and getting a man to His side against the man's will. Such people wonder why God would not extend to them the same gesture He gave to Paul by wrestling them out of sin against their own will. But this is a delusion, a wrong interpretation of events which naturally leads to wrong expectations. Many forget that Paul was already very zealous for God even as an unbeliever. He merely lacked the knowledge of Christ to pursue correctly and that was what the Damascus road encounter equipped him with. We forget that Paul himself said that when he was confronted by God, he was not disobedient to the call implying that it was his choice to go ahead with God or step back after he was released from the road to Damascus. We forget that many have had experiences that matched Paul's and yet did not serve God. God knew that the Gentiles of his day and future generations needed Paul to fully translate Christ into day to day experiences. Despite these, God still insisted that Paul's call would be accompanied by much suffering, including stoning. How many of those that want Paul's call also want his experiences? God has made it abundantly clear that He wants every man to be saved, that He has no pleasure in the death of the wicked and that there is nothing else for man to pay to bring this salvation about. Some scriptures highlight these truths:

> Say unto them, as I live, saith the Lord God, I have no pleasure in the death of the wicked; but that the wicked turn from his way and live; turn ye, turn ye from your evil ways; for why will ye die, O house of Israel (Ezekiel 33:11)

> For **whoever** will call on the name of the Lord will be saved" (Romans 10:13)

> Who will have all men to be saved and to come unto the knowledge of the truth... who gave Himself as a ransom for all, the testimony given at the proper time (1 Timothy 2: 4, 6)

*For the grace of God that bringeth salvation hath appeared
to **all men** (Titus 2:11)*

How many have taken advantage of these truths? Or why
would God go any further when we are yet to follow Him up to
the point where He is. God's position on the matter of saving man
is unambiguous. He makes no distinction among men, He has
no favourites and no unloved; He wants all men to have access to
salvation. I have seen many people who, possibly on account of their
estate in life or even just an unfortunate incident, believe that God's
love does not extend to them. Many of these people sincerely believe
that God is not interested in them or in what they do. For as much as
they know, God does not care. They blame their past, their relatives,
their background and all the usual factors we blame for our unsavory
experiences. Consequently, such people usually turn their backs on
God because of their perception that God is already against them. But
this, again, is a fallacy. Given God's position on the matter, we know
that such attitudes are part of the devil's gimmick to keep people away
from coming to the decision to choose God, and thereby allowing
God's help to come to them. God loves you, He loves me, and He loves
every one of us. Our commissions and omissions, the devil's attacks,
other men's mistakes and a number of other factors can combine to
give us unsavoury experiences, but none of them can detract from the
fact that God loves us. It pains Him when we suffer out of ignorance
or any other reason. He sets Himself to deliver us from sin and pain.

But God will wait for our choice. He will not override us. Sitting
idly thinking He should save us 'Paul-style' is not useful. Paul did not
sit idly waiting for God to save him; he was actively out for God, only
that He did not have the knowledge of the justification that comes
through Jesus. God met Paul, blazing with zeal as he travelled on the
road to Damascus to ensure that those that 'profaned' the Name of God
were brought to book. Paul himself noted that as to the righteousness
which is in the law, he was blameless, even without knowing Christ
(Philippians 3:6). The devil uses anything, including arguments turned
upside down, like the one that tells us that He should save us the way

He saved Paul, to keep us away from facing the choice. Sometimes, the devil tells a man that his 'tiny' choice makes no difference; that life is (and will continue to be) rough anyway, or he makes him believe that were God as interested as He 'pretends' to be, He could override his will and save him. Meanwhile, such men love the sin in their lives and are deeply not convinced they have any real need for salvation.

One brother once taught that the coming of Jesus was not God's remedial programme. His argument is that Jesus has always been God's 'Plan A'. But instead of declaring Christ the Head from creation, God instead put out Adam knowing that the devil would pounce on him with a view to destroying God's work and plan for the earth. Even though I believed this then by faith, I had difficulty understanding how it could be. My challenge was that I could not see the sense in creating an Adam that would fail, only to go out seeking for remedy through Jesus, and that, after so many years. And I am sure whatever you may think of that doctrine, you will agree that looking at the depth of misery and suffering among men, the idea does not seem a good one. But after a long time of searching the scriptures, I began to understand God's plan in the light of the necessity of availing every man an opportunity for choice. And that was when the brother's teaching began to make sense to me. I realized that many of us would have been very happy if Adam made a good choice and we are all sinless and eternally happy with God. The challenge though is that Adam's choice would be nothing more than Adam's choice. It is not my choice and it is not your choice. I realize that when God said He needed man in His own image, He was particularly careful about getting a creature with the power of choice. And that choice should not be exercised for man through an agent, as Adam would have been to us if he had made the choice for righteousness on our behalf. Each man must make his own choice. So Adam was not a mistake. He provided the opportunity for every man that came into the world to (individually) make his own choice as he lives the present life.

Our present life presents us with an opportunity to choose. A father cannot choose for his son nor can a mother choose for her daughter. No person chooses for the other. And when each man has made his choice, he retires into eternity to enjoy or endure the consequences of his choice. You then begin to see that it would have been morally wrong for God to punish or acquit any man on account of the choice of any other. Adam's choice should not in any way determine what consequences I face. So contrary to the conventional view that Adam was responsible for man's suffering, the reality is that he was merely responsible for his own suffering. Adam chose and left the scene. Every other man is given the opportunity to make a choice for himself. It was not Adam that told Cain to kill Abel; in fact, Adam must have been thoroughly grieved to see Abel die the way he did. Nor was it Adam that told Job to be upright and eschew evil. Job enjoyed protection and warm relationship with God despite the fact that he was a descendant of Adam. All the time, we see horrible fathers giving birth to noble sons and vice versa.

If God's intention to have a kingdom of intelligent and willing subjects with choice emanating from knowledge is to be realized, then it is absolutely necessary that each man be made to choose. I was once persuading a man to be born again, but citing Genesis 6:6 where scripture notes that it repented God that He had made man, he argued that God is not really as omnipotent (all-powerful) and omniscient (all-knowing) as we ascribe to Him. Otherwise, according to him, God would have known Adam would go the way he did, and stopped him. I reminded him that the Bible (in Revelation 13:8) called Jesus the Lamb of God that was slain before the foundation of the world. And that means that even before God called forth light, He had slain Jesus as redemption for man whom He knew must fall. But why the struggle to redeem when the fall could have been prevented? Well, Adam does not mean all men. Adam is just a man; though the father of all men, he is not all men. Today, we bear sons and see them deliberately refuse to toe life paths that we have treaded and proven despite our persuasion and best intentions. If Adam had chosen God, would his children also have chosen God? If Adam's choice of God had qualified his children, could it then be said that Adam's children were given the liberty of choice? Not really. No man is an appendage of his fathers. If a man is denied opportunity of choice, how could he be judged? He can claim that his judgement is not borne out of his choice. Adam's fall bequeathed a difficult nature upon man and made it difficult even for those that have chosen God to stick to Him. But Jesus came so that He may release the power to be to all them that have chosen Him. But the coming of Jesus did not take away the responsibility of choice from man - each man still has to choose. Actually, in coming to Christ, all that we come to Him with is choice, nothing more. He provides the rest.

And it is only when we understand this that we will see that it made sense for God to allow Adam to choose first and then beget children afterwards, each of whom must be brought to the point of choice. The present age is for this same reason; to provide us with opportunity to choose. Now Jesus said that in eternity, we will be like Angels, neither marrying nor given in marriage. What this implies is that in eternity, multiplication will cease. By that time, God would have gathered all the people who willingly chose Him and yielded their wills to Him, allowing Him to rule over them. He will not need to get new persons who will be making choices again. In eternity, there would be no choices. The opportunity for choices ends here on earth, just as the entry of new persons who will be required to choose also ends here.

Everywhere, the scriptures note the role of choice; not only about Jesus but also about anyone who ever followed God. Abraham had the wherewithal to build fortified cities and become a lord of his own day, but He **chose** to dwell in tents alongside Isaac and Jacob (Hebrews 11:9). Reason: they saw that the current world was without foundations and whatever is built on it would perish with it. By believing God, they saw the land which is infinitely superior to the present one, which houses were not made with human hands. And they trusted God faithful enough to bring them into it. Joseph was a slave and then came his master's amorous wife with an enticement, 'lie with me and your worries will be over'. No one would ever have known, and the woman would have protected Joseph and helped ensure he lived well. In any case, his master did not even care to know of anything that happened in the house except to demand and receive his meals regularly. But Joseph chose to see the One who sees in darkness and for that reason shunned the woman, withstanding her pressure. For this he was sent to prison. In prison, he chose to lighten up other prisoners and bear their burdens, asking for their welfare daily as he went about telling everyone about the God who has the destiny of all creation in His hands. Likewise, Moses grew up in Pharaoh's house and had the opportunity of being the Prime Minister in Egypt, but he **chose** the suffering of the people of God and to be identified with them over and above the fleeting pleasures of Egypt. It was again a choice. David was anointed King, but the renegade Saul was still on the throne. And worse still, Saul decided to abandon all the policy, administrative and logistical challenges of administering Israel in order to pursue and eliminate David in the wilderness. Somehow, David came upon him tired and asleep. It was an opportunity for David to slay Saul. But he chose not to. David's men, having known all the circumstances of their master and that of Saul, saw a quick end to a cause where their boss was innocent, a vindication of the just and the appropriate reward of the wicked on his own head. So they requested of him that he should permit them to strike Saul; and made him a promise; they would not have to do it twice. But David **chose** to let Saul live because of the Name and anointing of the Lord upon him. He chose to remain in the wilderness instead of the throne. His decision was at the risk of his person and his future. He preferred to wait for God's time. That decision was to consign him to continue living as a fugitive for only God knows how much longer.

Daniel chose to eat vegetables instead of guaranteed dainties from the wealthiest royalty of his day. It was risky, for if the king found out, he and those that aided and abetted such violations of the king's order would be in serious trouble. Later, he chose to flout the law not to pray to any other god except the king of Babylon for 30 days. He knew the risk; being served as a meal to lions. His Hebrew brothers were even more daring when told to bow down to Nebuchadnezzar's golden image, 'we are not careful to answer you regarding this matter' (Daniel 3:16). The fire (which they could see) was so hot that it killed the soldiers detailed to throw them in. But they had already made up their minds. Their choice was firm. For them, God was the one to fear.

Everyman that we hear of in the scriptures made a choice. We acknowledge and emulate those who made wise choices. We also learn from the sufferings of those who did not (1 Corinthians 10:6). This is God's way of justice. It is important that even the devil comes to acknowledge that anyone who enters into God's kingdom did so by choice. And that choice was made here on earth. It needs to be clear that God did not override any man's choice and drag him into life, or ignore any man's choice and force him into death. Whatever a man gets in this life and the life to come must be a function of his deliberate choices. Indeed, all that would have life with God in eternity are people who **chose** to have life and have Him here on earth, people who chose and desire eternity so seriously that they would dare strong challenges here to have it.

b. Looking Upon the Brazen Serpent

The Lord Jesus used the experience of the Israelites in the wilderness to illustrate the path from sin to salvation. He said, just as Moses lifted the serpent in the wilderness … so shall the Son of Man be lifted, so that whoever looks upon Him shall be saved …" (John 3:14; Numbers 21: 5 – 6). The Israelites murmured bitterly and God was displeased with them and therefore allowed serpents into the camp. Several thousands died from the venom of very poisonous snakes. Despite being the one offended, Moses prayed for the Israelites and next, we see God give them a therapy, a very strange one. He asked Moses to make a brazen serpent and hang same on a high pole where every Israelite could see it. Then he was to inform the Israelites that whosoever got bitten by any of the live serpents should look upon the molded serpent upon the pole and the person would live. By implication, whosoever is bitten, but fails to look upon the brazen serpent, will die.

Admittedly, there is no known logic between being bitten by a live snake and looking upon a molded one. Let us just imagine a man bitten by a snake (say in a limb). The first natural response is to find some band and tie up the limb at a position higher than the place of the snakebite in order to prevent the flow of the poison through the bloodstream to the rest of his body. This is first aid. The nurse usually would look for a potent anti-snakebite drug. If the man has such a drug in the house, that will be useful, otherwise, he is taken to a knowledgeable doctor. Those who live in serpent-infested areas would often arm themselves with machets and other weapons for defense. In the wilderness, the man who arms himself with a machete will always look down, living in fear as he scans the ground for any threats. Being armed with a weapon and looking out for serpents would also mean looking away from the serpent on the pole. Interestingly, the serpents were not afraid of the weapons nor could they be kept away by being careful. They were ubiquitous. It was not those that were careful that survived. Everyone was vulnerable no matter the amount of care he exhibits; the snakes were everywhere. If, when bitten, a person's eyes remain on the ground as he struggles to kill the snake that bit him, nurse his wounds or even tries to be careful so as not to be bitten by another, he would die. Likewise, the snake-bitten man who went about looking for drugs and other remedial measures would die.

Here was God's therapy: look upon the serpent hanging on the pole and live; look away from it and die. As it were, there was no life in the brazen snake hung upon the pole. What gave it life was the Word of God. God says to look upon it and that is all the life it has got. So whoever will look upon that serpent on the pole would not do so because it is logical or reasonable, he would do so simply because God said to do so - that is what we call 'faith'. Counter-intuitive as his action may seem, such a person who looks will live. Those who would not look at the bronze serpent would merely be responding to the reasoning of their heads and trusting their capacities to handle their lives. So instead of obeying the simple (apparently unreasonable) instruction, they would look for any of the reasonable, conventional ways of dealing with snakes and snakebites. Doing the latter amounts to trusting in themselves and the things they can see, and of course, they would die. Nobody actually wants to die. So those who chose not to look but do other things are not necessarily those who want to die. They are merely those who have not come to trust that God's word is true and is enough to save them from death. They doubt God; and unfortunately, they die. And here, you would agree that the important thing is the result. Whoever fails to look, despite the reasonableness of the other actions he takes, would die. But whoever looks, despite the unreasonableness of the logic behind his looking, would live.

> And Jesus said, "Just as Moses lifted the brazen serpent, so shall the Son of Man be lifted so that whosoever shall look upon Him shall have life" (John 3:14 &15).

At least two things are critical in getting life from this instruction. The first is the ability to see, and the second is the willingness to keep one's eyes up. Many of us take sight for granted but there is much more to seeing. First, we note that there are people who do not have eyes and so lack the capacity for vision. But even for those that have sight, there are things which seem very easy to see; and yet others that are more difficult. For example, while we can see trees around, it is very difficult to see microorganisms. Again, someone could be pointing in a particular direction and insisting that he can see something. Yet despite our looking in that direction, we are unable to see what he saw. Now if a man for any (or a combination) of these reasons is not able to see the brazen serpent, he would die.

The ability to see should never be presumed. Many Christians are languishing in slavery to sin and the devil because they simply cannot see. There is the assumption among many of us that once a person is born again, he can see. But neither the Lord Jesus nor the early Apostles assumed that. For Paul, the matter of sight was a prayer point. He prayed for the Ephesians that the 'eyes of their understanding being enlightened, that (they) may know what is the hope of (the Lord's) calling, and what the riches of the glory of His inheritance in the saints' (Ephesians 1:18). Why pray to see? Note that the people for whom Paul was making this prayer were already born again. What was wrong with the sight of the Ephesians? One may ask. The sight referred to in this context goes beyond natural sight. It is revelation, internal sight, the sight that comes by faith and is able to see what is decreed and happening in the spiritual. It is the ability of a 'normal Christian' to understand what the Lord wants from him, what He has provided for him and how such provisions could be reached and used to ensure continued victory on earth.

In natural seeing, there are two requirements – there must be sight (the eyes must be good) and there must be light (it must not be dark). When any one of these two is lacking, one cannot see. The same goes for spiritual seeing. So when Paul prayed for the Ephesians to see, he was asking that God would give them good sight as well as clear light. One of the reasons we will not take good sight for granted is because the Lord Jesus mentioned that there could be problems there, even in the spiritual. Hear Him:

> The light of the body is the eye: if therefore thine eye be single, thy whole body shall be full of light. But if thine eye be evil, thy whole body shall be full of darkness. If therefore the light that is in thee be darkness, how great is that darkness! (Matthew 6:22 – 23)

He quickly followed up with another assertion in verse 24:

> No man can serve two masters, for either he will hate the one, and love the other; or else he will hold to the one, and despise the other. Ye cannot serve God and mammon.

See the instruction in verse 25:

> Therefore I say unto you, take no thought for your life, what ye shall eat, or what ye shall drink; nor yet for your body, what ye shall put on. Is not the life more than meat, and the body than raiment?

How do these relate? First, it is important to note that the opposite of single (if thine eye be single...) should be double or multiple. But after noting the benefits of a single eye, scriptures did not use double or multiple for the opposite, it rather used evil (but if thine eye be evil...). Is it not strange that the Lord is saying that one's eye has to be either single or evil? Herein is an important spiritual principle. From verses 24 and 25, we see that the Lord was actually referring to **focus** – the object of attention for the eye. The light of the body is the eye. That eye should be single, focused on only one thing. In that verse 22 and 23, it did not tell us what it should be focused on. We were merely told that it is important the eye be focused on only one thing; otherwise, the body would be full of darkness. And at whatever point the light in a man is darkness, it is great darkness indeed. In verse 24 we get to learn that this focus is also the same as service. And it is impossible for that service to be rendered on to two masters. Then Jesus told us the two masters that are perpetually in contention for the attention of mankind – God and Mammon, and insisted that each person must keep to one.

There are several other implications of looking up to God, but they all imply and require trusting Him alone for all things. In verse 25, the Lord Jesus quickly outlined what this whole business of looking and focus could imply when He said *"Therefore I say unto you, take no thought for your life, what ye shall eat, or what ye shall drink; nor yet for your body, what ye shall put on. Is not the life more than meat, and the body than raiment?"* Men continue to face the big challenge of food, clothing, housing, security, provision, transport, relevance, inclusion, and all the other necessities and desirables of life. Most, if not all, can be purchased, and people can be incapacitated if they lack the resources to purchase them. As a result, they form the basis for the oppression of Mammon over man. For their sakes too, human beings are forever distracted away from God. But the Lord insists that life is more than these. He also insists that it is not possible for a man to serve Mammon or run around daily for these things and be able to serve God. Specifically, one has to be liberated from the care of what to eat and drink, where to live, what to wear, how to be secure, among others, to be able to serve God well. God has to deliver a man's heart from concentrating on these things before that man can live his life for Jesus.

If God is not the object of focus for any man in all things, then He is not the object of focus for him in anything. Jesus seems to be insisting here that it is either all for God or nothing for Him. Whenever a man tries to set his eye on two masters, it becomes evil. And everyone, at one point or the other, is bound to be confronted with circumstances that challenge his focus. But David says "Unto Thee lift I up mine eyes, O Thou that dwellest in the heavens" (Psalm 123:1). And twice we saw what he did when he met Saul vulnerable. Meanwhile, Saul had never hidden his intent to kill David. In fact, he was in the wilderness in both occasions with an army to kill David. But David would rather trust the Lord to handle Saul at His own time. If any declares that he looks up to God alone, he is expected to act likewise.

We should also be confident of God's providence. Interestingly, God's provision is infinitely superior and more satisfying than whatever a man can provide. That is the reason why our prayer needs to constantly be 'Lord, help us to see!' In Genesis (21: 9 – 21), Abraham was grieved about sending Hagar and Ishmael away, but circumstances demanded he did. So he provided all he could for the lady and his dear son. What did he provide? A bottle of water and bread; and the duo headed to the dry desert. Hagar and her son were almost dead from thirst after just a little time. Then, she prayed and God came into the picture. God **opened her eyes and she saw** a well of water. As against, Abraham's water bottle, God's provision was a well. Without God's intervention, she may have died of thirst. But taking advantage of God's provision required that she saw. You must see, and you must see clearly. Several people have seemingly come to God, worshipping hard, working conscientiously in the house of God, doing whatever they are told is necessary, but they are yet to see anything. They do things in response to instruction, but do not understand why. It appears as though God does not talk to them or help them to see the glorious inheritance awaiting them. So they have little internal motivation for the things they do. They struggle to keep up with other believers and perennially need to be encouraged to keep trying, and that it is not all in vain. Many such persons are fighting for heaven, but really do not imagine how and why heaven is better than the earth. There is something that every man that closely follows God must have to see. Some of us have heard of the goodness, glory and mercy of God; but we are yet to see them. Many have heard of God's provision, but as individuals, we have not partaken of it. We cannot even bring ourselves to see how God would do, in our own lives, some of those things we hear of.

It is very crucial that everyman asks to see. Indeed, God is eager and pleased to answer the enquiring heart that wants to see what it is He intends to do, particularly if the purpose of the enquiry is to have a sure basis for following Him and not just mere curiosity. When the Angel came to Gideon and announced that he was highly favoured and that God was with him, Gideon did not take it for granted (Judges 6:12). Gideon's response to the Angel, in effect, was, 'If God is with us, how come we do not see any of the things which our fathers saw that showed that God was with them? Are the manifestations of the presence of God different in our days from what they were in the days of our fathers?' Thereupon, he insisted on 'proofs' of God's presence. And God mercifully obliged him in each case. In Judges (13: 7) Manoah's wife saw an angel and received message of a wonder boy they would give birth to and nurture. She told her husband. But Manoah did not want to assume, he prayed, insisting that God re-sends the same Angel that came to his wife so that he himself would also see. If he would be a partaker of the divine mercies of God through a son, if he would make input into the life of the child to be born, then it was imperative that the message he received be not hearsay. And again, God obliged him. But in these days, we see a lot of believers who rely on hearsay for their spiritual meat, whose whole spiritual lives are formed on the basis of the experiences and sights of others. How dangerous! It is imperative that I see. Salvation and deliverance from sin come from seeing the One who has been laid as a substitute for me, having a direct experience of His love and coming out with a witness of what I saw. A brother, Andrew Wommack, has argued that the reason Eve was deceived was that she did not hear the instruction of "thou shall not eat " directly from God. He posited that when we hear directly from God, it is harder to be deceived. This, according to him, is the reason the devil did not go to Adam.

These days, there are many theological evangelists and ministers, who expose and expound the word of God, but a number of them are without experience. Brother Watchman Nee told the story of a pastor who went to see a poor lady parishioner of his. The man was highly educated in doctrines and procedures. After labouring to explain the mystery of the Godhead and the love of Jesus to the woman, he asked if she had any question or clarification. The beloved sister simply responded that she honestly did not understand any of the 'deeper' mysteries that he shared but that the much she knows is that when it is prayer time, she simply kneels down by her bed, stretches forth her hand, and that the Lord Jesus physically holds the hands while she talks with Him. The learned preacher blushed in shame and went away without another word. Unfortunately, many, very many have come to substitute eloquent preaching, counseling, pastoring, different church activities, and even evangelism, for a changed life. We have come to think that preaching about Jesus means the same as knowing Jesus. We measure our spirituality with all manner of indices that are altogether unrelated to personal walk with God or the evolution of righteousness in our lives. Some measure prayer time, praying life and without knowing it, replace Jesus with prayer, boasting about our exploits in the place of prayer and tying God's graces in our lives to our praying. We compare our knowledge of God with others' by relating them to our bible studies and prayer. But, in our battle to overcome sin, and enjoy an effective walk with God, there is no substitute for experience. A man's theological knowledge can do little to help him from being under bondage to several manifestations of sin, but the woman with divine life, whose hands Christ holds would not stray. Head knowledge avails nothing in regard to overcoming life.

The next condition for seeing is the willingness to look up and keep our sight up. Apostle Peter taught how to show the kind of willingness that would yield result: as newborn babes, desire the sincere milk of the word .... (1 Peter 2: 2). Prophet Isaiah also wrote, "if ye be willing and obedient, you shall eat .... (Isaiah 1: 19). We choose the extent and pace of our walk with God. One's progress in the life and knowledge of the Lord Jesus depends on the force of encounter one has with Jesus, the disposition of one's heart and the quality of the Word of God one desirously or otherwise feeds on. While some encounter automatic or rapid change in different aspects of their characters upon turning to Christ, the change is slower in others. Passion makes all the difference.

For example, while we are able to see the shortcomings in the behavior of a believer, we are completely unaware of what battles he is having with the Spirit of God or of the many night cries he is raising to the throne of grace as he laments his shortcomings. He laments because God continues to place the righteousness of Christ before him and he can see how far away he is from that righteousness. When the believer's blockwork 'misaligns' with the foundation, the Holy Spirit instructs, whips, remonstrates and uses whatever other instrument available to bring the man back to build in line with the foundation. Before long, he records victory. The unwilling believer or an unbeliever does not enjoy such a guide, he does not use or have the bible as a compass; he does not utilize or have the righteousness of Christ as a covering and to look up to. So most times, even his assessment of his own shortcoming is based on what the society accepts, not the righteousness of Christ, which is God's baseline. Expectedly, such unwilling believer would keep dwindling in his walk with God until he loses his faith completely.

So who or what are we supposed to see when we look up? We are supposed to see Christ, who hung on the tree for us, as God's complete answer to everything about life here on earth and in eternity. Christ took up human nature in order to fully pay the price for the redemption of all mankind and provide access to the Godhead for all that believe. God does not accept any other sacrifice, any other arrangement or any other good works for sin. Christ is enough and no man can add to what He has done. He lived a perfect human life to fulfill all the requirements of righteousness. He died on the cross because there was need for atonement for the sin of man. He was bruised so that all that pertain to human ailment can be restored. He rose from the dead so that those who trust in Him can have access to the riches of heaven for actualizing the purpose of God on earth. He lives to ever make intercession for the sins of the people so that looking on Him, God would not charge us with iniquity. He gave us the Holy Spirit so that we can be continually purified and guided in the way of righteousness. The Holy Spirit also makes it possible not only to know what God wants us to be and to do, but gives us the power to be and to do it. He prays through us. What more can a man add? God expects that we should just trust that Jesus is enough. This is why scripture's approach to righteousness is 'looking on to Jesus, the author and finisher of our faith' (Hebrews 12: 2). Such looking up must preclude whatever a man can bring to the table. There is nothing. It must be Jesus alone as the basis for God's mercy, the source of everything that is going to come to us, the propeller of the life of God in us and our reason for living.

God laid the foundation of Jesus and whoever builds anything outside of Him perishes, even if what he is building is good. When God said in Matthew 3: 17, 'This is my beloved Son, in whom I am well pleased …" He actually meant that nothing else outside Jesus brings Him joy. For anything therefore to be acceptable to God, it must be found in Jesus; in who He is, in what He has done and in what He shall yet do. Jesus hung on the pole in order to provide the answer to all life's questions. God's answer to all matters – it makes no difference whether such matter pertains to salvation, deliverance, victory over sin, victory over demons, stability of life or resources and material blessing – it is Jesus and Jesus alone. When I am bitten by the bug of sin, I do not need to search for how to cover it up, or undo what I have done. What God demands of me is to realize that there is nothing in me that can please Him, I am given to sin and would sin anyway. So I should beg Him to forgive me for Jesus' sake and plead the blood of Jesus to cleanse me. As someone once pointed out, the law was not given for man to keep. The law was merely given so that in struggling and failing to keep it, man would see his own inadequacy, limitation and impotence and be willing to cry to God for help. And when one cries to God, God does not only show him Jesus, He gives him Jesus. Jesus is not only righteous; He is actually God's righteousness. He is the sufficient requirement for all righteousness. He does not only resurrect lives, He is the resurrection Himself. When Lazarus died, He raised him up from the grave; when He Himself died, He also rose from the dead. I should simply submit myself to Him and accept His forgiveness. I should believe that His sacrifice is enough to pay for whatever I may have done. I am not going to impress God by doing anything special. Accepting that Jesus' righteousness is enough for me is sufficient to please God. This is a very simple solution; yet, difficult for many to accept, because it does not fit into the mode of life that we have been taught by the world system.

c. Eating Jesus, the Tree (Fruit) of Life

When God calls us to Jesus, He is not trying to get us back to Eden, He is rather offering us what Adam never had. The scriptures say, "Just as by disobedience of one man, all sinned, so by the obedience of one man shall all be made righteous" (Romans 5:19). Jesus is the fruit of life that was in the garden, which Adam never ate. By coming to Him, we partake of that life that is above sin. Adam needed to make a choice between life and death, between sin and righteousness. Christ is a choice for righteousness and life already made. He came with the remedy for sin. Sin can only be overcome by a divine life that puts to death the body of sin. But death is not enough to overcome sin because death flows from sin. After one has died, he also needs to live again. That is the essence of resurrection. This time, he lives in the newness of the life of Christ, which we refer to as being born of the Spirit. Only that which is born of the Spirit can overcome the world, sin and death. Many believers have made attempts to mortify their members, but are unaware of the provisions made for rising again to life. These are yet to understand what their inheritance in the Lord Jesus is, and so severally fall prey to sin still.

Jesus summarized our relationship with the world and with Him when He said, "In the world, ye shall have tribulation, but be of good cheer, I have overcome the world" (John 16:33). What did Jesus mean when He said of Himself, "I have overcome the world'? We often refer to His death on the cross and the resurrection that followed it as the key issues in the overcoming. In His death, Jesus conquered death, which is the highest manifestation and consequence of the curse of sin. But in His resurrection, He introduced us to a new life, a glorious life that constantly overcomes and which cannot be overcome by sin again. This does not mean that sin cannot tempt it, but it sits high above sin and for as long as it constantly looks up to Jesus and draws life from Him, it cannot fail. This is a point that many believers do not ever get to. But it is promised in the Scriptures. Jesus died that the body of sin might be done away with. So we must daily arise to take up our cross and follow Him. But He also resurrected so that we might live in the newness of life (Romans 6:4b). So while I must recognize the need to carry my cross daily, I must also recognize the exciting new life that should come after the work of the cross in my heart has been accomplished. There is a new life which I am supposed to live daily and that new life is over and above sin. There are a number of believers who know the pain of taking up the cross, but do not know the excitement of living in newness of life. This can be drudgery. These Christians are acutely conscious of sin, all the time. They live their lives struggling not to offend God and man. And when they preach to other people, they also emphasize the necessity for holiness. Their argument is that holiness entails man's ability to avoid whatever contaminates. So they recommend good works.

The resurrection of Christ is not only an illustrative abstract; it is a spiritual reality to which every believer should enter. Paul understood this well when he said, 'But if the Spirit of Him that raised up Jesus from the dead dwell in you, he that raised up Christ from the dead shall also quicken your mortal bodies by His Spirit that dwelleth in you' (Romans 8:11). The resurrection of Christ from the dead is not only useful to the believer spiritually; it is supposed to also be a physical experience. When He rose from the dead, Jesus moved through walls unhindered, signaling the reality of his new body. When Philip was caught up by the Spirit and carried around different towns and cities to preach the gospel, God was again demonstrating the working of the new body. When Paul was bitten by a venomous snake in the Island of Malta and men panicked because they thought his life was in danger, he simply shook it off into the fire and did not bother to take any further precautions. There is a quickening of the body, soul and spirit that we should inherit because we have given our lives to Christ. And scriptures encourage us to keep our minds focused on things associated with that quickening (Romans 12: 1 – 2). We should be concerned about propagating the righteousness that we have in Christ to the rest of the world, and not just be content struggling not to sin. We are excitedly walking with God daily to bring about His will on earth, not frantically praying to keep demons and the devil at bay in our lives. When a believing young man sees a lady who exposes her body in the name of fashion, he falls into either of two modes – praying and fasting in order to prevent himself from committing sin or he is challenged in his spirit to take her up in prayer so that she may be delivered from the power of darkness that has held her bound. The former is the mode many Christians live in, but the latter is the mode of the resurrection life. It is an exciting world, where the concern ceases to be about how not to provoke God, but about ways of expanding God's purpose on earth through the help of the Spirit. This is what resurrection offers us; and it encompasses our spirit, soul and body. It is not limited to the spiritual; it is a physical experience as well.

When a man has come to this point, the body of sin has been taken away and replaced with the body of Christ. About the body of Christ, the Scriptures writes, "Sacrifice and offering thou wouldest not, but a body hast thou prepared for me … then said I, Lo, I come, in the volume of the books it is written of me, to do thy will, O God" (Hebrews 10:5 – 7). We know Jesus was in existence before He came into the world. But for Him to come to the world, a body had to be prepared for Him. The body was prepared so that He would come to do the will of the Father. The believer who has entered into the ressurrection experience wears the body of Jesus, to do the will of the Father. God did not only redeem our souls, He also redeemed our bodies for his work here on earth. The body we wear as believers, therefore, is for us to do the will of the

Father, not to satisfy the demands of sin. As heathens, we inherited a body that was under the curse of sin from Adam. Believing in Jesus entitles us to receive His body, the body that was prepared simply to do the will of God. Sin has no victory over the body of Christ, so when I take up the body of Christ, sin should have no victory over me. This is the reason we insist that while the unbeliever is under compulsion from sin, the believer can only be lured into sin. He must, of his own accord, agree to sin before he can sin. The body of Christ neutralizes the power of sin over us. That is the reason the bulk of the work left for us to do is to renew our minds.

CHAPTER 14

COLLABORATING WITH GOD TO DEMOBILIZE SIN

a. Renewing the Mind

The Lord Jesus said to His disciples in John 15:3, "Ye are clean by the words I speak to you ..." Interestingly, thinking of the men he was addressing, one is amazed and wonders how God could refer to those men as clean. Was it Peter that would deny Him a few hours later or Thomas that would not even believe Him in the first place? (Matt 26: 69 – 75; John 20: 24 – 29). Who among them really looked clean? James and John had, just a little while before, infuriated the rest by their selfish requests – the demand to be placed at the immediate sides of Jesus in His kingdom, at the expense of others. Thomas had told Him, "Lord we don't know where you are going..." (John 14: 5). All the disciples of Jesus had big character or habit problems; not one of them looked like a material for big spiritual work. None looked clean. Even after His resurrection, He gave them appointment in Galilee. According to Bible account, when they saw Him, they worshipped, but some **doubted** (Matt 28:17). When the Lord was ready to depart, after having brought them back from their backsliding fishing expedition, their question was, 'Lord, are you now going to restore the kingdom to Israel?' (Acts 1:7), showing how little they understood the purpose of the man they had been following for three years. Yet the Lord said, "Ye are clean". So cleanliness is very much about the Word of God. The Lord seemed to be suggesting that just hearing and repenting at the word of God and placing faith in its ability to heal and restore us, cleanses us from sin. Indeed, the 'clean' action that can please God must emanate as a response to the Word of God; it must be action of faith. Otherwise, it is not righteousness. And to show that Jesus meant every word He spoke, He left the entire work of propagating the gospel to these apparently weak men. So we note that overcoming sin is by faith, the faith that comes from hearing the word of God. That faith is ignited when the word of God affects the setting of the mind.

Every man grows with a certain mindset, influenced by his environment and experiences. There are varieties of mindsets that many of us got from long years of interacting with the environment, with people and from our personal experiences. For example, the experiences of some people taught them that they must pay for whatever is good that comes to them. Others learnt that the world is a dog-eat-dog scene where the strongest eats up the weakest. Some learnt that sin is so pervasive that it is impossible for any man to live outside its control. Some grew up believing that money is the answer to all things and that they are dead without money. Some men were taught by friends and relatives that women are things to be used, while some women learnt that they can only survive by living off a man who, in turn, is free to use them as he wishes. Some were taught that those who wait for things lose out at the end and that they must go out and grab things for themselves and by themselves. So there is no place in their lives for waiting, let alone waiting on an impersonal God whom they cannot see. Some grew up with the mindset that you must assert yourself for others to recognize you; else people will always trample on you and on your rights. Different folks have different mindsets emanating from their trainings and environment and each person's response to a particular circumstance depends on the mindset he has acquired over the years. Unfortunately, all through childhood, the training we received was to equip us with these ways of perceiving things invented from and controlled by the self-life.

When a man gives his life to Christ, God sets out through the Holy Spirit to release grace to him. The believer latches unto this grace and begins the ever continuing work of renewing his mind. God has his own way of looking at everything and He is keen that His children acquire the same mind. So the process of sanctification involves gradually wiping off and disabusing a man's mind from everything he had received in training and replacing these with God's perspective. God is very keen that we do not take positions born of the flesh, of training or of experience. We need to take positions based on the Word of God, or what the Scriptures termed to be 'whatsoever is born of God (1 John 5:4)'. He knows that any reaction based on what we obtain from the flesh can also be overcome by the flesh, but whenever we act based on the Word of God, we overcome the world, sin and the flesh.

A man's progress with God depends largely on the state of his mind. This mind digs into the reflexes of the brain and programmed behaviours. But it also involves volition. In fact, the most important part of the mind used for following God is volition. God wants us to take volitional actions initiated by contemplations based on evidence of His dealings with us, and the vanity of things around us. This is the foundation of a productive walk with God and until a man is able to bring himself to this point, God cannot reveal more of Himself to him. Jesus illustrated this when He said, 'if any man will do His will, he shall know of the doctrine...' (John 7:17). Settling the 'if' in doing God's will is important if one is to proceed to knowing of the doctrine. But the moment this decision to follow is accomplished, God then begins to teach the man, step by step, what He requires at each point. He will use a variety of means, but principally, He engages the Word of God. The scriptures begin to make meaning to the mind of the fellow and as he braces himself to make changes in his life, by the grace of God and based on the revelations he receives, God opens up new vistas to him. One of the major outcomes of this process is a brand new and different perception of things. The man is helped by God to see things the way they really are and he realizes that some of the things he thought were useful, actually were unnecessary or altogether harmful. He sees the ways of the natural man as anti-God and vain as they really are and he makes up his mind to take on God's approach towards issues in life. He begins to see not only what God instructs him to do, but why God instructs those things. Spiritual virtues like patience, humility, love, temperance, kindness and peace all begin to make sense, and he receives the ability, not only to appreciate them, but also to apply them where necessary. He does not need any man to preach to him about the vanity of the present life and why he should not tie his heart to it. Such vanity becomes a reality he can touch. Then he begins to appreciate why Paul said, '...for to be carnally minded is death' (Romans 8:6). As he applies the word of God in his daily life and relies on prayer, waiting on God to reveal what he should do before he takes the leap, he also experiences the overcoming life through the efficacy of the Word of God as it is written, "And they overcame him by the blood of the Lamb and by the Word of their testimony ...". Then he also realizes that given the vanity of the present life and the need to be fruitful for Jesus, he must be in the company of those who "...loved not their lives unto the death" (Revelation 12:11).

Loving not their lives unto death is critical for another reason. When Jesus said that whoever hates not his life will not be able to follow Him, it is not because He Himself hates men's lives and wants them to be wasted. It is primarily because He knows that a major tool of the devil is to frighten men with threats to their lives. This may not be outright threat to physical existence. It may be threat to means of living, threat to options in life, to growth, to love and to the conveniences of life. Whenever a man clings to any of these, he creates a foothold for the devil to threaten him. As in the case of the Lord, 'the prince of this world cometh', but he must have nothing in us (John 14:30).

b. Dividing the Light from Darkness

Like in any other matter, a person can reverse his decision and stop from following Christ. We refer to this as backsliding. Backsliding defines a man who once was very convinced about what he has seen and heard of the Lord, but who at some point in his life begins to be lukewarm or even completely denounces what he believed in. While it is abnormal, nearly all believers, at one point or another in their lives, experience some form of uncertainty and wavering in their faith. Only very few run with the same (or increasing) steam all their lives. In fact, the Lord Jesus, while discussing matters of the end of the age wondered if He (the Son of Man) shall still find faith on earth when He shall appear (Luke 18:8b). Several illustrations He gave during His earthly ministry bore the mark of His appreciation of the challenge believers are likely to face as they progress in their walk. One such story is that of the ten virgins (Matthew 25: 1 – 13). In the story, the bridegroom came at midnight, at the peak of darkness and immobility. Expectedly, prior to his arrival, everyone slumbered and slept – none was awake when he arrived. When in the book of Revelation, the Lord visited the Church at Ephesus, He said, "Nevertheless, I have this against you, that you have left your first love. Remember therefore from where you have fallen; repent and do the first works ..." (Revelation 2: 4 – 5). Similarly, Paul talked about Demas who forsook him, having loved this present world, and has gone on to Thessalonica. And through history, we have seen men being on fire for God for a while, and dying out completely afterwards. But even among those that do not completely die out, many just tag along without the joy and oil of the Holy Spirit. Such persons largely remain unproductive for God. The cause of this unfortunate scenario is the focus of this section.

In 2 Corinthians 4:6, Paul likened the salvation we have received to the emergence of light at the time of creation, "For God who commanded light to shine forth has shone in our hearts ..." And indeed, anyone who has ever had the experience of liberation from sin and the salvation that is in Jesus knows that the only thing that can be compared with it is the dawning of the light from heaven upon a soul previously enveloped in darkness. For those that received genuine salvation, the initial entrance of Jesus into our hearts at the point of salvation was as overwhelming as the flooding of bright light and warmth in a dark, cold and damp room. There was this out-of-this-world feeling and heavenly joy that followed us for many days and weeks or even months and years in some cases. Everything seemed possible and we sometimes felt like flying. We delighted in attending to anything related to God and found joy in the most menial of responsibilities we did for the faith. We embraced threats from men without fear and had warmth in the place of fellowship with God. Love for men simply surged in our hearts as we needed no preaching to do good to others. We had peace within ourselves and with our environment. We seemed to have faith to move mountains. We had no problem spending hours in reading and meditating on the Word of God and prayers. Preaching the message of Christ was a delight and even though we had very little understanding or preaching capabilities, we were eager to share whatever little experiences we have about our salvation with others. We would have nothing to do with unfruitful works of darkness in any way they may want to show up. Our values changed drastically and showed up in our carriage, dressing and mannerisms. Our words were seasoned with grace and everyone knew we were changed men. Our world was indeed recreated in light in every sense. But after a while, those things seemed to evaporate and we found ourselves struggling to even pray. Gradually, we realized that there were no differences between us and the unbelievers around us. We appear to have settled back to 'normal', the way of ordinary men and it seemed God is very far. Righteousness became plain drudgery, something we did, not because we were convinced of them, but because we fear that God would be angry with us should we fail. We developed long lists of dos and don'ts but seemed to fail to keep most of them. At that point, our righteousness became mechanical and sin appeared very enticing.

Many sincere believers have wondered what happened to them that brought about such situation. Others struggled initially and thereafter gave up, hoping that the fact that they gave their lives to Christ at some point should be enough to get them into heaven. Yet there are those who are convinced their current situation was manifest destiny and their relationship with Christ was never meant to be smooth all through.

But none of the above is correct. The reality is that what happened to many of us is what happens each time light shines forth. We look at the account of the creation of light in Genesis 1.

*"Then God said, 'let there be light'; and there was light. And
God saw the light that it was good; and God divided the
light from the darkness. God called the light Day, and the
darkness He called Night. So the evening and the morning
were the first day" (Genesis 1:3 – 5)*

Interestingly, this account shows that all through the first day,
God did nothing else than putting on the light and separating it from
darkness. Given the enormity of creation and the quantity of the things
we now know that God created, this seems to be so little a part of
the work to warrant a whole day out of the six. We will appreciate
this more deeply if we remember that the gathering of the seas, the
appearance of dry ground, the creation of grasses, herbs, seeds, and
fruit trees all happened in one day (the third day) as well. Again, the
calling forth of every single living creature in water happened in one
day (the fifth day) and the population of the entire earth with animals,
including man also happened in one day (the sixth day). So how come
creating light alone took a whole day, enough time as it took to create
the millions of animal species on the face of the earth?

We remember that Genesis 1 started with the pronouncement
that the earth was without form and void, and darkness was upon
the face of the deep (God did not have to create the darkness; the
absence of the presence of God is darkness already). This darkness
was therefore already there when the light was called forth. It appears
then that the moment God announced the Light and it came forth,
the already existing darkness immediately swooped on it and wanted
to snuff it out. We get the same impression when we read the account
of John about the Light and its interaction with darkness at the point
of creation. *"And the Light shines in the darkness, and the darkness did not
comprehend it"* (John 1:4). The word 'comprehend' as used in the above
verse is translated 'overcome' in some other versions of the Bible. The
Message Bible specifically put it as "The Life-Light blazed out of the
darkness; the darkness **could not put it out**". "Could not put it out"
means the darkness attempted (or even struggled) to put it out, but
was unable to do so. So the darkness tried, but could not. The Genesis

account put it as "God **divided** the Light from the darkness". Gospel of John chapter 1 verse 4 says that the light shone in the darkness, but the darkness could not overcome it. Speaking forth the light was one thing, dividing (or keeping) the light from (the threat of) darkness was another. Even for God, deliberate attempt had to be made to keep darkness away from the Light. Dividing the light from the darkness meant that God deliberately had to confine the darkness to certain limits so as to create space for the light to operate.

While we admit that the shining forth of light immediately dislodges darkness, there is also no doubt that putting forth the light takes energy. Darkness is natural; it is always there, it does not need energy. Take away light and it just takes the space, no need for effort. But light takes energy to bring forth and retain. We pay bills to get light; no one needs to pay any bill to create, sustain or utilize darkness. Wherever no work is done to bring about and maintain light, darkness naturally takes over the space. Scriptures said in Isaiah 60 that darkness covers the face of the earth and gross darkness the people. That is God's way of describing man in the different cultures and civilizations of the earth. The darkness that has covered the people does not need any work to sustain. Most cultures, including great civilizations, simply grow in darkness. And from what is seen in the scriptures referred to above, darkness does not sit back in the face of light. Even though light overpowers it whenever it shines forth, it continues to fight relentlessly to push back the confines of light. And often, if the energy with which the light is sustained or the source of the light, is compromised or gets weak, we see darkness speedily retake the position from where it was chased away by the light. Two issues therefore emerge from these. First the light needs to be **divided** (made separate) from darkness. Second, the separation needs to be sustained and the source of light refueled if the separation would remain. And technically, this is where many believers fail.

We have seen great revivals fade after a while. The move of God among a people often starts like wild fire, but with time and without any spectacular occurrence, we see the move fizzle away. Many nations that were originally born and sustained by God seem to be covered by darkness now. Nobody had any meeting to say, 'See we have had enough light, we think it is time we try some darkness'. No. The darkness rather simply emerges after a while. In the same way, a believer gets light into his heart. Somehow, after a while, he just realizes that the steam is no longer there. He is struggling with darkness. In some instances, the problem is that the initial dividing that should have been done in the life of the believer did not happen or was not sustained. Many believers take the light for granted and assume that it should remain there and is inherently capable of pushing away the darkness. We make no deliberate attempt to keep separating what was obtained from our experience at the point of salvation from what existed prior to being born again. Deliberate measures were not taken to ensure that we clearly define what are on and off limits. We merely basked in the euphoria of the new life and forgot that 'the spiritual was not first, but the natural, and afterward the spiritual (I Corinthians 15:46) and that " ...as he who was born according to the flesh then persecuted him who was born according to the Spirit, even so it is now" (Galatians 4:29). What we obtained in Christ came long after we had been slaves to sin and darkness for many years. And the darkness would not just sit back and watch the light grow. As Ishmael mocked and "frustrated" Isaac, so must darkness mock and struggle to frustrate the light in us. Unfortunately, many of us were not taught on time to separate the light from the darkness. Sarah stood up and insisted that Hagar and her son must be put away because both cannot partake of the same inheritance. They are strikingly different and contrary one to another. The scriptures says that they lust one against the other (Galatians 5:17). The moment anyone of them indicated something he liked, the other was sure to stand up and insist otherwise. Isaac was younger and less experienced, yet he was the rightful and legitimate heir. Without Abraham, Ishmael could easily snuff life out of Isaac. I could imagine the pain on Abraham's bosom as he munched the issue of putting Ishmael away. God had to wade in and ask him to go ahead and do it. It was in the interest of the promise.

Many of us were neither taught, nor learnt on our own, to separate the light we received from the darkness that surrounds us or that has been within us. Neither did we invite God to do so for us. So we retained a number of our old habits and relationships. They seemed harmless initially; except for the occasional contradictions they presented to us based on our new convictions. Our lifestyles did not change; we did not consider acquiring new ways of doing things. We were honest and in earnest, but did not consider the kind of thought and mindset we carried. Some of the things taught us in school and by the society still formed the basis for our actions. We visited the same places to do the same things we did before. We indulged in the same set of habits and mingled with the same set of friends. We laughed at the same jokes. Our meals (including their timing) and our leisure activities remained the same. Sometimes, we had a nudge in our hearts that we needed to re-examine those habits, but we waved it aside, figuring that the light we received was strong enough to chase away any darkness. We indeed could not imagine our being swayed by the worthless lives and aspirations we saw our colleagues and friends living by. Heaven was real in our hearts and therefore we believed we had grown beyond those. We did not need to worry about the trappings of the present world. Our thinking was that whatever seemed to be out of place would somehow sort itself out with time. Some of us were not even fortunate to receive sound teachings on the basics of the faith then. Someone told us it did not really matter that much because as we read the bible on our own, it will continue to open and we would get all that we needed for running the race.

But things did not quite turn out that way. It did not take long before we found that the light in us was becoming dim, and that darkness was overcoming us. Darkness was fighting back, and it started in our hearts. The coldness, the struggle, the uncertainty and doubts about a lot of things, all seemed overwhelming. Myriad of doctrines seemed to be hurled at us, many of which added to our confusion. Some of the believers we looked up to and could have gone to for help seemed to suffer from the same ailments. Some even backslided. So we did not know who to turn to. The presence of God seemed far-fetched and far in-between when it comes. Our confidence and faith seemed to dry up. The Word of God became tasteless and prayer was drudgery, often with no knowledge of what to pray about.

Darkness fights back, and fights dirty. Those struggles in our faith are indicators that it would not passively sit by and get dislodged. Even if this is your situation now that you are reading this, it is not yet late. Just call upon God with all earnestness to help you identify the sources of darkness in your life and separate the light in you from every tinge of darkness. This is the beginning of victory. Dividing the light from the darkness involves identifying the drags on our spiritual lives and allowing God to deal with them by Himself. For some, it might be something as small as the feeding pattern; for others it might be relationships and friends, yet for others, aspirations and careers may stand in the way. These sometimes do not look like darkness, but they facilitate the re-emergence of darkness because they do not allow us to settle to living in the light continually.

The second measure we need to stem backsliding is the need to sustain the light. Every light needs powering, a source of energy, for it to continue to shine. Without the state's central supply, or a fuelled generator, electric bulbs would have no means of giving out light. Nor can the light that comes to the earth remain except the sun continues to burn at extremely high temperatures. The same way, no man can, in and of himself, sustain light within him. There must be continual empowerment from the light that lights the world. There is only one true Light; and it is He that lights up every man that comes into the world (John 1:9). We must be sustained through continual contact with Him and Him alone. Any righteousness which we think we can have or do by ourselves is already a threat to our keeping in touch with the light. Needless to say, that is dangerous.

c. ... And Finally Brethren

Sin is powerful, but there is Someone much more powerful. Attempting to overcome sin outside of the One who has conquered sin, death, and darkness is futile. A sin-free life is possible and provided for, but he that would have liberty from sin must hate even the garment stained by sin (Jude vs 23). It is written of the Author of our salvation "You have loved righteousness and hated iniquity; Therefore God, Your God, has anointed You with the oil of gladness more than Your companions". Just like Him, we have to love righteousness, sometimes when it seems that righteousness is against us, just as it seemed to be against Him when it took Him to the cross. We also have to hate iniquity, even when it appears as though it is helping our personal or corporate causes. When Peter raised the sword against the servant of the High Priest that was among those that came to arrest Jesus, the Lord did not keep quiet because the fight was for Him. He knew that the fact that the sword is for Him presently does not make the sword correct. So He rebuked the sword and brought healing to the person wronged. May we be deliberate about loving righteousness and hating iniquity! Living a victorious life is a matter of choice. There are many believers who, though aware that they are not living correct Christian lives, desire and welcome the subtle pleasures they derive from what they do. Such cannot give up their sins – and the Holy Spirit cannot take anything that is not completely given up. But because we cannot give up by our own powers, we then have to earnestly desire deliverance and cooperate with the Holy Spirit to bring it about in us. We can approach the Lord today for mercies – and He will abundantly grant it. According to Him, "it is finished", and we can experience the reality of sin being finished if we come in complete surrender to Jesus, who alone has the capabilities against sin. Even if you have suffered defeat against sin in the past on account of lack of knowledge, there is hope. The Lord yet speaks and can speak to you on how to mend your broken fences. He may require that you take some time off the pressures of life to listen to the Spirit of Truth. And while we walk, may we remember the words of victory in the book of Revelation saying,

"Then I heard a loud voice saying in heaven, 'Now salvation, and strength, and the kingdom of our God, and the power of His Christ have come, for the accuser of our brethren, who accused them before our God day and night, has been cast

down. And they overcame him by the blood of the Lamb and by the word of their testimony, and they did not love their lives to the death ..." (Revelation 12:10 – 11).

Sin, death, hades, the flesh, the devil and all that are associated with them have been judged. Upon the cross, Jesus judged sin and the flesh. He also told us that the prince of this world has been judged. Upon His second coming, he will consign all of them, including everything and everyone confusing us now, into the lake of fire. In the book of Revelation chapter 20, verses 10 and 14, it is written:

The devil, who deceived them, was cast into the lake of fire and brimstone where the beast and the false prophet are. And they will be tormented day and night forever ... Then Death and Hades were cast into the lake of fire. This is the second death"

The fight against sin is not forever. So may we hold on to the testimony and the blood of the Lamb. May we not love our lives as to provide a platform upon which sin will hold us to ransom. Maybe you are not even yet born again, but you are tired of being tossed around by sin. You are yet to come in contact with the Light of the world, the source of overcoming life. You can bend your head right now and ask Jesus into your life. Determine to have nothing to do with the works of darkness henceforth and ask the Lord for the grace to live for Him. The Lord who called us is faithful and will continue to shower the grace to overcome to all those who will receive the gospel of peace and hope with sincere hearts.

Printed in the United States
By Bookmasters